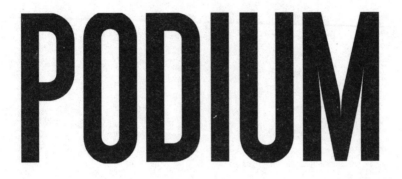

D0317983

PODIUM

WHAT SHAPES A SPORTING CHAMPION?

BEN OAKLEY

SOUTH DUBLIN COUNTY LIBRARIES	
SD900000123980	
Bertrams	19/06/2014
	£12.99
	TF

BLOOMSBURY

LONDON · NEW DELHI · NEW YORK · SYDNEY

Note
While every effort has been made to ensure that the content of this book
is as technically accurate and as sound as possible, neither the author nor
the publishers can accept responsibility for any injury or loss sustained as
a result of the use of this material.

Published by Bloomsbury Publishing Plc
50 Bedford Square
London WC1B 3DP
www.bloomsbury.com

Bloomsbury is a trademark of Bloomsbury Publishing Plc

First edition 2014

Copyright © 2014 Ben Oakley

ISBN (print): 978-1-4729-0216-0
ISBN (ePdf): 978-1-4729-0218-4
ISBN (EPUB): 978-1-4729-0217-7

All rights reserved. No part of this publication may be reproduced in any
form or by any means – graphic, electronic or mechanical, including
photocopying, recording, taping or information storage and retrieval
systems – without the prior permission in writing of the publishers.

Ben Oakley has asserted his rights under the Copyright, Design and
Patents Act, 1988, to be identified as the author of this work.

A CIP catalogue record for this book is available from the British Library.

Acknowledgements
Cover image © Shutterstock
Inside photographs, chapters: 1 (first) © Johannes Eisele/AFP/Getty
Images; 1 (second) © mooinblack/Shutterstock; 3 © AFP/Getty Images;
4 (first) © Kaliva/Shutterstock; 4 (second) © Julian Finney/Getty Images;
5 © Bryn Lennon/Getty Images; 7 © Tom Dulat/Getty Images;
8 © Natursports/Shutterstock; 9 © thelefty/Shutterstock; 10 © Anthony
Correia/Shutterstock; 11 © Alexander Hassenstein/Getty Images;
12 (first) © Neale Cousland/Shutterstock; 12 (second) © Phil Walter/Getty
Images; 15 © Christopher Halloran/Shutterstock; 16 © Radu Razvan/
Shutterstock; 17 © Warren Little/Getty Images; 18 © Bruce Bennett/Getty
Images; 19 (first) © Stu Forster/Getty Images; 19 (second) © Neale
Cousland/Shutterstock; and 21 © Pascal Rondeau/Getty Images.
Commissioned by Kirsty Schaper

This book is produced using paper that is made from wood grown in
managed, sustainable forests. It is natural, renewable and recyclable. The
logging and manufacturing processes conform to the environmental
regulations of the country of origin.

Typeset in 9.5 on 12 Palatino by Saxon Graphics Ltd, Derby
Printed and bound in Great Britain by CPI Group (UK) Ltd, Croydon, CR0 4YY

10 9 8 7 6 5 4 3 2 1

Contents

Acknowledgements

This book was stimulated by the initial prompting of BBC journalists Kevin Bishop and Paul Harris to write short online pieces for the BBC Sport website in the build up to London 2012. Thank you for getting me started. Then further down the line a range of friends, acquaintances and work colleagues critiqued and enhanced individual chapters thereby providing the oxygen of feedback to help keep me going. In no particular order I owe huge thanks to Jo Austen, Sarah Reid, Kate Peters, Martin Rhys, Anne Pankhurst, Linda Ellis, Jacky Hinton, Caroline Heaney, Gary Anderson, Mark Hirst, Martin Toms, Natalie Walker, Luke Austen, Ben Lyttleton, Uschi Moore, Nick Townsend, Victoria Cooper, Paul Mansell, Duncan Truswell, Kieron Sheehy and Andy Williams.

Sporting champions Matthew Pinsent, Martin Cross and Lesley Paterson consented for the use of my dialogue with them in discrete parts of the book – I am very grateful to them for allowing me to use their voices to bring particular topics to life.

And finally Sarah Oakley has coped with me often displaying 'grumpy writer syndrome' and beyond. I'm eternally lucky to have her ongoing love and support, and for her capacity for helping ensure that things fall into place.

Part I

Explaining the path to the top

1 Behind the lines

The London 2012 Olympic final of the women's judo. In the audience, British Prime Minister David Cameron and visiting Russian Premier Vladimir Putin, the latter a huge judoka fan – this event has been carefully chosen.

In the wider audience, millions of avid viewers across the world, keen to see an eagerly awaited contest which has captured the public imagination and will lead to a virtual standing ovation on Twitter as one of the most popular online replay moments of the 2012 Olympics. On the bright yellow mat, two young women are going for gold. Two young women at the height of their powers who are the best in the world at what they are about to do. But only one of them can win. One is from Ohio, USA. The other – just to add a bit more spice – is a local London girl. To hot it up even further, the USA have never in the history of the Olympic Games won a gold at judo, and Putin knows this!

The London girl, Gemma Gibbons from down the road in Greenwich, had spent part of the day having her hand heavily strapped. 'It hurt a lot,' she confessed after the contest, 'but I was told I was fine and encouraged to get on with it. I'm grateful they didn't tell me otherwise – I'd have been worrying about it'.[1] As she suspected, the medical team had decided not to give her all the facts. She later revealed, 'They knew it was broken but decided it wouldn't get any worse.' It must have been the toughest of calls for the medical team. It took her four months to get over the injury.

Few people watching that epic final would have realised that Gemma was fortunate to have made the British team. Earlier in the year, she lost out on selection in her favoured under-70 kilos weight category. She had to adjust her training to gain weight, enabling her to compete in the heavier under-78 kilos category.

In her semi-final earlier that day, she had endured five minutes of stalemate before the contest went into a nail-biting golden score situation in which the first score determined the winner. Summoning all her strength, power and skill, she spectacularly threw the French world champion to secure her place in the final. An emotional Gibbons held her hands to her face as she knelt, then slowly stood up, looked upward and mouthed the words, 'I love you, Mum'.

Eight years earlier, Gemma had lost her mother, Jeanette, to leukaemia. It was Jeanette who had introduced Gemma to judo. That moving moment touched millions as it was replayed frequently as one of the iconic images of 2012. The backstory of Gemma Gibbons was coming to the front of the action.

In the final she faced American, Kayla Harrison. Twenty-two-year-old Kayla's backstory was not so much touching as downright shocking. Her long and sometimes tortuous path to this final had been poisoned by the sexual abuse of her former coach, Daniel Doyle, which started when she was just 13. She recalled in retrospect, 'I mean, it was definitely grooming … I moved to the club when I was eight years old. From a young age, I had a very keen drive to please people.'[2]

A *Time* magazine interview revealed that her mother finally discovered the abuse through one of Kayla's friends and reported Doyle. In 2007, the former coach pleaded guilty to 'engaging in illicit sexual conduct in a foreign place'. Some of the abuse took place while they were abroad for judo tournaments. He is serving a 10-year prison sentence.

Kayla moved to Massachusetts to join a new father-and-son coaching team, the Pedros. According to Jimmy Pedro Junior, the traumatised 16-year-old 'was somebody who had no self-esteem … She was somebody who didn't know if she wanted to go on with life or not'. His assessment signalled the difficult journey ahead. 'I hated judo,' confessed Kayla. 'I hated the Pedros. I didn't want to be the strong girl. I didn't want to be the golden girl, I didn't want to be the one who overcame everything.'

Eventually, the Pedros' coaching, together with the support of her judoka peers, helped her on her path to elite success. That is why she publicly acknowledged that she owed any success she had to the Pedros and her teammates.

As she progressed through the rounds in London towards the final, she drew constantly on an inner hunger to succeed and a well-developed, tough mind. She repeated her own mantra. 'This is my day, this is my purpose.'

In front of a packed and loudly partisan home crowd, Harrison beat Gibbons in the final. America had its first gold in the sport. The lives of the two young women would never be the same again.

What was it Muhammed Ali said? 'The fight is won or lost far away from witnesses – behind the lines, in the gym, and out there on the road, long before I dance under those lights.'[3]

It's not just their passion for combat at the highest level that Harrison and Gibbons shared with the legendary World Heavyweight Champion. It's also their ability to overcome challenges and work single-mindedly towards their dream. Their determination, persistence and years of training had got them to this point, something the watching millions would have little concept of.

They also shared other similarities. Their respective mothers' influence since Jeannie, Kayla's mother, had – like Gemma's mother Jeanette – introduced her to the sport. Kayla's and Gemma's coaches also played similar functions as motivational role models. The British coach Kate Howey won her first Olympic medal (a bronze) as a competitor at the Barcelona Olympics, which inspired Gemma and many other youngsters in the UK. A year earlier, in the same Barcelona venue – the Palau Blaugrana – the US coach Jimmy Pedro also became a judo legend in the USA with a bronze at the World Championships.

Not all champions share so many coincidences, but there are some patterns in each sport – and individual attributes from childhood and beyond – that shape champions' paths.

It is how developing champions deal with these hidden, complex and unspeakably tough paths to the top, which are driven by complex motivations and punctuated by critical events that is the focus of this book.

Paths to the top

All too often we focus on polarised and oversimplified explanations of champions' success. In judo, for instance, a focus on genetic and physical attributes would put Gemma and Kayla's success down to their supreme agility, power and speed. At its most extreme, single genetic characteristics are used to explain success, so that Ian Thorpe's flipper-sized feet have been claimed to be the secret of his success in swimming. It suggests some champions are freaks of nature without recognising that physical attributes are not down to one gene, and need to be honed and combined with the right mindset.

More recently the quality and quantity of practice (in particular 10,000 hours) has been the focus of simplified explanations of success.[4] We now know this not to be the case, but this approach lays success at the door of the athlete's learning environment. It claims that the learning of detailed movement patterns and the ability to sustain quality practices account for Gemma and Kayla's success. For instance, if we examined how they trained, and were able to track their progress from an early age to look at how they were encouraged to persevere we might be able to provide a plausible explanation of how their agility, power, speed and above all champion judo technique, was learned.

This kind of naive oversimplification has been used to suggest that successful graduates from tennis or golf academies are not naturals but more freaks of extreme nurture.

The familiar compromise, of course, is to say it's a mixture of both natural characteristics and the learning environment. But, for me, that is not enough. I want a deeper understanding. Champions' paths are punctuated with a variety of potential roadblocks and a complex interaction between a range of physical, social and mental factors (including motivational influences) that keep athletes going. In my quest to explain this complexity I draw on some of my own experiences as a former Olympic coach at the Seoul and Barcelona Games and as an academic.

But, as Muhammed Ali urges, we need to delve deep behind the lines. In looking beneath the surface for what shapes champions, I wanted to view whole careers, not just the snapshot that is represented by Gemma and Kayla in their early to mid-twenties.

Champions' paths by numbers

Initially I was probably subconsciously influenced by the *Moneyball*[5] phenomenon in looking for neat representation of sporting careers by numbers. I experimented by graphically representing the career progress of tennis player Andre Agassi and athlete Kelly Holmes to see what their paths looked like. For Agassi we have his Association of Tennis Professionals (ATP) world ranking history and for Holmes her annual personal bests (PBs) in the 800m discipline to use as data. My experimental mapping of their progress paths are shown in Figures 1.1 and 1.2.

What does this tell us? First, each path is distinct and different in shape. Second, neither path is a smooth linear line of gradual progress to the ultimate goal of world number one or Olympic gold. Both paths are zigzags full of steep progress with plateaux and deep downward ravines. It is all too easy to let the path metaphors tumble out – 'the path to Everest is long', '… negotiating foothills before the summit' and referring to coaches as 'guides' and so on.

I was intrigued. What explained Agassi's fall from number 1 down to 141 and his climb back again? Why did Holmes's career stutter early on? I went to their autobiographies in search of answers (of course, being aware of potential autobiographical bias).

Describing the detailed ups and downs of individual champions is most definitely *not* the focus of this book. But I'll answer the above questions.

I learnt that both had slightly fractured childhoods, though I was not yet able to interpret the impact of this. But in their career paths I began to see that it was how Agassi and Holmes responded to key negative episodes in sport and in life, and the ways in which their desire and need to compete was reignited that made the big difference. Now I needed a broader sample from which I might pick narrative examples to illustrate the issues addressed in this book.

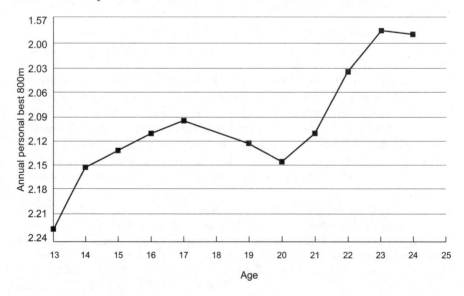

Figure 1.1 Kelly Holmes, career performance over time.

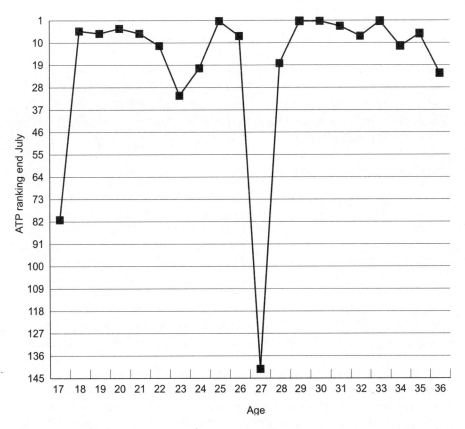

Figure 1.2 Andre Agassi, career performance over time.

Agassi's fall and rise[6]

His plummeting rankings had little to do with tennis strategy or physical condition, but rather life events disturbing his contentment and mental state. A failing marriage to Brooke Shields, the distractions of injury, illness in close friends' families and his general disillusionment with tennis. A symptom of his state of mind was his taking crystal meth. This was not someone who was struggling with prolonged injuries, or match strategy, or having a crisis with his service action; the bad results were caused by Agassi's inability to find the motivation and focus required for top-level competition. Or rather, it was his inability to have a fruitful life away from tennis – to mentally separate tennis and the rest of his problems – that caused him to lose interest and drive.

The two-year journey back to the top was again largely mental. Perhaps his description of an inspirational meeting with Nelson Mandela ignited an altruistic spark, and suddenly his tennis motivation was reinvigorated from his desire to generate income for the charter school he was developing. It was a tad ironic that someone who had voluntarily ducked out of school at an early age for the sake of tennis was now pursuing the dream of providing education for others.

He also moved on from his divorce to pursue Steffi Graff. Agassi's tennis trademarks – the ability to hit fizzing backhands up the line and return a serve better than anyone else in the world – never went away. What did desert him for a period was motivation, concentration, clear goals and world-class fitness. During Agassi's various crises his problems were hidden to the outside observer, locked away in his mind.

Holmes' stuttering start[7]

If you were looking at the early career of Kelly Holmes from the age of 16 to her early 20s from a physiological perspective you would expect a more or less straight line to reflect her response to increased training. That didn't happen. The influence of significant others, life events, career aspiration and athletics passion all came to the fore and mingled in different ways over time. It was during her early years as a mixed-race youngster with an absent biological father that Holmes developed a close bond with her mother, together with an independent streak that set her on her way.

The catalyst for her athletic development was a teacher who urged her to join the local running club after winning a few races. Soon she won the national schools 1500m championships, competed internationally and was introduced to her long-term local coach. Around the same time, an enthusiastic Army careers officer ignited her dream of joining the army as a physical training instructor (PTI), which distracted her from the full-time pursuit of her running. Two other life events entered the mix at the age of 17; a first major asthma attack and an emotional crisis when she believed her mother was abandoning her and moved out of the parental home. 'Independence' is a word that features strongly in her book.

Barcelona proved a turning point for Holmes, just as it did for the coaches of Gemma and Kayla. Watching the Barcelona Olympics on TV as a 22-year-old, she saw a former junior athletics rival, who she used to beat regularly, competing. Affronted, she was prompted to return to committed athletics training. Soon she progressed to national and international events and showed strong improvements in her PBs. She was back on track; a track that would eventually lead to double gold in Athens, although it took her a decade to get there.

A quest to explain

My initial use of autobiographies to help explain the shape of champions' paths grew from two to twenty-one over many months of research. I met with the co-author[8] of Steve Redgrave and Ben Ainslie's books to check how autobiography writing works – most athletes carefully correct manuscripts so they can be considered authentic. It helped, when refining my choices, to have some criteria

Steven Gerrard: negotiated rejection by England selectors at U15, early injuries and more recently a transition to playing a deeper anchor role in midfield

to determine which champions' stories to read. What do the top sportspeople listed in Table 1.1 (see overleaf) have in common?

My focus has been on the autobiographies of *serial champions* – who have had sustained success and (apart from Messi, Wiggins, Gerrard and Bolt)[9] have retired from World Championship or Olympic sport. A focus on serial champions means their stories are long-term accounts of being at the top for a while. This longevity helps when looking back at the influences that shaped their success. Disappointingly, in my autobiography sample there are fewer women's than men's, so I made a conscious effort – as in this chapter – to enhance the scope by also including intriguing examples from women's sport, even though some athletes might not have yet published their stories.

I've also found in my search that lessons from other champions' career-defining achievements, such as Mo Farah (distance running), Chris Froome (Tour de France cycling) and Andy Murray (tennis) help explain a number of points I consider in this book, even though their paths are not yet complete.

There are differences between team sport and individual sporting paths, not least in the subjective nature of team selections, which I have reflected in parts of the book. I am also acutely aware of the tangible differences in group dynamics and group momentum in teams compared to an individual champion competing within, say, an Olympic squad, but my use of autobiographies from rowing, football and rugby help to address this. I sought out other career defining examples from basketball, American football, baseball and cricket to provide further balance.

Table 1.1 Champions' autobiographies/biographies read: listed broadly chronologically.

Athlete	Sport
Seb Coe	Athletics (800m and 1500m)
Jonathan Edwards	Athletics (Triple Jump)
Tanni Grey-Thompson	Athletics (Wheelchair track events)
Michael Johnson (2 books)	Athletics (200m and 400m)
Cathy Freeman	Athletics (400m)
Andre Agassi	Tennis
Steve Redgrave	Rowing
Steven Gerrard	Football
Chris Hoy	Cycling (Track)
Chrissie Wellington	Ironman (swim/cycle/run)
Jonny Wilkinson	Rugby
Ben Ainslie	Sailing
Matthew Pinsent	Rowing
Victoria Pendleton	Cycling (Track)
Michael Phelps	Swimming
Roger Federer	Tennis
Kelly Holmes	Athletics (800m and 1500m)
Ian Thorpe	Swimming
Bradley Wiggins (2 books)	Cycling (track and road)
Lionel Messi	Football
Usain Bolt	Athletics (100m and 200m)

I also interviewed coaches and experts and consulted the research literature from genetics, physiology and psychology to coaching and sport science. Blending this has been fascinating in trying to answer the big question: what shapes a sporting champion?

There are a number of influences I want to cover in responding to this question. I have used a chronological approach, discussing formative childhood years through difficult transitions to senior level right up to considering specialist issues such as how champions' redirect their motivational 'rocket' in retirement.

By neatly dividing influences and mental aspects into chapters lies a paradox. While aiming to provide clarity and insight with 23 or so neatly segmented chapters I'm also working against my overall argument – that understanding champions' paths is down to a complex holistic interaction that we are only beginning to understand. I'm mindful of one or two chapters being taken out of context, and American essayist Henry Mencken's words resonate: 'for every problem, there is a solution that is simple, neat, and wrong'. So, I'm issuing my own health warning not to take each chapter as a factor in isolation. We don't exactly know how the 20 or so variables featured interact with each other.

Why do some athletes make it and others do not?[10]

In 2012, Dave Collins and his colleague Aine MacNamara published a paper with the provocative title of 'The Rocky Road to the Top: Why Talent Needs Trauma'[11] (note another 'path' metaphor!) in which they argued that 'talented potential can often benefit from, or even need, a variety of challenges to facilitate adult performance'.

They observed that having overcome negative episodes is more common in athletes that reach the top, and also considered that appropriate interventions can enhance an individual's resilience. The story behind the success of Kayla Harrison and Gemma Gibbons might seem to partly support such a theory.

The negative sporting episodes faced by athletes include the transition from junior to senior competition, changing coaches, relocating, injury and performance dips. These and many others are identified later (see chapter 12). It is how athletes interpret and deal with these challenges along with how they optimise physical (e.g. genetics, conditioning) and mental aspects such as nerves/confidence that shapes their paths.

Final thoughts

You may have noticed even at this early stage of the book that there is one word that is surprisingly underused: 'talent'. The word and its derivatives are often used carelessly without a passing thought, which is why I use it sparingly. Here is how leading psychologist Dean Simonton from the University of California expressed the use of the word:

> Talent has a somewhat strange status within psychology. On the one hand, the concept is commonplace in everyday psychology. Teachers often speak about some of their students having more talents than others, and coaches freely use the term to describe the differential performance of their athletes.[12]
>
> Moreover, conversations among diverse people, including psychologists, will often contain statements like 'I have no talent for mathematics' or 'you have a genuine talent for business'. Talent is frequently counted among the personal capacities responsible for the exceptional performance of a violin virtuoso or Olympic champion or of a 'maths whizz'.
>
> On the other hand, recent psychological research has increasingly cast doubt on the very existence of talent.[13] Instead of being blessed with innate gifts, the individuals who demonstrate world-class performance in any skill domain are simply those who have engaged in a great deal of deliberate practice.[14]

The word is used in many different ways, some implying that talent is a natural gift, a personal inherent capacity someone is born with (i.e. genetics). If you adopt the perspective that practice is the main way of explaining success 'natural' talent might be regarded as a myth.

In this book talent refers to an individual's *potential* for success. For example, in swimming, the person swimming the fastest in their age group is often considered the most talented. This alone may not indicate potential – beyond this simplistic use of the term other characteristics may contribute, such as anthropometric (e.g. height, weight), motor (e.g. speed, coordination) and psychological (e.g. motivation, stress resilience) aspects. To that we might also add the swimmer's continued exposure to expert coaching and practices, their social environment (e.g. family) and elements of chance and good fortune.

So while 'talent' is used sparingly, two other words are used a great deal. This book often refers to 'psychological' and 'mental'. As Usain Bolt said: 'mental strength was a tool in every single race, it was as important as a fast start or a powerful drive phase'.[15] This reflects my growing belief that at the absolute pinnacle most athletes operate at similar physical levels and it is how people approach their preparation, performance and indeed their life outside sport that often determine who ultimately steps on to the podium.

2 How could I have got it so wrong?

My earliest interest in how champions emerge took me for a second time to China. I wanted to know how Chinese sport was preparing for the Beijing Olympics, and was seeking to confirm my beliefs that a wide pool of athletes training together confers an advantage. My beliefs about sporting success have taken rather a leap since then; this chapter explains some of those transformations.

My first visit in 1986 had been as a naive young visiting coach with the newly formed Chinese Olympic windsurfing squad. In my second visit two decades later the sporting landscape had changed with preparations for a home Games in Beijing: the arresting visual images of my trip have stayed with me. It was a bitter, freezing day in January at the Chengdu Sports School. I was wearing about six layers and the moist low cloud, often a feature of Chinese winters, lingered around the colourless buildings.

The facilities and training I saw reinforced my simple mindset at the time: a high population size and large numbers of well coached athletes almost inevitably lead to special individuals who have what it takes to become champions. A sort of numbers game.

This was largely confirmed when I walked into a 50m pool – I'd never seen such a wide pool: it was almost square – and the pool's width was full of swimmers training. I was staggered by the sheer volume of swimmers in one pool. Their efforts were given a spectral ambience by the mist of chlorine infused condensation rising from the relatively warm water, it was –8°C outside.

From the pool I went into another building and as I climbed the stairs the unmistakable clatter of sponged bat on hollow ball rose to a machine-gun crescendo as we got closer. China dominates world table tennis. But this was table tennis training on a grand scale with lines of tables filling the cavernous hall. A coach shouted loudly and everyone changed their routine from backhand to forehand, some with coaches feeding the shots to the athletes and other pairs whacking the ball to each other. It was astonishing to watch on a number of levels: the speed of play, the young age (under 10) of some of the athletes and the sustained repetition of one shot. We'll talk about the nature of practice later in the book, but this was a striking illustration of how a motor movement is grooved deep into the brain with repetition – and I'd only glimpsed part of a training session.

Finally, on that memorable first day, I walked into an aircraft hangar of a gymnastics hall. I felt like a visiting ant. The immense space made the hall impossible to heat, but the young athletes went about their different gymnastic elements in the near freezing temperature. Up in one corner of the hall was a countdown clock of some sort. My interpreter revealed that it was displaying the number of days until the quadrennial National Games later that year in Nanjing City. China's 30 provinces and regions each send a team to compete in Olympic sports and cultural events. Chengdu is the capital of Sichuan province and this sports school would supply many of the athletes for their team. In terms of prestige for athlete and coach, success at the National Games – with 10,000 athletes participating – seals your status at the apex of the Chinese sporting pyramid. From what I'd seen I could only guess at how high the standards must be, as the best athletes from each province constantly pushed one another to ever higher levels. In many sports the standard would be similar to European or World Championships.

Suddenly a heated discussion was taking place between my interpreter and a senior coach. Rather perplexed, I was led to a corner of the hall where the senior coach robustly asked a tall, lithe gymnast to perform her rhythmic gymnastics routine for the overseas guest. It was clear her heart was not in it but she took to the floor nevertheless as the coach fiddled with the small CD player. She was ranked among the top 10 in the world. I'd never viewed this discipline at such close quarters before and the coordination between her movement and the tossing and manipulation of the hoop was breathtaking. I now realised why the hall needed to be so tall – to accommodate the hoop's looping trajectories. All the while this was done with her performance face – a fixed smile – on despite other body language giving away her dampened enthusiasm.

Pyramid thinking[1]

My initial thinking and beliefs stemmed from a popular and often quoted idea that uses the pyramid analogy; in fact in printed sports policy documents it is often presented as a one-dimensional triangle. Elite sport performance and champions are viewed as being at the apex. Their success, according to this way of thinking, is largely predicated on the numbers lower down the pyramid at what is often called the base, or foundation, level. For example, you might hear the leader of a new initiative say something like:

> what we're trying to do here is develop a broad base of participation and attract a diverse range of young people to try the sport: if they like it, we can guide them towards clubs and coaches who can help them take things further.

Then go on to suggest: 'Who knows, we might attract champions of the future'.

So pyramid thinking follows the logic that if you attract large numbers into a sport and provide appropriate funding, resources and experiences to help athletes – normally youngsters – to develop then you are likely to develop champions. As athletes progress up the pyramid, fewer and fewer are involved and resources are more precisely targeted. In China resources are targeted at sports schools.

Intuitively, it is a simple and appealing theory. When applied as a way of thinking about national sports 'systems' it helps explain what I saw in China. A broad base of participation in table tennis or gymnastics, both a strong feature in Chinese schools, refined with the help of funding specialist coaching facilities such as at Chengdu, combined with exposure to top-class competitions. Result: international success.

The collegiate (university) sports system in the United States is likewise largely based on high numbers and fierce competition. Some view it as almost a Darwinian journey towards the top of the pyramid, both in terms of individual athletes' progress and the survival of the college teams involved – an ESPN sports report was titled: 'College sports: survival of the fittest.'[2] This broad collegiate system represents a very strong penultimate layer of their pyramid with numerous young student athletes coached to high levels. It is the reason why the USA will always produce champion athletes in global sports such as basketball, athletics, swimming and women's soccer, because sporting scholarships provide hubs of top-level athletes.

My initial belief in pyramid thinking started to unravel when I looked more closely at evidence beyond China or US colleges. For instance, in windsurfing the small nations of New Zealand, Greece and Israel dominated the Olympic Games between 1984 and 2004 – countries lacking high numbers of athletes. To investigate pyramid thinking further at a national level is fairly simple. You'd expect countries with larger numbers of players or athletes in a particular sport to broadly speaking be more successful on the world stage. We will consider tennis and rugby union since there is reasonably good data on each sport and they have an international spread (admittedly tennis more so than rugby union).

Tennis professionals

In tennis the number of players in a country who have gained tennis professional ATP/WTA world tour ranking points represents a 'top slice' through the pyramid of players near the apex; it could be said to represent the cohort of professional athletes who have committed to chasing their champion's dream.

In Table 2.1 I compare Spain, USA and Great Britain in terms of total number of players, those with ATP/WTA singles ranking points[3] and those close to being champions (i.e. the top 30).[4] Some interesting comparisons emerge.

Table 2.1 Comparing Spain, USA and Great Britain: numbers of tennis players, ranked professionals and those top-ranked.

Country	Number of players[5]	Total number with ranking points	Number top ranked (top 30)
Spain	1,900,000	124	5
USA	19,500,000	236	6
Great Britain	2,900,000	93	1

An economist might comment on the low efficiency of 'producing' champions in Great Britain and USA compared to Spain. In particular, Spain's conversion of players from those with ranking points to top-30 level is high. National pyramid thinking in tennis is somewhat challenged by this simple research. In this case the numbers game does not add up.

The rugby base

The sport of rugby union is rich in data describing the number of players active at different levels, supplied by each country to the international federation.[6] Let's take a look at the base of the pyramid in different counties. We'll focus on New Zealand, Australia, England and Samoa and their efficiency at the time of writing (see Table 2.2).

If national pyramid thinking is valid in rugby, the highest standards and tallest apex should be represented by the England team. England, with so many teenagers (732,000) and adults (156,000) playing rugby, should dominate world rugby year on year. England has 15 to 30 times as many male teenagers and about four or five times as many men playing the game compared to their Antipodean rivals. New Zealand appears to be the most efficient in producing a top world ranking with a modest player base. Tiny Samoa sometimes comes close to beating the larger countries while drawing on a tiny pool of players.

So there is more to national success in sport than just numbers. Certainly, it helps if you have a lot of people to chose from (i.e. a large 'talent pool') but it is what happens on players' journeys towards the top that shapes national success: things like coaching knowledge, scientific support, sustained motivation, quality practices and appropriate competition opportunities.

Rugby union – in its seven-a-side format – returns to the Olympic Games in 2016, which is encouraging national coaches to examine more closely the transition of players from successful 19/20-year-olds to champion adults. Bizarrely, almost a century ago the United States became the most successful nation in Olympic rugby history, having won the gold medal in both 1920 and 1924. They didn't have many players then, and the same is true now.

Table 2.2 Total number of players at different levels of the rugby pyramid for selected countries compared to world ranking.

Country	Total number teenagers (boys/girls)	Total number adults (male/female)	World ranking (m/f)
New Zealand	40,000/4000	28,000/900	1/5*
Australia	19,000/no data	39,000/1700	4/2*
England	603,000/129,000	131,000/25,000	3/1*
Samoa	1800/200	7700/250	7/0

* Women's world rankings only available in the seven-a-side format[7]

So looking at the numbers in tennis and rugby challenged my pyramid thinking. There was much, much more to follow.

Talent identification beliefs

As well as visiting China I also looked towards Australia as a nation that knew how to develop sporting potential. For instance, as you can see from Table 2.2 opposite, the Australian rugby team's record in both the male and female game is pretty strong compared to the size of its talent pool. Its performance in other sports has also defied population odds. Mark Peters, the CEO of the Australian Sports Commission, suggested in 2007 that specialised testing for talent was the only way to sustain their search for success:

Compare the statistics, Australia has a population approaching 21 million, the United States of America has a population of over 300 million and China's population is over one billion. If you look at the numbers and the potential for sporting talent within the population, Australia, compared to these nations, should not be competitive, however, we seem to defy the odds and rank high in world sport … The role talent identification plays in our ongoing sporting success is critical.[8]

Peters was proudly promoting the new *Talent Identification and Development Programme*. Little did he know that Australia's Olympic team was in serious decline, falling from fourth in the medal table at Athens to tenth in London eight years later.

In 1996, Great Britain also had a traumatic time: at the Atlanta Olympics they managed just one gold medal, and that was from rowing legends Steve Redgrave and Matthew Pinsent. At the time there was a view in London that Australia may have had the answer with their talent search programme. Here's an example from the London *Financial Times* in 1997

Youngsters with stars in their eyes[9]

The country's talent identification scheme has run since 1991. It identifies the children who could potentially be the next Ian Thorpe of swimming or Cathy Freeman of running.

Annually Australia's 2,000 high schools are invited to participate in the talent search and some 800 reply. Experts then visit the school and eight tests are conducted on children around the age of 14 with 10,000 children taking part. About half are invited back for more testing. The second stage of testing is based on more scientific measurements.

Those who are identified in this second stage are then inducted into the chosen sport for three months and, if they continue to show aptitude, they spend one or two years in intensive training.

Since 1994, 2,077 athletes have been placed in these further training programmes and around one in three remain. In particular, 40 per cent of the national rowing team has come from this programme.

The talent scheme is best at identifying potential champions for athletics, cycling and rowing but the programme has also identified the participants for the 2000 women's weightlifting team. The manager of the programme Deborah Hoare says 'It makes sense for us to target the "softer" events'.

Once upon a time I too held the belief that talent can be identified at a young age through a number of standardised physical and technical tests. It is still a widely held idea. Published research evidence, however, has shown it to be a myth.

Scepticism towards testing children for talent was kicked off largely as a result of some inquisitive researchers in Scotland.[10] In 2002, Angela Abbott and Dave Collins were sponsored to monitor the pilot stage of a new testing programme, which Scottish sports leaders hoped might transform the opportunities of the nation's youth. A new computer-based programme had been imported from the designers of the Australian talent search scheme (see above) that points a child towards specific sports after a series of physical tests based on a model of desirable characteristics for each sport. Nine test measurements were taken: height, weight, arm length, a catching task, a throwing task, a vertical jump and agility/sprint/ endurance running tasks. The pilot in Scotland tested almost 2500 10–14-year-olds and 390 of them were retested a year later to see how consistent the results were.

Among the numerous findings was a particularly striking one that relates to the unstable nature of performance results a year apart when adolescents are in their growth spurt (see Figure 2.1). The test–retest rankings illustrated dramatically demonstrate how the endurance running task, indicating aerobic capacity – a pretty important factor in sporting potential – of children (aged 11–12 yrs), varies considerably and is 'unstable' across just one year.

For example, a youngster who was ranked 12th in the group dropped to 47th the following year, while another, who was 55th, rose to almost the top of the group, and was ranked 4th. It seems unfair if the programme uses such physical results to identify those suited to certain sports. The report's authors explain their finding:

> The instability observed on the physical factors over time is not surprising since physical maturity is known to differ greatly between individuals during adolescence ... research has also shown that the performance capacity of an individual will be directly influenced by their physique, therefore the instability observed on the performance tasks is also not surprising. The unstable nature of these physique and performance scores, as compared to what is required, indicates there are serious flaws in the assumption that a sport that is 'suited' to a child will remain appropriate into adulthood and that talent identification processes can be based upon this concept.[11]

Needless to say the programme was not adopted after such strong findings: though a lot more research into talent development was stimulated by this initial work.

For example, a team from Belgium drew attention to the fact that sporting champions in adulthood do not all possess a standard set of skills or physique;

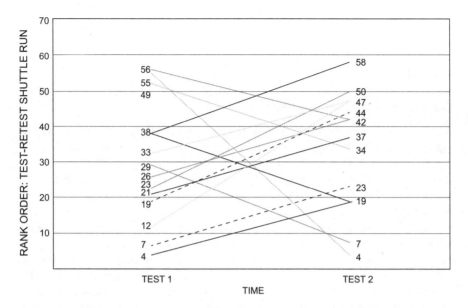

Figure 2.1 Childrens' aerobic capacity test rankings compared between one year and the next among a Scottish pilot programme.

Abbott, A., Collins, D., Sowerby, K. and Martindale, R. (2007) *Developing the potential of young people in sport,* A report for Sport Scotland, Edinburgh: Sport Scotland, p. 9.

for example there is a great variety of specialised attributes, along with height and weight differences within a sport squad. Success can be achieved in idiosyncratic ways through a unique blend of skills, attributes and capacities. This effect has been termed the 'compensation phenomenon' and suggests that deficiencies in one area of performance may be compensated by strengths in others.[12] Lionel Messi, holder of multiple world football player of the year awards, is far from tall (he is 1.69m/5ft 7in tall) or muscular, but makes up for it by being incredibly skilful, quick to accelerate and having excellent balance and poise. He says, 'being smaller, [he has] learned to control the ball better on the ground, and be more agile and faster than the bigger players in order to keep the ball.'[13]

If physical attributes and skills are so varied in adults, it seems a waste of time trying to use the results of physical screening tests *before puberty*. It is worth noting that none of the champions' autobiographies in this book mentioned a childhood talent identification scheme largely based on physical testing. My beliefs obviously needed considerable adjustment. In fact, the gradual realisation that pyramid thinking and talent identification among children were unfounded partly stimulated this book.

So if physical testing in adolescence is largely discredited, how were many of the champions discussed in this book were identified to go on for further training? The answer lies in their competition performances and age-group competition in particular. Among our sample autobiographies, three out of four champions were among the top juniors in their country before their 19th birthday.

Champions and age-group competition

Age-group competition represents talent identification based on sporting performance. But what are your chances of making it to the top if you are selected for, say, an under-13 (U13) national squad?

Some have number-crunched the predictive power of age-group sport. One study[14] looked at individual Olympic sports and reported that among the Athens 2004 Olympians only 44 per cent were reported to have made their international competition debut within their sporting discipline's youth or junior age categories. Most (56 per cent), made their first international appearance in the senior age category with a mean age of 22 years. In cycling, for example, one-third of participants in junior World Championships went on to participate in major elite competitions. This ratio of 1 in 3 making it from junior to senior international level has also been observed in a national investigation across soccer, volleyball, swimming and judo.[15] It has been concluded 'that exceptional success and performance by juvenile athletes appeared to be neither a necessary nor a sufficient prerequisite for later success'.[16]

Applying this to South African rugby, Ross Tucker explains how many players have played at the highest level in South Africa at the age of 13, the age of 16 and the age of 18. The conversion of top 13-year-olds to top 16-year-olds is relatively low at 31 per cent. It gets much better from 16 to 18 at 76 per cent – three-quarters of top young players who play at U16 level also go on to play at U18 level. The chances of making it from U13 to U18 level is basically 1 in 4, i.e. not too good. The U16 to U18 transition is much more reliable.[17]

All this evidence suggests that the more you can delay the selection of talent, the more efficient your system is likely to be. England's football captain Steven Gerrard was selected for the national team at U21, U18, U16, but significantly not at U15 level, partly because he was a late developer, compounded further by a birthdate (30 May) late in the selection year (see chapter 8 for more on birth date).

Age group selections before puberty (i.e. before 14–16 years) are, therefore, very poor at predicting future success and in a way the significant aspect is the deselection process and the fate of the overwhelming majority of the players who are *not* selected.

More awareness of these processes and statistics, at the very least, points to reducing the status and importance that *adults* place on age group competition. We cover further selection myths and compromises partly drawing on my experience as a national squad selector in chapter 8.

Your beliefs about sporting ability[18]

Now let's consider your own beliefs about sporting ability. Your beliefs can affect not only your own behaviour but also that of developing athletes you interact with.

Take a look at this short questionnaire, which uses a Likert scale (1–5 agree/disagree) named after the American psychologist who developed the rating scale. Complete this so that you can begin to understand your own beliefs about sporting ability.

To what extent do you agree or disagree with the following statements:

(1 = strongly disagree, 2 = disagree, 3 = neither disagree or agree, 4 = agree, 5 = strongly agree).

Statements	1	2	3	4	5
We have a certain level of sporting ability and we cannot really do much to change that level					
If you put enough effort into it, you will always get better at sport					
To be good at sport you need to be naturally gifted					
To be successful in sport you need to learn techniques and skills and practice them regularly					

Adapted from Wang C. K. J., Liu W. C., Biddle S. J. H., Spray C. M., Cross-cultural validation of the Conceptions of the Nature of Athletic Ability Questionnaire Version 2. *Personality and Individual Differences*, 38 (6), (2005) pp. 1245–56.

Responding to these statements begins to reveal your views on the fixed or changeable nature of sporting ability. Most champions believe they can progress in sport by continual learning and persistence – a 'learning orientation' – but this view works best when it is shared by those around them, including parents and coaches in their formative years.

Perceptions of ability and a learning orientation

American psychologist Carol Dweck is a professor who has researched intelligence and development in educational settings. She proposed two clusters of beliefs that underpin people's actions, which she termed 'fixed' and 'growth' beliefs. Those with fixed beliefs feel that, to a greater or smaller extent, attributes like intelligence or sporting ability are difficult or impossible to change. The converse, growth beliefs, are based on the extent to which attributes like sporting ability are flexible and open to learning/change – this is what I call a 'learning orientation'.

Questions or statements used in questionnaires, a sample of which you have just considered, draw on Dweck's work. Fixed views of ability are represented by a tendency to agree with the following items:

- We have a certain level of sporting ability and we cannot really do much to change that level, and
- To be good at sport you need to be naturally gifted.

Learning orientation views of ability are represented by a tendency to agree with the following items:

- If you put enough effort into it, you will always get better at sport, and
- To be successful in sport you need to learn techniques and skills and practice them regularly.

But how much do beliefs influence behaviour? Dweck's research compared beliefs and behaviour in children. She and her colleagues found that:

- Children holding a *fixed* view are more likely to have negative reactions when faced with setbacks (e.g. harder tasks).
- Those with a *fixed* view are more likely to pursue outcome (ego) goals that focus on end-results.
- Those with growth learning orientation views have been shown to endorse process (task) goals which support their development.

For example, a child who thinks people are either sporty or non-sporty is holding a fixed view of ability, and is more likely to focus on their results on a sports day they participate in – an outcome goal. In contrast, a child who thinks that effort and practice is the key to success is more likely to focus on performing the detailed aspects of events on the sports day as best they can – a process goal.

Dweck's research has implications for champions' paths, since beliefs about ability underpin many coaches' or teachers' approaches to their work and to supporting athletes' development. As we shall see, what coaches and others say and do has a significant impact, particularly on children in their early sporting experiences.

Dweck has not explicitly researched sport but she has referred to the field in her writing and conference speaking. For example, in a short online piece titled 'The Mindset of a Champion' she says this about the hot topic of talent identification:

> Many of the scouts in the sports world scouted for naturals, people who looked like superstars – were shaped like superstars, moved like superstars. If they didn't look the part, they weren't recruited. Yet ... Muhammad Ali actually did not have the build of the natural boxer. He did not have a champion's fists, reach, chest expansion, and heft. (...)
>
> Within ... fixed beliefs ... potential is easy to judge. You just look at the person's gifts right now and project them into the future. Talented now equals talented in the future. Not talented now equals not talented in the future. Boy, that was easy!

Yet within growth beliefs, potential is hard to judge. Sure 'natural talent' buys you a lot, and if you're accomplished now, you've got a leg up on others. But after that you cannot know where someone might end up with years of passion, discipline, and commitment – and good instruction.[19]

This chimes with what I have just been talking about: the inappropriate use of physical testing of adolescents and overemphasis on age group competition under the age of 16. Instead it emphasises what most of us know already: that attitude and hard work can get you a long, long way in all aspects of life, including sport. It's interesting that Dweck talks about talent giving you a 'leg up on the others'; this initial small advantage gives great encouragement for youngsters to continue training and follow their passion. A small initial advantage can be magnified through a number of other effects, as we'll see throughout this book.

Champions' learning orientation

Researchers tend to be curious people who like to solve a puzzle. In Norway Yngvar Ommundsen saw the puzzle as 'what effect do different Dweck-like ideas on beliefs about physical ability have on youngsters approach to physical education (PE)?'

He found that a growth-learning orientation belief predicted a particular learning stance toward sports, including the tendency to take an analytic stance toward one's activities (useful in potential champions). For example, these are typical phrases that the research suggests people with a learning orientation might say:

- 'If the activities or exercises are difficult to understand, I work out another way to approach them.'
- 'If I can't do an exercise, I'll often ask for help to figure out how to do it.'

As opposed to a fixed belief:

- 'When the activities or exercises are difficult, I tend to do the easy ones and sometimes I give up.'
- 'I don't like other people seeing that I can't do something so I figure out a way of keeping a low profile'.

I think you'll agree that if people behave in this way in their youth it is likely to have a pretty strong impact on their development path. These findings in sport and education regarding the effect of belief on behaviour and learning are not just limited to individual children: they seep in everywhere. Notably on how we guide, mentor, coach and even label young people.[20]

The 'talented' label and the power of words

Beliefs are partly fostered by the kind of praise and feedback people get from parents and coaches with whom they are in close contact. Dweck and a colleague carried out an influential experiment in 1998 about praise and feedback using mental reasoning puzzles with children. The research article by Mueller and Dweck has a bold assertion as a title: *Praise for Intelligence Can Undermine Children's Motivation and Performance.* Substitute 'sporting talent' for 'intelligence', and you can see that it's a bold statement – what did they discover?

Their approach was to take 400 11-year-olds, one-by-one, and give them a series of simple puzzles. After each round of puzzles, each student was given their score plus different praise:

> A third of the students were praised with: 'You must be smart at this' (fixed intelligence praise);
> another third were told: 'you must have worked really hard' (process related praise i.e. learning related).
> The remaining third were a control group and no praise was given.

The striking finding was that the group praised for their intelligence (a fixed belief) consistently showed in the region of a 15–20 per cent decline in performance on a retest at the end of the session while those praised for their effort (a learning belief) increased their scores by 20–25 per cent. The control group was relatively stable in its performance within about a 10 per cent range (I have grossly simplified the results for reasons of brevity). [21] This would suggest that praise about aspects such as 'effort' is more effective, and this has relevance to feedback in sport. It is wasteful and counterproductive calling someone 'talented': they need feedback and reinforcement about the process of what makes them good at what they do. Once someone gets the 'I'm talented' label and they start believing that they have special gifts, it can doom them to failure unless they realise that the learning orientation side of things is what is going to convert potential into greatness.

In fact you can view Dweck's explanation of this fascinating experiment via YouTube (search for 'Mueller and Dweck 1998'). This helps make sense of my brief description here. Figure 2.2 below represents a useful summary of Dweck's overall findings on ability beliefs after many years of research.

In Figure 2.2 (opposite) I particularly like the summaries of what each mindset leads to in terms of challenges, obstacles, effort, criticism and success of others. Dweck published a very successful book (*Mindset*, published by Robinson Press in 2012) which has recently been influential in the talent development and coaching worlds.

Final thoughts

I started this chapter by asking how I could have got it so wrong. Well, despite being immersed in sport all my life, moving in athletic circles has taken time to

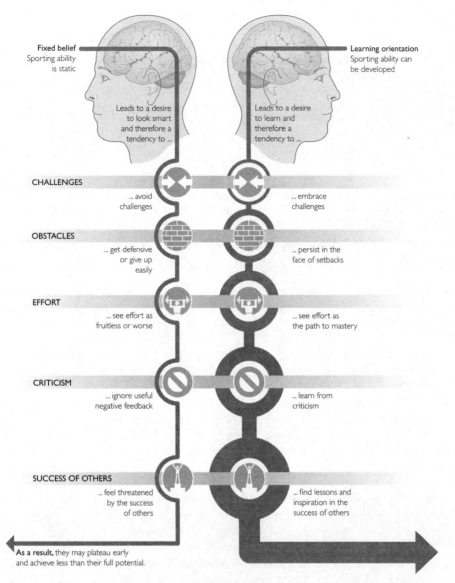

Figure 2.2 The relationship between ability beliefs and achievements

have an effect. My three initial pyramid, talent identification and age group beliefs have been challenged over time with travel, reading and benefiting from others' research.

We are beginning to understand what shapes sporting champions, but if my experience is anything to go by, first you have to challenge your own firmly held beliefs.

In the chapters that follow we start to uncover two questions: 'what do we really know about champions and genetics?' and 'what role could parents play in supporting their child's development as a potential champion?'

3 Champion DNA?

We gravitate towards biological explanations of champions' success because physical attributes are tangible and appear simple. We can see 'natural' abilities such as speed, power or the grace of an athlete's movement.

Here is Spanish tennis ace Rafa Nadal in his autobiography talking of Roger Federer:

> He just seems to have been born to play the game. His physique – his DNA – seems perfectly adapted to tennis ... You get these blessed freaks of nature in other sports too.

I aim to convince you in this chapter of the place and context of physical and genetic explanations of sporting success and how they should be seen as interacting with other influences elsewhere in this book. It is only since about 1980 that the DNA or genes, that Nadal refers to, have featured in polarised arguments. The age-old nature versus nurture discussion.

Nadal's claim of his colleague being 'born to play the game' may be right in one sense since his comment was made with reference to his own battles with injury. We start our look at genes by investigating their role in predicting human height: an important component of physique in many sports. If you are tall you cannot contemplate gymnastics, diving or weightlifting – size matters. I've chosen height since it is easily understood, and we know some sport squads such as basketball or volleyball need tall players to be competitive.

After this we move on to look at three examples of the very latest research on the role of genes in sport: genetic influences on injury along with responses to aerobic training and performance at altitude.

Perhaps in 50 years' time, if genetic testing were to become commonplace, sporting autobiographies might begin to identify some of the genetic markers of their authors. Right now though in autobiographies there is plenty of talk in champions' accounts of their physical attributes: height, weight, lung capacity and in the case of Ian Thorpe, large feet (viewed as advantageous for swimmers).

Genes and height

Intuitively we know that our height is largely inherited from our parents. But perhaps the amount of height variability among your own siblings or others suggests it is not a straightforward process of inheritance. Stature is part of all of us and helps illustrate the complexity of using genes to explain a physical attribute. Yet it is also an example of a physical feature that may predispose an athlete to certain sports – showing sporting genes at work.

Australian Institute of Sport (AIS) staff have measured male and female elite athlete heights over the years and identified those sports which have a preponderance of very tall or short athletes (see table 3.1 below). There are no big surprises on the left hand side.

On the right side of the table the tall or short athletes that feature in this book are included in rank order with four of the best rowers and swimmers of all time dominating the leader board and Kelly Holmes (a middle-distance runner) and Lionel Messi (footballer) featuring in the short list (pun intended). We'll come back to the taller, giant-like champions in a moment.

The trends identified over time are revealing. Athletes' height is becoming more and more extreme at both ends of the spectrum. For example, in the NBA the percentage of players over 2.13m (7ft) until the 1980s was about 3 per cent but since 2000 this has risen to 9+%.[1] Taller champions are increasingly emerging in other sports such as sprinting (e.g. Usain Bolt) and tennis (e.g. Novak Djokavic, the Williams sisters). At the other end of the scale the benefits of being small in some sports have encouraged specialisation. David Epstein, in *The Sporting Gene*, explains that elite female gymnasts in the last 30 years have shrunk on average from 1.6m (5ft 3in) to 1.45m (4ft 9in). Being small confers advantage in being able to spin and rotate more readily. Likewise in springboard diving you also see shorter than average athletes.

Table 3.1 Sports identified by AIS as populated by very tall or short athletes and corresponding examples from this book'.

Sports with tall athletes (i.e. male>1.86m and female>1.74m)	Sports with short athletes (i.e. male<1.71m and female<1.61m)	Tall athletes featured in this book (in rank order)	Short athletes featured in this book
Basketball	Long-distance running	Usain Bolt 1.95m	Kelly Holmes 1.60m
Volleyball	Weightlifting	Ian Thorpe 1.95m	Lionel Messi 1.69m
High Jump	Diving	Steve Redgrave 1.95m	
Netball (women)	Gymnastics	Matthew Pinsent 1.95m	
Rowing (heavyweight)		Michael Phelps 1.93m	
Swimming (sprint)		Bradley Wiggins 1.90m	
		Andy Murray 1.90m	

The scientific concept of morphological optimisation in sport is something the AIS have thrived on over the years. This idea is about there being distinctive body shapes in some sports that represent the optimised physical characteristics. It is one of the underpinning principles originally used in the talent testing of younger athletes in the 1990s referred to in chapter 2, i.e. if you are this shape and size, you may well be suited to this sport. If you are a giant, then the sports in Table 3.1 are clearly an example of morphological optimisation in action. Take a look at what the English Institute of Sport have said about what makes the perfect swimmer.[2]

Height

Height is especially important in swimming because the taller the swimmer, the less body length distance (BLD) needs to be covered in order to complete the race distance (e.g. a 1.76m tall swimmer will have to cover 20cm more BLD than a 1.93m tall swimmer over a 400m race). Additionally, the taller the swimmer, the faster he or she is able to swim without suffering maximum wave drag. Alternatively, shorter swimmers will encounter maximum wave drag at slower race speeds, thereby reducing their swimming efficiency.

Arm span

In general, the longer the arms are, the more efficient the swimmer will be. This is because in most cases, the greater the reach, the greater is the distance travelled per stroke, so fewer strokes will be taken to cover any given race distance.

Foot size

Anyone who has worn flippers when swimming will know that they enable you to produce more power from the leg kick, and therefore swim faster; having large feet has precisely the same effect. Additionally, we know that ankle flexibility is very important in swimming, in order to get the most benefit from the 'whipping' action, thereby creating extra power and propulsion.

Lung capacity

Important especially for distance swimmers, as the larger the lungs are, the more oxygen is taken in, which is ultimately transported to the active muscles to help produce energy. Additionally, having large lungs helps swimmers to take fewer breaths during races, so that stroke disruption is minimised, and more time can be spent swimming underwater during turns, which can be significantly faster than on the surface.

The swimmer Ian Thorpe does pretty well on all these physical attributes; and since these characteristics are genetically determined it is no wonder he has been labelled, and indeed talks of himself, as a natural:

Ian Thorpe: one of the heaviest ever swimmers, yet hugely flexible

> I was naturally talented with a strangely flexible body and, yes, big feet...[3] I also have unusually big shoulders and legs, which should give me a power advantage and make up for the fact that I don't sit as high in the water as some of the lighter guys[4] ... I was 105 kilos (16st 7lb), at Athens which made me the heaviest swimmer ever.[5]

Notice how he foregrounds his flexible body as a real strength. Ian Thorpe is therefore a very large but flexible, powerful swimmer who is considerably heavier than the norm (i.e. 'the heaviest swimmer ever'). In pictures of his childhood podium moments he towers over his peers, and this early physical advantage set the foundation for what followed

Height is important in many sports since it tends to give you longer levers (i.e. swimming and rowing) and greater reach (i.e. court sports such as basketball, volleyball etc.). Stature in itself has been the basis for increasing the talent pool in some relatively minority sports. For example, when the organisation for optimising British Olympic success, UK Sport, advertised a search for mature 'sporting giants' and 'tall and talented' athletes using a talent profile they used criteria such as:

- exceptionally tall (men over 1.90m and women over 1.80m);
- competing in any sport at a minimum of regional level; and,
- mentally tough and competitive.

Gold medallist rower Helen Glover emerged from this initiative and went from rowing novice to 2012 Olympic champion in four years, and was also World Champion in 2013. Height, and thus by implication genes, matter. But also notice the last point 'mentally tough and competitive' – a psychological attribute.

So if genes are important how precisely do they contribute to height? Here lies the problem – it is extremely complex. The benefit of my not being a geneticist is that I have had to make sense of it myself in plain English, while synthesising the work of researchers. We are all made up of about 20,000 genes, depending how you define a gene (each gene comes in slightly different versions, called variants or alleles). It is now recognised that genes can interact with each other. For example, if gene A contributes a 0.2 factor to height, gene B a 0.3 contribution, when they interact together they may contribute a higher factor than the simple sum (i.e. 0.2 + 0.3 may equal more than 0.5). That makes it more complicated from the beginning.

To date 47 genes have been identified that account for 5 per cent of the differences in height.[6] That is rather a lot of genes to investigate for not much variation. By further exploring the slight genetic variations in the population, scientists have been able to demonstrate that 80 per cent of the height differences between us can be accounted for by over 100 different genes and hundreds of thousands of gene variations.[7]

So not only are there many genes, but also many variants within each gene and subsequently a mixture from each parent. I have not even mentioned the environmental influences – in this case the quality of your nutrition as a growing child. Nutrition will influence maximum height achieved (against the genetic potential), early nutritional deprivation will stunt growth so that genetic potential is never realised, but nutritional deprivation after late puberty will have no effect. This is a great example of an environmental stimulus: the impact of elite training as a child grows is also likely to be significant but as yet this is not fully understood.

You can begin to see that if it is this complicated for a relatively simple phenomenon such as height, then the range of other physical attributes that make a champion (e.g. weight, aerobic capacity, muscle types – fast and slow twitch – lung capacity and so on) will be even harder to clearly ascribe to genes. Any explanations that point as evidence to one or two genes are missing the point: what is happening, even for height, is a very, very complex genetic interaction.

One of the difficulties is the way in which genetic studies are reported. Take this from the respected *New Scientist*. The headline suggests one thing, 'Endurance running is in East Africans' genes'[8] but the science in the magazine article suggests another:

> The athletes do show differences from the population as a whole. But they are not so overwhelming to say that this is the reason for their success … and no single gene for endurance running emerged.[9]

However, there are some promising avenues of recent research which resonate with all of us and point to where we might be headed in the future.

How do you respond to training?

Canadian Claude Bouchard is slowly turning received wisdom on its head: it was assumed that training makes everyone fitter. Now after 30 years' work Bouchard and others are proving that how fitness levels develop is partly dependent on genes.

Identical twins have the same DNA. Scientists love to study those who have come from the same sperm–egg combination since it means they can investigate to what extent our genes and other influences determine talent. Bouchard and colleagues in Canada explored this further. In one experiment he found that when inactive people were trained in exactly the same way for 20 weeks the improvement in aerobic capacity among twins was almost identical when compared to the randomness of the general population. He suggested that peoples' baseline aerobic capacity (VO_2max) and the way people respond to training was due to genetics. By comparing families, Bouchard was able to determine that genes determined about 50 per cent of that variability and the presence or absence of 21 specific genetic variants.

After further probing he established that one in seven people after a period of sustained training only manage to improve their VO_2max by 8 per cent, not so good, while a smaller proportion (one in twelve) responded to training far better by improving their test score by 28 per cent, far better. Not only that but they could even predict which group someone would fall into (i.e. good responders/ poor responders) with sophisticated screening of the 21 genetic variants. Those who carry 9 or fewer would not make it as an endurance athlete while those carrying 19 or more variants had the innate attribute of benefiting from training.

So it is fair to say that those who inherit the best responding genetic profile have the *potential* to raise their endurance capacity to champion levels. Many people have the potential but only a few realise it. Conversely if you do not have the 21 genetic variants it is unlikely you would ever make it in an endurance-based discipline. What genes indicate is not an absolute measure but the increased probability of a phenomenon.

So it is likely that virtually all the champions in this book are genetic 'responders' to training. Those champions whose events could be considered to fit the 'endurance' label include ironwoman Chrissie Wellington, athletes Seb Coe, Kelly Holmes and Mo Farah, Tour de France winners Bradley Wiggins and Chris Froome and rowers Steven Redgrave and Matthew Pinsent. Of course, endurance capability underpins virtually every other sport – how important do you think Federer or Murray would say endurance is after playing over four hours of tennis?

You might be starting to think about the implications of all this for genetic testing – we'll address this, but we first need to cover two further interesting developments.

Oxygen: in sickness and health

How efficiently we use oxygen is decisive both in sport and for those who are severely ill. The lungs deliver oxygen to the blood, the heart pumps that blood and blood vessels deliver the oxygen to the brain and muscles via tiny capillary networks. This sickness-and-health line of enquiry is what interests Hugh Montgomery and his team based at University College Hospital, London. He is credited with discovering one of the first 'fitness genes' in the mid-1990s.

Training is all about the body system's adaptation to increased demands. In 1994 Montgomery looked for a training environment in which people were all being pushed hard in training and in which variables were kept reasonably constant, for example: uniform age/gender, diet, living conditions and coaching style. The choice of studying 17-year-old-army recruits in their initial training was a creative masterstroke. He even did internal scans of recruits to see what happened to their hearts through training.

A remarkable finding emerged, in which those recruits with one particular gene variant experienced three times as much heart-growth through training than others who had another gene variant. A number of other studies of this one gene followed, including another piece of leftfield thinking some 10 years later.

Imagine the scene high on the slopes of Europe's highest mountain, Mont Blanc, in France. Here Montgomery's team waited over a number of days almost four kilometers above sea level in the Gouter mountain hut (3807m). Using great tact they politely asked sweaty, probably smelly, tired climbers as they arrived if they could take mouth swabs to test for the two gene variants – they took specimens from the 284 climbers and then recorded which climbers made it to the summit 1000m further up into the clouds. When the results were analysed one gene variation showed 100 per cent summit success while the other showed only an 87 per cent success rate.[10]

The gene they were tracing was called ACE or angiotensin-converting enzyme. The ACE gene has about 110 variants. ACE activates a hormone, which helps to maintain blood pressure and promotes the growth of the heart in response to exercise. One common gene variant carried by about 25 per cent of us, known as ACE 'D', makes more enzyme than the other common version, ACE 'I' (carried by another 25 per cent of us). The difference between the two variants is so marked that it was the athletes with ACE 'D' who experienced the heart-growth finding while it was those with ACE 'I' genes, associated with efficient use of energy and oxygen, that comprised the 100 per cent successful Mont Blanc group of climbers.

In elite sport those with ACE 'D' perform better in speed and power orientated sports, such as weightlifting or sprinting. The 'I' variant, in contrast, is more prevalent among Caucasian endurance athletes in endurance sports such as long-distance running, road cycling and rowing.

Montgomery, wondered whether ACE 'I' might also be advantageous to those suffering serious illness. For example, he found that those who were very ill with acute respiratory distress syndrome (ARDS) were five times more likely to survive than those with the ACE 'D' variant.[11] His work has also been extended to seriously ill children and premature babies whose conditions were linked with depleted oxygen use. 'Our work on athletes is feeding back into the clinic,' says Montgomery. 'How efficiently we use oxygen is decisive when we are desperately sick.'[12]

Once again the media reporting of a genetic discovery is unfortunate. It reinforces beliefs that a gene holds all the answers. For example, take this one about the ACE gene: 'Brazilian football star Ronaldo's breathtaking dribbles ... can be due to the "fitness gene" that scientists have recently identified'.[13] Its popular labeling as 'the fitness gene' (singular) distracts from the roles of other genes and the wider implications of Montgomery's work.

Injury propensity

If Rafa Nadal is reading this he might be interested. Most of us have suffered an injury of one sort or another and, in some, it often seems to be the same repeated injury that blights a sporting career. We know that considerable practice and training volume is needed to be a champion. Intriguingly, South Africans Ross Tucker and Malcolm Collins have presented strong evidence that injury propensity can partly be identified through genes. Therefore you'll never reach the top if your body can't sustain a high training volume. For example, you may have extraordinary stature and aerobic capacity to be a fine swimmer like Ian Thorpe, but if you are in a higher risk category for shoulder injury then you are unlikely to be able to train enough to get to the top.

A little more detail. The Anterior Cruciate Ligament (ACL) is well known and feared in sport. It is not something that any would-be champion wants to hear a medic talk about. It is frequently only mentioned in the context of pain and injury. The ACL is part of a very complicated joint: the knee. An ACL injury ranges from a slight tear to a rupture, and since knee stability is fundamental to most sporting movement, it can be a serious obstacle to sporting progress. Tucker and Collins have looked in detail at the ACL along with tendon (shoulder and Achilles) ruptures. They have identified genes that influence the structural proteins, the building blocks of tendons/ligaments. They found genetic variants that are prevalent with those who have less risk of injury (a sort of protective function) and those who are connected to increased risk of injury. These genetic markers apply to chronic injuries (i.e. a long-developing syndrome) as opposed to acute conditions (these are severe and sudden in onset).[14]

It is still early days in this research and it is likely that other markers might be identified for other types of injuries such as stress fractures. However, Collins and most other experts in this field warn that genetic screening is not yet sophisticated:

> One of the risks that can take place if you go down the road of trying to determine your genetic ability based on our current understanding is that you will be given the wrong information ... we're only identifying a very small handful of genes so if we now send DNA to test for one or two of those genes it measures nothing, it is only a very small component which contributes to the whole.[15]

These three research examples demonstrate that it is a complicated field, not helped by simplistic media reporting. There are some interesting developments that directly relate to elite performance. But when I consulted an expert in genes and human disease he cautioned:

> We have been continually disappointed to find a significant number of the major 'associations' between disease and genes turn out to be false leads. Despite having huge groups of many thousands of individuals, many associations between genetic variants and physical performance characteristics may simply turn out to be similar false dawns for many complex reasons.[16]

It is indeed too early to draw firm conclusions. However, there's just one more important factor to consider, something called epigenetics.

Genes × environment = epigenetics

This heading will become clear soon. In the early decades of genetic research DNA was considered to be our destiny – this is no longer true since it is now realised there are also interactions between genes and the environment. Consider two environmental factors in a champion's development: high training volumes and exposure to very stressful situations (e.g. competition). These may interact with particular genes in a way not yet fully understood. Dr Jeff Craig speaking on ABC (Australia) explained it this way:

> Our genes are just lengths of DNA; they don't do anything by themselves – they need something to turn the gene on and turn the gene off. This is where epigenetics comes in. Epigenetics literally means 'above' genetics and it refers to the tags that sit on top of our DNA … It's like having a dimmer switch. A light bulb in a socket doesn't do anything by itself; it needs power, an on/off switch and a dimmer switch to turn it up or down.[17]

The idea that chemical reactions that switch the genes on and off could play a part is rather hard to study in humans. Instead, one of the first experiments to establish this was on rats (bear with me!).

Canadian research considered the connection between a mother rat's attentiveness to her offspring and the 'success' of her offspring. Those mothers who scored highly for attentiveness (i.e. licking and grooming behaviours) reared young that were more curious, bolder and dominant. A part of the pup's genes activated by the grooming attention from her mum was identified as related to the stress hormone cortisol. Therefore an epigenetic chemical change had been detected as a result of an environmental stimulus. And that change stayed with these pups; they were more robust and could cope better with stress both as youngsters and in later life.[18]

What does this mean for humans? The phrasing of genes 'multiplied by' environment implies that, for us humans, genetic dimming switches are turned up or down depending what happens to us. So what young athletes are exposed to at home, with coaches and perhaps even what they eat, might trigger as yet unknown genetic adaptations. Hopefully in years to come we'll know more about these dimmer switch interactions between environment and genes, but I suspect that two things will be at the forefront of how genes respond to extreme stress, trauma and long-term training.

Final thoughts

The story of a 24-year-old champion's path to the top illustrates some final thoughts of these three introductory chapters.

British 2012 Olympic Gold Medallist, Joanna Rowsell

Joanna, tall at 1.80m (5ft 10in), was academic and studied hard at her local secondary school but wasn't originally particularly 'sporty'. Despite this tag she always showed up for the 1500m on sports day and beat everybody without any training.

Then the cycling talent scouts came to her school. She was 15; she was curious. She did the sprint, laps and static bike tests and guess what? Although the scouts did not let on at the time, she had the highest power output for a girl of her age that they'd ever seen.

She commenced training. Both before and after school she'd train, often in darkness, and most weekends were spent competing around the country. 'My dad would drive me, which I think was pretty tiring for him. He'd have to get up early every day of the week for his job at HSBC' (the bank), then stand in the cold all weekend watching her race.

She did well in her exams but delayed taking up a confirmed place at university. The Olympics seemed a remote dream even when she joined the British Cycling Academy at 18, only intending it to be a 'year out' as a professional cyclist.

For five years before the 2012 Olympics, she lived in Manchester taking part in the academy programme; a full-time training commitment every day, 8 a.m.– 10 a.m. on the track and then up to five hours endurance training on the road in the afternoon.[19]

Joanna's progress to gold took nine years of hard work in which she realised her genetic potential (height and more importantly, cycling power output). In this case she found her sport through physical testing as a teenager, unlike any of the other champions in this book (largely because such testing was rare in Western Europe pre-1998). She also had the support of her father in her early years of racing around the country. She then had the passion and deep seated hunger to succeed and to train full-time for five years without injury blocking her progress.

Perhaps those sports disciplines that are measured in seconds (cycling, running, swimming, rowing, triathlon, canoeing), centimetres (jumping, throwing) and grammes (weightlifting) have a more direct link to genetic potential since they are largely concerned with optimising physical performance. Other team sports or skill-based sports have physical components, but also a complex set of skills and strategy that need to be refined. This is a crude distinction but does illustrate a potential difference in genetic influences of champions from different disciplines.

The final part of Joanna's story suggest that this book's focus beyond physical and genetic potential is warranted. She had a condition called alopecia (the hair-loss disorder, *alopecia areata*) which made her go bald – not easy for a teenager. As a result she was very shy and her self-worth must have been affected, so originally she focused intensely on her exam work. Working hard was the only thing that distracted her from worrying about the future. Then cycling came along and it provided a compensatory outlet at which she could achieve. She had extra drive as a result of her condition since it probably provided a way of reaffirming self-worth. 'I worked through any worries I had about my hair and I focused solely on [training hard]. It made me who I am.'[20] (For more on the impact of negative life episodes see chapter 12).

I'm beginning to detect different types of paths to the top (e.g. Joanna Rowsell and Kelly Holmes). Think of five champions you know of: to what extent is it possible to broadly categorise different routes to the top?

Part II

From child to elite athlete

4 How do champions' paths differ?

When do champions' early steps in sport start diverging from those of the average person? The appeal of sporting champions' stories largely lies in the transformation from the ordinariness of early lives to what follows. The majority of champions' childhood experiences are like the girl or boy next door until they start training in earnest. We may even see similarities to our own childhoods.

To explore how champions start out and begin diverging from the rest of us we will compare developmental biographical stories. There is also plenty of research about different routes to the top; combining both enables us to identify a marker that starts to discriminate between different champions' stories: the age they start training in earnest and their first global podium moment. Using this there are five discernable genres of champions' stories:

1. The *extreme nurture* story: Andre Agassi and others, particularly in tennis, gymnastics and golf (e.g. Tiger Woods), who specialised in a single sport above all other activities at an early age, frequently before the age of 10. Agassi almost exclusively specialised in tennis from the age of 7 and left mainstream school to concentrate on tennis when he was 14. While extreme nurture as an approach is increasingly questioned in the West it is now becoming more popular in the East – take a look at China (in Olympic sports), Korea (womens' golf) and Eastern Europe (tennis).
2. The *early champion story*: Michael Phelps and Ian Thorpe provide examples of early champions. Phelps and Thorpe specialised in swimming relatively early, became world champions by the age of 15 and 16 respectively and soon started breaking world records. Almost every sport has its early champions who quickly rise to the top and subsequent World Championship/Olympic participation at 18 or 19 years of age. Not just in individual sports but in teams. Look at football: Lionel Messi (Argentina), Michael Owen (England) and Wayne Rooney (England), among others, energised their national teams in their early appearances. Top-level performance before the age of 16 years is generally limited to a few sports, such as swimming, gymnastics and ice skating.
3. The *gradual progress* story: the majority of champions, including Usain Bolt, have this more gradual narrative of slow progress. Three out of four champions' autobiographies used in this book describe this more typical drawn out sporting journey. Unlike the extreme nurture and early champion

stories, these athletes sampled a range of sports as youngsters (this is known as 'sporting diversification') and achieved podium success after the age of 19 or later (see chapter 5 for further discussion of sampling and diversification). Usain Bolt's story is an interesting one. Remarkably he ran his favoured 200m event just 0.8 sec (4.2 per cent) outside the then senior world record at the age of 16. In a moment we explore why it took him five more years of stuttering progress to finally achieve senior success in 2008.

4. The *fast-track* or *transfer* story: this is a relatively new phenomenon in which mature athletes with a diverse sporting past are identified and transferred into other sports. A striking recent example is that of British rower, Heather Glover, who, four years prior to winning Olympic gold in 2012, had never picked up an oar. Hence the fast-track tag. Notably, athletes with this unusual type of story, to date, have not had time to write autobiographies! This type of story will, I predict, become more commonplace as adult identification and coaching of potential podium athletes becomes more widespread. Think of all the excellent athletes that do not get offered professional contracts in soccer or American football who might thrive in other sports if given the opportunity.

5. And finally, the *late bloomer* story: these are not so common, and depend partly on what age you think constitutes 'late blooming'. Remarkably, Chrissie Wellington started competitive triathlon racing at the age of 27 and by the age of 30 had won the first of four world Ironman titles – now, that is what I call a late arrival on the scene! She too, like the *gradual progress* and *fast-track* stories, had a diverse range of sporting experiences in her younger years. Champions blooming at such an age are unusual and are different to those one might talk about as simply being late developers whose maturation was delayed.

Usain Bolt's stuttering progress to gold

Despite making it look so easy when he wins gold medals, this champion, like many others, faced some difficult twists and turns to get to the top, which is why it is worth looking behind his world records. Yes, being 1.95m (6ft 5in) and lightning fast at the age of 15 meant his genes had given him the physical attributes to be a potential winner, but his own account of the challenges he faced over the next five years is a fascinating insight into what shaped him. Some of the main difficulties he faced are very commonly found in other champions' paths, making some tentative generalisations possible from his progress to the top.

Let's start with what he calls his 'greatest ever race': which medal or world record race do you think sticks out for him? Surprisingly, he identifies his 200m World Junior Championship victory in 2002, aged 15, because of the mountain he had to climb at that tender age against athletes up to four years his senior.

He also had the challenge of it being staged in Kingston, Jamaica in front of a 30,000-strong home crowd hungry for his success – his mother, with grandmother alongside, had to convince him not to pull out when Bolt was in tears of self-doubt weeks beforehand. His mother and grandmother prompted him to 'Do your best. What ever you do, we'll accept it. We'll be proud'.[1]

Bolt experienced massive pre-race nerves and anxiety, and could hardly put his shoes on or put one foot in front of the other, so overcome was he with tension. Bolt calls it '[his] first Big Moment ... [he] had not collapsed under the weight of Jamaica's expectation'.[2] It taught him a lot about, in his words, his mental strength being a tool in every race.

After this staggering 200m success under intense pressure as a 15-year-old (the only Jamaican gold at the championships) let's examine what happened next. The countdown of the next five years to his Beijing triple world record and gold medal triumph illustrates how negative episodes and challenges shaped his path.

Aged 16: Moving away and adjustment

Bolt moved away from home for the first time living with a trusted mentor. He started training full-time at the Kingston High Performance Centre and struggled to keep up, saying his body was in shock from the extra workload. Bolt also faced many distractions, having moved from 'living in the sticks' to the capital city; balancing his play with his athletic preparation is a continuing theme of Bolt's career.

Despite winning the senior trials for the World Championships in Paris, he had to rest up and put his training on hold while he recovered from conjunctivitis of the eye. He still went to Paris without competing, in order to gain experience. Remember Bolt was still just 16.

Aged 17: Tension, injury and an unsettling diagnosis

Bolt expressed alarm and grumbled at his coach's training regime as reoccurring back and leg pain continued into his second year of training. Then, a pulled hamstring meant Bolt spends much of the Olympic year (2004) in rehabilitation. He realises the challenge that injury represents. Injuries 'are about self-discovery as well as recovery: learning in the mind is as important as understanding the body'.

Bolt describes how he had to learn about pain thresholds, patience and inner strength through bitter experience. He also learnt something about himself that 'in times of physical stress, [he] picked up doubts'.[3] He sounds like most 17-year-olds would do under duress; confidence can slip away as quickly as you grasp hold of it.

Although selected for the Athens Olympics, negative thoughts dogged Bolt in every training session during the build up. He flew to Germany to visit back injury specialist, Dr Hans Muller-Wohlfahrt. Scoliosis of the back was the unsettling diagnosis; curvature of the spine compounded by his right leg being half an inch shorter than the left. An imbalance particularly ill-suited to running around left-hand bends at close to world record speed on an athletics track! Think about which leg needs to act as if it is longer around a bend.

Although, pre-injury, Bolt ran the world's fastest time at 200m that year, he attended the Athens Olympics low on both confidence and conditioning. In his qualifying heat at the Games, Bolt did not have the heart to fight for fourth place, which would allow progression to the next round. It is amazing to hear this now, but Bolt admits giving his place away to finish fifth. Much negative press followed in Jamaica, and this was hard for an emerging 17-year-old billed as the nation's next sprinting wunderkind after his earlier World Junior Championships success.

Aged 18: Changing coach

Bolt's Athens Olympic experience forced him into a decision about his coach. In consultation with his mentor, Bolt approached a new coach, Glen Mills. Mills used a new slow, gradual development approach as part of a four-year plan, including revised medical support for Bolt's scoliosis. For most of the first year Bolt ran in modest level meetings to rebuild his confidence. At the World Championships in Helsinki, he progressed to the 200m final but a fourth place in the semi-final meant Bolt got lane 1: the worst possible lane draw in the final for a tall rangy athlete. Bolt led coming out of the turn but muscle cramps cause him to pull up and finish last. Seemingly not a good outcome.

Mills, with masterful coaching, made it a hugely positive experience by providing skilful feedback and praising him for the ability he showed in coping with lane 1. As they met track side in the stadium afterwards Mills grinned widely congratulating Bolt on the first part of the race, 'you discovered the heart of a champion'.[4] Tellingly – Bolt remembers the moment vividly in his autobiography even naming a chapter with those words, 'the heart of a champion'.

Aged 19: Gradual progress tainted by Jamaican fans' derision

Bolt began to challenge his American 200m rivals harder but this was tainted by being widely booed by Jamaican fans when he pulled up again with hamstring problems in front of his home crowd Kingston. Bolt's fans' derision at his efforts was a catalyst for huge self-doubt. Coach Mills also faced public criticism for allegedly squandering Bolt's talent. Together they steered through the crisis and Bolt learned another important lesson about who he was training and competing for: Mills implored him to not 'worry about what other people think'[5] and do it for his own motives. Athletes can easily get caught up in media hype and national expectation and this was an important episode in helping him understand exactly why he was pursuing his sport.

Aged 20: Learning from defeat and taking responsibility

One race changed everything for Bolt: the World Championships 200m final in Osaka, 2007. Tyson Gay ran past him off the bend to take gold, and Bolt took his first major senior medal, a silver. At 2 a.m. the night after the race, Bolt couldn't sleep and wanted to know why he was beaten after initially leading. He knocked on the door of his bleary eyed coach … once awake, Mills told him straight 'You're slacking off in the gym [conditioning]'.[6] From then on Bolt did everything that was asked of him in training and started to build the strength that would allow him to burst off the bend and maintain his high knee lift. Each year brought another lesson and this one was about the priority of focused conditioning work in the gym, particularly important with his back condition.

We associate Bolt now with his success at the blue ribbon Olympic 100m event. But such was his focus on cracking the 200m event and his enormous height being considered by many, including Mills, as a disadvantage, that even aged 20 he had not run the shorter distance as a senior. Bolt continually pestered his coach to let him try the 100m, and his coach reluctantly agreed, provided he could better a target of 10.30 seconds at a small meeting in Crete. He flew to the Greek island and achieved 10.03 seconds. The world of 100m running never looked the same again.

Aged 21: History beckons

After focused winter months of gym work, training for both distances and five years of zigzagging gradual upward progress, Bolt ran a new 100m world record in New York during May, announcing his arrival in his new event. Beijing beckoned and the rest is history, 10 years after he chose athletics over cricket as his main sport at the age of 11.

The social environment of living in Jamaica meant that his physique would inevitably mean him being directed towards one or other of two national sports: athletics or cricket. Usain Bolt's path to the top is a good illustration of the combination of physical, mental and social factors and his own set of key episodes along the way which moulded how he thought about conditioning, defeat, injury, national expectation and mental tools. Without finally taking personal responsibility for his conditioning and learning from these key episodes he would have been vulnerable when facing his final steps to the summit.

The fast-track path

Now let's turn to examples of those with a faster trajectory than Bolt's 10 years to get to the top. Measuring how rapidly an athlete makes it to a senior World/Olympic podium[7] after they specialised in their sport is a way of comparing the speed of development between different champions. Kelly Holmes made it to the podium 13 years after starting dedicated training (see chapter 1); Usain Bolt took 10; Chrissie Wellington took three years. Here we consider the fast-track story in more detail, since it illuminates some of the fallacies of counting how long it takes to succeed. It also highlights further truths about what shapes champions.

On 1 August 2012, Heather Glover achieved her Olympic rowing dream. However, it was not just her dream fulfilled: it marked the first gold medal for the host nation, Great Britain, which had nervously awaited a podium-topping moment. Glover's fast-track four years is at the shorter end of the time continuum it takes to become an Olympic gold medallist.

Let's remind ourselves of the full criteria used in UK Sport's talent transfer scheme, whcih Glover was a part of. The call for applicants for this scheme asked for those who were:

- aged between 15 and 22 years old;
- exceptionally tall (men over 1.90m (6ft 2in) and women over 1.80m (5ft 9in));
- competing in any sport at a *minimum* of county/regional level;
- quick, agile and skilful *and/or* fit, powerful and strong;
- mentally tough and competitive;

up for a once in a lifetime opportunity to become part of Britain's sporting elite.

Note the combination of physical (i.e. genetic) and mental characteristics. The physical can be measured accurately provided puberty has worked its maturation magic. Mental characteristics can only be identified in the initial interviews, and even then to a fairly minimal extent. Think of how a job interview has a limited ability to identify a person's inner abilities but later, while in a job role, a new employee reveals their true self. In sport talent transfer, there is greater certainty of the right athletes being identified when pressure is applied in training and competition, i.e. a few years after physical identification tests.

Helen's sporting credentials suggested she was physically very able but had not found her elite niche and had focused instead on qualifying as a PE teacher. Glover attended a prestigious sporting school, Millfield, and as a result participated in a wider variety of sports than many: as a junior she ran county cross-country (for Cornwall) and internationally for England; played tennis for Cornwall; swam for Cornwall; captained the county hockey team and was part of a national satellite squad for hockey – an impressive record. Yet she'd not progressed further in any of these sports:

> [She] only started rowing in 2008 when [she] got through the Sporting Giants scheme where [she] was basically chosen for being tall and sporty ... [UK Sport] tested 4,500 of [them] in groups of 200 at a time. [She] remembers sitting in a room in Bisham Abbey in 2007 and someone saying: 'A gold medallist in 2012 could be sitting in this room. Look around you.' [She] thought: 'Right, I'm going to make that me.' [She said] 'It was quite surreal.'[8]

Glover's experience of making gold with four years of training questions the 10-year theory which originally derives from the research of Anders Ericsson in the early 1990s. The appeal of the 10-year message is its simplicity. You can become a champion with a strong work ethic, the right opportunities and the right environment. Subsequent authors, including Malcolm Gladwell, have suggested that talent is 'overrated' or a 'myth', downplaying the importance of natural giftedness; this line of argument suggests it is more about determination, hard work and quality practice.

The 10,000 hour rule, as it is also known, roughly equates to 10 years (20 hours x 50 weeks x 10 years) of perspiration to get to the top. Little wonder this theory – and books that have derived from it downplay talent – these accounts emphasise graft and are popular in the business community. But does it still add up?

It is a truism that we all improve with practice, but advocates of the 10,000 hour rule go further: it is the quality of practice that is important. Few would disagree that the ability to work persistently at weaknesses and respond to feedback and setbacks while refining the different components of your sport is more important than just playing a lot. It also follows that excellent coaching is needed, as well as a deep-seated desire to continually improve – i.e. a learning orientation combined with a strong drive.

However, there is controversy about the precise quantity of practice needed, since the 10,000 hour rule was derived from Ericsson's research, in which he asked top musicians in 1993 to retrospectively recall their practice behaviour. It is a shame therefore that the catchy memorable 'rule' is now widely quoted and used to determine youth training policy despite it being a falsehood.

How the magical 10,000 hour number was invented and now wrongly guides some elite football training

The author of the original research, Anders Ericsson, from Florida State University is irked. In 2012 he issued a blunt rebuttal saying that the 10,000 hour rule was invented by author Malcolm Gladwell, who cited his research as a stimulus for provocative generalisation to a magical number. He says that in fact, 10,000 hours was the *average* of the best group of musicians he studied and most of this group had accumulated substantially fewer hours of practice at age 20.[9] His argument is partly contained in the title of his rebuttal: 'The Danger of Delegating Education to Journalists'.

So the original researcher is very annoyed at the generalisation of his research to a magical 10,000 hours, yet in many sports it has been used to justify approaches to youth training. For example, in football, the whole 2011 'Elite Player Performance Plan' of the English Premier League, which determines how top young players aspiring towards a professional contract are prepared, is based on the 10,000 hour fallacy.

As a result, in English football academies contact time with coaches has trebled, with the aim of reaching the magic 10,000 hours by the time players turn 21. What this does is increase downward age pressure to somehow identify the best young players at an increasingly younger age to accumulate the magic 10,000 hours in formal training. Identifying potential at any age before physical maturity is at best extremely difficult, some would say impossible.

The danger is that those youngsters selected specialise at a very young age, and structured coaching rather than spontaneous playing with friends becomes the focus. Is this single sport specialisation and commercial interests to nurture players going too far? Some think so.[10]

The use of contested research aside, let's come back to what Helen Glover's story demonstrates.

Athletes can change from one sport to another if they have sufficient physical capabilities, sporting experience and mental tools. The best athletes can reach international level in a very short time – sometimes in less than two years. Other cases include Rebecca Romaro, whose transformation from British silver medallist rower to gold medallist cyclist took place between two Olympic Games – Athens (2004) and Beijing (2008).

My question is: 'to what extent is the fast-track story most likely to occur in sports measured in *seconds* and/or in which *physique* and conditioning is paramount where the number of athletes in a country is limited?'

In Australia, the Australian Institute of Sport (AIS) had some success bringing new athletes into women's sprint cycling in 2002. Then in 2004, with the introduction of skeleton (the ice 'sled') to the Winter Olympics the AIS wanted to identify women with the potential to qualify for the 2006 Torino Olympics within two years. An ambitious goal.

Talent transfer may indeed suit sports in which there is a limited pool of existing competitors – therefore when any new Olympic discipline emerges, scientists start thinking, 'what if'? In the case of skeleton sliding, sprinting ability over 30m is a key part of the talent profile of the sport as it launches them down the track. In Australia, Michele Steele a surf life-saver who excelled at beach sprinting was identified and immersed in training and competition environments. She qualified for the Olympics within 14 months, finishing 13th at the 2006 Games. From being 'on the beach' to on Olympic ice in 14 months is a staggering transformation. The UK has specialised in transferring those with sprinting speed into women's skeleton sliding – such transferred athletes have made the podium every Olympics since 2002. In a relatively small sport with only 17 venues worldwide, better to find speed and teach sliding rather than vice versa.

Meanwhile UK Sport is also seeking to transfer athletes in a number of other programmes. One initiative is called 'Fighting Chance' – aimed at the relatively new Olympic combat sport taekwondo. It is expanding the talent pool of a small sport by recruiting 16–26-year-olds from existing combat sports that use kicking and those displaying 'lightning reactions and decision making' and 'desire and determination for success'.

Michelle Steele: from the beach to Olympic ice in 14 months

Taekwondo is obviously not a sport measured in seconds: tactics and detailed movement patterns need to be learnt. There have also been initiatives to find suitable very tall athletes to develop in handball and volleyball, sports in which Great Britain has very few players.

It seems that early talent-transfer successes were initially related to sports measured in seconds and where physique is paramount, but it is now an evolving field as the taekwondo, volleyball and handball examples suggest.

Helen Glover and other examples of a rapid rise to gold demonstrate that determination and the necessary mental tools can combine with potent effect as long as the athlete has learnt how to compete, move and train to at least regional level before transferring. Glover has embarked on her second Olympiad and has already won a World Championship gold since her 2012 success.

Final thoughts

It is tempting to view the five genres of champions' stories as the definitive paths to success. That would be far too neat a categorisation since, while there might be similarities at the start, after a few years each athlete's path follows its own largely individualised, complicated and dynamic course.

Each athlete has their own complex story as different influences interact; no two biographies are the same, even in athletes in the same sport, born at the same time and in the same place. Instead, the focus in the rest of this book is on identifying a number of the key episodes, attitudes, behaviours and chance factors that shape their paths as we started to do in looking at Usain Bolt's path to gold. Understanding how champions learn from and respond to key episodes is illuminating and is explored further in chapters 10, 12, 13 and 15.

The foundation of all champions' stories is how they take the all-important early steps in sport and what sets them on different paths. At one end of the continuum are those who specialise in one sport all year round from under the age of 10 (e.g. Tiger Woods, Andre Agassi) while at the other are those who play many sports, often becoming good at a variety before eventually in late adolescence choosing which one to pursue further (e.g. Chris Hoy, cycling). These crucial early steps and the implications of some of these early sporting decisions is the focus of the next chapter.

5 From playground to podium
Playing then specialising

One of the most respected rugby coaches in Britain and a former international player, Ian McGeechan, explained his early sporting experiences:

> There was nothing structured about my early sporting career. I had the classic street-games background ... you would just play whatever sport was appropriate ... in whatever version ... on whatever surface was available ... the opportunities for practising ball skills, for sharpening reactions, were endless. I would ... see how many times consecutively I could hit the target [kicking]. I would also bowl for hours against a lamppost, entirely on my own. We even used to play football and cricket on the cobbles. Imagine the reactions you needed for that ... I used to play tennis for hours, hitting the ball against the wall.[1]

In this chapter we explore the playground to podium[2] journey and the optimum period for youngsters to specialise in a sport to the exclusion of others, alongside four important motivational 'nutrients' that young athletes need for healthy development. At one end of the scale we have champions in sports like gymnastics or swimming in which children specialise early, often under 10 years of age, while at the other, champions in many sports like Ian McGeechan (rugby) or Chris Hoy (cycling) specialise in late adolescence (16–18 years) or beyond.

There is a tension, however, for youngsters, parents and coaches; I will show that it is less risky – in terms of overall physical and mental well-being – to delay specialiation. But if you want to be an adolescent star, starting earlier will put you ahead of your peers and increase the chances of *early* success. The 'normal' or average age of specialisation among champions is around mid-adolescence (14–16 years), of course, like any average, there is a whole lot of variation either side of this but it is a useful reference point. For example, Usain Bolt's choice to concentrate on athletics over cricket at the age of 11 can be viewed as earlier specialisation than many other champions, but by no means extreme.

Playfulness

Larking around, game playing, using imagination and having fun – you may fondly remember, as Ian McGeechan did, your early experimentation at sports played both alone or with others. This is prompted by children's own interest and parent's willingness to let them get on with it, provided they are safe. It basically develops strong enjoyment of the sport, which underpins later passion and specialised training.

A prominent researcher in this area is Canadian Jean Côté. He terms this early play and sampling 'deliberate play' and 'spontaneous practice' and places it at the heart of enjoyable early experiences in sport. Activities such as backyard soccer or street basketball/hockey use adapted rules and are set up and monitored either by children themselves or adults. Côté says these activities, 'are intrinsically motivating, provide immediate gratification and are specifically designed to maximize enjoyment'.[3]

A Irishman now living and working in Kenya agrees. Picture this, on a chilly autumn day in 2012, Father Colm O'Connell, an Irish priest, sat next to a 23-year-old Kenyan of the Masai, named David Rhodesia (800m World Record holder and 2012 Olympic champion): they were watching the Munster team O'Connell supported play in rugby's Heineken Cup. Why? As coach to numerous Kenyan running champions over almost 40 years, Father O'Connell was on a tour of his homeland with the protégée he had coached to success in Kenya and beyond. This gently spoken man is an iconic figure in Kenyan running coaching. He outlines his own approach to guiding young people:

> Very often when you have a young kid who is enthusiastic and they go out and run when they are at primary school, they're running out of sheer enjoyment, teamwork or representing their school and they have that very basic motivation. Now, when they come to me maybe to do a little bit more formal training in the programme [as a teenager] you have to be very careful to try to retain their original reason for becoming athletes, for wanting to join the sport rather than becoming too regimented in your training – and suddenly that can turn off kids.
>
> I want them to kind of lock in to the enjoyment and the concept of doing what they feel is instinctive; what they *like* doing. That must be very central to their lives before they start formal training.[4]

Father O'Connell is pointing us towards the value of young peoples' early training still being playful, not being too regimented when they start, and finding ways to still feed off their instinctive passion. He, Côté, and others claim it is children's playfulness that makes their early engagement with sport so much fun.

Child development experts say that spontaneity and free experimentation help to develop adaptability and creativity in a safe, low-risk environment. A number of studies have identified a variety of playful activities' importance in skill acquisition and motor learning.[5]

Across the Atlantic, Michael Johnson agrees, but he calls it 'athleticism':

> Most of the kids who come into my ... performance centre have already started to specialise in one sport as early as age 10, so they lack the athleticism that we kids from the seventies developed from playing multiple sports.[6]

I hadn't fully appreciated it when I started coaching but basic movement skills such as running, jumping, throwing, catching, kicking, bouncing, striking, rotating, falling and even sliding (think of baseball, clay court tennis and ice sports) underpin many sports. They are gradually built upon and progressively linked into sports from play. It has been called the development of *Physical Literacy* (i.e. learning to move and a vocabulary of movement). Some argue that movement skills are similar to learning to write. First children learn sounds, then form words, then learn to link words into sentences; finally, they learn to develop these into writing.[7] As children gradually link together movements, they learn to become physically competent in a range of situations – even on McGeechan's cobblestones.

Parents have a key influence on all this. Statistics suggest that more active parents are likely to have more active children. Children of two active parents are almost six times as likely to be active as children of two inactive parents.[8] It is the parents who largely provide the opportunities to make a range of playful and sporting opportunities available; easier said than done in places where facilities may be limited or child safety is a concern. Where you live has an impact. Contrast an inner city with limited open spaces and against smaller spread out towns or rural villages (see chapter 9 for more on the geography of success).

School physical education (PE) also contributes a large part to introducing a range of sports. Most champions' both name and laud their school PE teachers for inspiring them, often finding them clubs outside of school to help satiate their early sporting passion.

Sampling many sports brings longer term benefit

So far we have used examples of renowned coaches and scientists to explain the benefits of playfully sampling a range of sports. Sampling sporting interests, also termed 'early diversification' by researchers, does not hinder becoming a champion in sports in which peak performance is reached *after* maturation. Jean Côté says that the gradual progress model leads to longer careers and to more sustainable development of the athlete.

Let's consider the cyclist Chris Hoy and his slow steady development. Chris has described his early years of sampling five sports to a high level and the choices he made (see box opposite). He specialised at the age of 17.

Those coaches earning their living in a specialised football or tennis academy might not agree with leaving specialisation until mid- to late adolescence but the evidence from Olympic athletes and champions like Andy Murray is becoming compelling.

In Germany, the biographical details and path of 1560 German national squad athletes across all Olympic sports were analysed.[9] An impressively sized sample. Specialising early favoured early success. Those who started early in their sport achieved adolescent success as a senior: this is largely to be expected. But what was unusual was the comparison of athletes at two different levels: world class (world top-10) and national (national top-10) athletes.

Chris Hoy's varied path to track cycling

Hoy participated in rugby and athletics, then did rowing. He was good at them all, especially rowing, which he loved. He found the trouble with rowing was being limited by his size. In rowing terms, he is pretty short at just 1.85m (6ft 1in). The best rowers in the world, as we know, are 7–10 cm (3–4 in) taller. He knew if he had any ambitions of taking rowing to a higher level, then he was going to have to be a lightweight rower (crew average 70kg (11st) with no rower over 72.5kg (11st 6lb)) but even then he would be rather short.

Chris Hoy: benefited from not being a child champion

He found he was most physically suited to cycling. After racing around the world on the BMX circuit from age 7 to 14, Chris transferred his skills to mountain biking, then road racing. Eventually when he was 17 he *found* track cycling and he was smitten with the experience.[10] By good fortune he lived in Edinburgh, a city that had hosted the Commonwealth Games and therefore had an international standard velodrome and cycling club

Chris Hoy's father emphasised the benefit of Chris not being a child champion:

> He [Chris] was never up there but he just kept plugging away. You've seen other kids who were winning all the time and when they get beaten they don't like it so they stop what they're doing. As long as they're enjoying it and they're doing pretty well, there is not a lot between first and second.[11]

World-class performers differed, showing more previous training in other sports (66 per cent of world performers trained in other sports vs 51 per cent national athletes). They also differed, showing over two years' later specialisation in their main sport at an average age of 14½. These findings support the idea that sampling a range of sports in formative teenage years has benefits later. Recent analysis in the UK backs this up.[12] The thinking from Jean Côté and others is that it may have:

▨ increased the probability of matching athletes with the sport discipline they are most suited for;
▨ eased the progress in their main sport due to more varied stimuli and experiences for learning physical literacy and movement skills, and
▨ reduced the risk of injury or staleness if one sport is the sole focus.

But above all, keeping sport fun and varied at a young age helps fuel later, more formal training.

Specialising early

How soon youngsters get into serious training depends on the culture and practices in a sport – the age profile of some sports is definitely lower than others – you don't see many Olympians over 30 in swimming or gymnastics. This is partly each sport's culture, but also something far more controversial: how much parents push their children.

The early specialisation sports are those in which peak performance can be reached before maturation (e.g. female gymnastics and figure skating). These sports and other examples feature *early champion stories* (see chapter 4) largely due to the young age at which individuals have started focused training. For example:

▨ swimming: Ian Thorpe, Michael Phelps, Ruta Meilutyte (Lithuanian 2012 Olympic Gold medalist).
▨ tennis: Boris Becker, Maria Sharapova.
▨ soccer: Lionel Messi, Michael Owen, Wayne Rooney.
▨ diving: Tom Daley (2009 World Champion and 2012 Olympic bronze medalist).

There is an ongoing debate about how young is too young to specialise in these and other sports.

The number of child prodigy parables in sport feeds stories such as Bill Finley's article in the *New York Times*, 'A Single Goal in Common',[13] in which it was reported that a growing number of coaches, parents and children believe that the best way to produce sports success is to have them play only one sport from an early age, and to play it virtually year-round. Yes, as we saw in the German Olympic study it does increase the chances of early adolescent success but athletes can be vulnerable later.

The way some sport is organised rather encourages this specialisation approach. In 2013, a dramatic documentary, *The Short Game*, followed eight pint-sized golfers as they prepared for and took part in the Junior World Golf Championships. If an under-10 category in a sport is staged and is called a world championships, the organisers are encouraging extreme nurture and early specialisation. This seems unnecessary. Previous winners of the under-10 category include Tiger Woods (1984) and, in a similar event, Rory McIlroy (2000).

Growing concern about the risks of early specialisation led two sports medicine organisations to issue statements about the evidence of such practices.[14] Their findings caution that 'risks include higher rates of injury, increased psychological stress, and quitting sports at a young age' and reiterate that 'limiting experiences to a single sport is not the best path to elite status'. The evidence mounts.

The fixation with early specialisation and the realisation of the hugely increased chances of early adolescent success that it brings, is spreading around the world. Rasmus Ankerson, among others, has highlighted the hubs of excellence for women's tennis in Russia (producing 25 per cent of the world's top players) and women's golf in Korea (producing 35 per cent of the world's top players). In highly technical sports like these and gymnastics, in which detailed motor skills take many years to perfect, starting early works. In his chapter titled 'Not pushing your kids is irresponsible' Ankerson sums up his position:

> There are different kinds of pressure. You can certainly push kids in bad ways, but you can also push them in good ways. I admit the balance is hard to find, but we often confuse egoistic and bullying parents with dedicated and engaged parents who are taking responsibility for establishing dreams and ambitions in their children.[15]

Getting the balance right is a personal and cultural thing as Chinese American Amy Chua expressed in her *Battle Hymn of a Tiger Mother* book: 'Western parents worry a lot about their children's self-esteem. But as a parent, one of the worst things you can do for your child's self-esteem is to allow them to give up.'

This quote and the broader themes of Chua's book caused considerable debate when it was published in 2011 – not 'allowing' them to give up sounded close to abuse to some readers. Perhaps a more palatable interpretation is: 'to support children through hurdles rather than always giving up' – this conveys a different sort of balance.

Among the champions in this book early senior success, achieved before their 17th birthdays, was achieved by only three athletes: Andre Agassi, Ian Thorpe and Michael Phelps.

However, the danger is that those who progress from early nurture and then made it to the top are the most visible today (e.g. the Williams sisters); even though most on such paths don't keep going as adults. The difficulty is in finding stories of those that *did not* sustain their success ... these athletes tend to disappear from view. Former tennis player, Andrea Jaeger, is now a nun dedicating her life to caring for children. At the age of 15 in 1980, she became a sensation at Wimbledon and rose to number 2 in the world the following year but withdrew from the sport, aged 19, partly as a result of a shoulder injury. It seems rather ghoulish highlighting those that are now comfortably getting on with something else in their lives. If you were to further explore in particular tennis, swimming, golf and soccer for examples of athletes who just succeeded in their teenage years you'd find many such cases.

Gogarty and Williamson's fascinating book about how the inner mental state often lies behind champions' success – *Winning at all Costs: Sporting Gods and their Demons* – portrays women's tennis as a particularly troubling sport for dysfunctional daughter–father relationships.[16] In one chapter it is claimed that the child's developing self can be taken over and exploited by some fathers.

By getting into their minds, such fathers colonise (or 'hypnotise') their daughters, making them extensions of their own desires. If the girls are lucky and talented, they may have the consolation of becoming famous and financially successful. But even for the lucky ones, what is the cost to their sense of self? As Jennifer Capriati discovered when she quit the game, ' If I don't have tennis who am I? What am I?'[17]

In other parts of Gogarty and Williamson's book they explore flawed football geniuses (e.g. Maradona, Garrincha, Best and Gascoigne), obsessional behaviour and specialist kickers (e.g. Jonny Wilkinson, David Beckham), most with an early specialisation past. All these stories of child prodigy or genius reinforce the idea that rising swiftly and smoothly from junior to senior ranks is 'normal' and encourages others to do the same. The difficulty is in separating out the causes of later problems – in the case of flawed football geniuses, Gogarty and Williamson point to dysfunctional earlier family lives that threaten children's self-worth as being an underpinning feature of problems later on in their lives.

But how common is it to rise quickly from junior ranks straight into senior success? Australian sports scientist Jason Gulbin answered this when he took 'A look through the rear view mirror' to examine Australian Institute of Sport athletes' development patterns.[18] He and colleagues asked 256 athletes, across 27 sports, and found only a small proportion (7 per cent) that followed what they called a 'linear trajectory' from junior competition *straight into* senior international level. So not many champions speed through junior programmes like Agassi, Thorpe and Phelps, who moved rapidly into top adult ranks – they are unusual outliers. Even though meteoric rises often grab our attention, it is more often the case that athletes take time to adjust, as you would expect, in the difficult transition from world-class junior champion to adult competition – look at Usain Bolt and Andy Murray.

The sampling versus specialisation debate will continue because, almost inevitably for those with the right attributes, starting early produces adolescent success in some sports, and this helps to perpetuate the practice. It's just that it also carries risks that a child under 10 cannot comprehend.

Four important motivational nutrients for young athletes

There is a powerful explanatory framework of motivation that helps explain young peoples' needs as they progress: *self determination theory*. This is used to explain effective and sustained behaviour and drive, not just in sport but also more broadly in many other fields. In outline, the four core nutrients that young developing athletes need for healthy development are:

1. Autonomy

During busy teenage years, while youngsters are making choices they are hopefully in a coaching and/or parental environment that supports autonomy in making decisions. For example, optimal situations have been identified in which athletes have responsibility, are provided with a rationale for tasks, with their feelings acknowledged and where they are allowed to pursue their own independent training.[19] Ideally personal responsibility and autonomy enable individuals like Chris Hoy, Ian Thorpe, Michael Phelps and many others to determine the path they follow. Without autonomy people tend to fall away and lose drive in the long-term.

2. Competence and recognition

All the champions in this book, without exception, had early success in most of the sports they tried. It is known that the perceived competence of children is a key factor in them taking sport further – if you're good at something you are more likely to keep going.[20] All our champions got strong feedback, both from their results and the reactions of others, to make them realise that actually they were pretty good at the new sport they were trying: it bolsters self-worth.

There are numerous accounts of people winning multiple events in their early school sports days, for example, Seb Coe won every athletics event he entered, aged 11. For others it may be making their first team selection against another school rather than a medal.

Early success becomes even more powerful when it is publicly recognised online or in print. Autobiographies are full of young teenagers scouring the latest edition of a specialist magazine in their sport (e.g. *Cycling News*) for the tiniest mention of their name in print for the very first time – normally a mention in a result listing. Club newsletters, school publications, local news sources or even the big time: a national publication. It is a big deal for a youngster trying to make sense of their place in the world and beginning to recognise their sporting identity.

Here is an explanation of a future champion's need for recognition:

> [He] would read through the entire list the first day [he] got it [*Swimming World*] and then read it through again the next day … [he] got a real charge out of looking in the magazine and seeing [his] name in its pages. So what if you had to skim through what seemed like ten thousand pages … And maybe it was listed in microscopic print, visible only by a high powered lens. There it was: M. Phelps.[21]

Recognition in print or other media means a lot to young people shaping their young identity. The inner drive to build self-esteem and relentlessly practise what you are good at is a powerful force in many young athletes.

3. Relatedness (the social aspect)

Some champions also describe an important social aspect of their early involvement – the need to fit in, belong and gain acceptance, termed 'relatedness' by Self Determination Theory. Michael Phelps, whose self-worth must have been unsettled by his childhood ADHD condition, said people in swimming made him feel like he could fit in, and involvement with older kids made him feel important and accomplished.[22] We often forget the social dimension of sport among youngsters and the strong sense of belonging and affiliation it can build.

As a national coach, I used to run week-long training camps for those teenagers with potential and, gradually, with experience I realised that the first hours of these camps were partly about youngsters catching up with each other and reaffirming friendships. That is largely why they loved the camps.

4. Healthy intrinsic motivation and drive

The enjoyable social aspect helps keep adolescents coming back for more, as do autonomy and perceived competence; this increases the chance of a healthy intrinsic motivation developing, and this encourages youngsters to keep practising through thick and thin.

Collectively when these four nutrients work together we can talk of an athlete who *self-determines* their sporting path. This sometimes combines with other aspects of personality (see chapter 11) and negative life episodes (see chapter 12), and collectively these ideas lie at the very centre of explaining what shapes and drives champions.

Final thoughts

A characterisation of champions' entry into sport is shown on the opposite page. Figure 5.1 represents an idealised gradual progress self-determining sequence of events as they move towards specialisation in their ultimate sport.

In practice, early steps in sport do not happen in these neat stages, but the diagram represents an outline of a healthy self-determined process. The reality, of course, is often different with a mingling of stages and perhaps other personality influences. Common features for some, but not all, successful athletes are that they will have early success (*competence*) that develops their self-worth; this makes it more likely that they will keep going; they hopefully make *autonomous* choices in what they decide to do and develop satisfying connections with others (*relatedness*). With luck they will live somewhere that means they can find a good coach who creates opportunities and inspiration for all this to happen.

Early successful momentum in sport and learning how to win – and lose – sets the scene for much of what follows in champions' paths. This early *self-determined* progress is unlikely to occur if potential champion's parents do not have sufficient resources, (particularly time) and interest to support their progress, especially when they start specialising and travelling away. It is the crucial role parents' play that we turn to next.

Figure 5.1 A characterisation of champions early self-determined path from playground to podium.

6 Winning parents
Getting the balance right

The burning question on parents' lips is how best to support a youngster who shows potential in sport. To what extent should parents be involved, be pro-active or push? Should parents take a back seat, offering support only when it is obviously needed? It can sometimes be difficult for parents making these decisions to get the balance right – the risks of pushing and encouraging a child to specialise too early in one sport are clear and well illustrated by the Andre Agassi *extreme nurture* story, which we'll consider in a moment. His unusual path shines a light on the motivational environment parents create. Parents can play an important positive role in modelling and shaping important behaviours that are used in sport: they are especially influential in children's early years, before the age of about eight.

I spoke to parents who had supported their children into international teams to establish how much they mirrored the thinking of respected authors in this field.

Extreme nurture

What can we learn from Agassi's story of his father seeking to optimise the likelihood of his son's success? His story, and those of the likes of Tiger Woods and the Williams sisters have become a sort of parable of American child prodigies benefiting from early and sustained training in one sport. The TV footage of a diminutive Woods, just short of his third birthday putting with comedian Bob Hope on a US national show lingers in the memory. Likewise Agassi recounts hitting balls with Jimmy Connors (aged 4) and Bjorn Borg (aged 8) – undoubtedly inspiring stuff for Andre, though worse was to follow. The incident described below illustrates the level of pressure and control exerted on Andre and the extent to which his father's ego was caught up in his son's progress.

His father, a former Iranian Olympic boxer, saw an opportunity when American Football legend Jim Brown showed up at their Las Vegas tennis club. Agassi's dad felt insulted by Brown turning down the offer of a game against his nine-year-old son, Andre. Their conversation escalated and Agassi's dad pledged $10,000 that Andre could beat the former professional athlete. Agassi's father went home to fetch the cash. He worked in a casino, and had calculated that his odds of winning were good. Eventually a compromise of a $500 bet was reached – Agassi's father won the bet.

Agassi's father knew his odds were good since Andre had benefited from, or been subjected to (if that is a more accurate phrase), a punishing practice regime as a child.

> My father says that if I hit 2,500 balls each day, I'll hit 17,500 each week, and at the end of one year I'll have hit nearly one million balls. He believes in math. Numbers, he says, don't lie. A child who hits one million balls each year will be unbeatable.[1]

Specialising early included being sent away to the Bollettieri tennis academy at the age of 13 to hit balls at a far higher level. This sustained practice environment combined with developing physical and psychological attributes made early success far more likely (see chapter 5).

The longevity of Agassi's career in professional tennis is incredible when you consider he started playing so young, but this is perhaps largely due to a reorientation of why, and for whom, he was doing the sport; a move away from his dad's aspirations and towards (aged 28) his own altruistic goals and a new purpose of raising huge funds for a charter school he wanted to build. His vision was to provide, through his charity, educational opportunities for those that might not have access to them. So every time he won a match (or was paid by his sponsors), he was funding others' educational dreams and ended up building a school with the proceeds. He managed to put the enjoyment and satisfaction back into the game that he previously said he had hated.

The abiding truth about achieving longevity of high-level performance, from Andre Agassi's story, is that the many lessons he learnt along the way – including physical conditioning, mental tools, life goals, controlling his perfectionist tendencies – were instrumental in buffering him against some of the risks of extreme nurture. He was able to draw on these resources to bring meaning, satisfaction and resilience into his sporting life. Not everyone is equipped to achieve this.

How can parents optimise the motivational environment?

Looking online at children's sport forums, parenting issues raise many of the central questions about how best to support children in the development of their sport? I've already partly answered this question by explaining four self-determining nutrients – competence, autonomy, relatedness and intrinsic drive – that young athletes need (see chapter 5). Added to this are ideas from Dr Steve Peters, a respected psychiatrist associated with British Cycling's and Liverpool Football Club's success. Dr Peters is also involved in many other sports and he has an interesting story to tell about parents and motivational environments. He has explained hardwired behavioural patterns, or habits, that are often learnt before the age of eight. He calls his parable the 'Fridge Door Syndrome', which he says affects most people in the Western world.

The Fridge Door Syndrome[2]

It is the first day of school and the young child is full of emotion. The teacher says to the child, 'Let's paint a picture for your parents.' After painting the picture the child runs home to show the parents. As the child runs up to the parents, the parent says, 'What is that you've got?' The child hands over the painting. The parent responds, 'This picture is fantastic, you are very clever, I am so proud of you, I want the world to know just how good you are,' and then puts the picture on the fridge door.

Let's look at the same scenario with a different approach. The child returns from school with the painting and runs to the parent. The parent responds with, 'Hang on', and moves the painting to one side and hugs the child. Then the parent says, 'I am so proud of you and you are clever and I want the world to know just how proud I am of you. Now, what is that you have got?' The parent and child now have a discussion about the painting and the parent compliments the painting and the child, and asks the child if they would like to put it on the fridge door because it is pretty.

In the first scenario the parent reinforces the message that *it is what the child achieved* that makes them proud. The child's worth is dependent on the painting. If this keeps on being repeated in different ways, a child learns that it is what you achieve in life that will make others see you in a good light: in the incident from Agassi's extreme case, by winning $500 for his dad in a bet.

The second scenario the child receives a different message that *they are worthy just as they are*. You are unconditionally loved and respected and you don't have to do anything to receive this. They were also asked if they would like the achievement posted on the fridge door – they were given some involvement in this.

Steve Peters' illustrative story is enlightening because many of us perhaps recognise in ourselves the likelihood of behaving as outlined in scenario one. If a child returns from competing in sport instead of brandishing a picture we, as adults, often blurt out 'how did you do?' or 'did you win?' You can see that if it is only the result that matters, it might encourage a certain way of thinking about sport and parental relationships. Peters summarises:

> It is of course always good to praise a child if it has done its best, whatever the level it has achieved. Of course there is a balance to be had … but all too many of us are fearful of how we do and what others think.[3]

Educational psychology supports the theory that performance is optimised by praising *effort* rather than performance outcomes (similar to Carol Dweck's ideas in chapter 1) – Parent: 'I can see you worked really hard at that'. The child self-evaluates – 'because I spent a lot of effort I'm proud of what I've achieved' so the motivation becomes intrinsically orientated and not based on the judgments of others.[4]

Champions aren't brought up in a particular way but a useful gauge, not always evident at the time, is to question the extent to which they have been motivated by a desire to please others. If this is so, it is likely to persist as they become adults, with detrimental implications, unless this imprint can be overcome or adapted later, as in the case of Agassi. It is obvious in Victoria Pendleton's autobiography that she was trying to please her dad in her early career, while it seems that Chrissie Wellington, though confident, still sought the approval of others – including her first coach.

How you interact with people in later life is thought partly to be shaped by the type of attachments you form to your primary carer as an infant. Primary caregivers who are available and responsive to an infant's needs allow the child to develop a sense of security. A child with a dependable caregiver benefits from a secure base from which the child can explore the world. More uncertain, erratic or distant interactions with infants influence future relationship, habits and dynamics.

Most athletes seem to have had fairly balanced building blocks from childhood, on which their personality develops. Donald Winnicott, English paediatrician and psychoanalyst, invented the phrase 'good enough' parenting[5] to describe the way in which the majority of parents are good enough to meet their children's needs. However, the trauma of early dysfunctional parenting, paradoxically, can lead to extreme compensatory behaviours and achievement in sport. Paul Gogarty and Ian Williamson's book *Winning At All Costs: Sporting Gods and Their Demons*[6] explains an example of a pattern of dysfunctional parenting suffered by football heroes Diego Maradona, George Best and Paul Gascoigne.

Football gods and their demons

The common sense view is that with good enough parenting, including loving parental guidance, children will adopt a relatively ordered and benign view of a safe and predictable world providing a secure psychological map for life.

If the process goes wrong with absent parents and unstable childhoods, a youngster might be left with incoherent experiences that, without parental love to make sense of their environment, spiral into overwhelming anxieties. Their self-worth is low and their view of the world is chaotic and threatening.

Youngsters such as Diego Maradona, George Best and Paul Gascoigne compensated for such negative childhood experiences by overdeveloping their physical skills in football, since this provided a haven where they as teenagers could start to excel and express themselves like nowhere else. This fuelled their endless practice and their need to excel propelled them by suppressing feelings of inadequacy and despair.

The metaphor of this inner 'need' being a rocket fuel is apt – the drive and hunger to rebuild self-worth through sport provides a powerful propellant. The exciting boost to self-esteem that the fuel encourages is compulsive – much like all three football players' later struggles with addictions that give a temporary and illusory sense of triumph and respite before depression, anxiety and phobias return.

This abridged version of Gogarty and Williamson's argument of complex cases highlights a process of how disruptive care and/or traumatic childhood events that undermine self-worth can *sometimes* fuel athletic achievement. It is not a simple switch, where if *x* happens in childhood *y* is the result. The football genius is an example at the far end of any scale and is not commonplace. We'll consider more everyday examples of negative childhood events possibly affecting self-worth and spurring motivational drive in chapter 12.

The box above re-emphasises the key role that parents play in creating stability. Parents do make a big difference. Next we examine three key roles of parents in sport: parents as *providers*, parents as *interpreters* of their child's sporting and life experience and parents as *role models* in showing how to behave.[7]

Parents as providers

We've already heard earlier in this book an example of parents as *providers* when the cyclist Joanna Rowsell, talked of her father's dedication in taking her around the country. Parents provide the resources of their own time, transport, equipment, attention and finance. Ian Thorpe and Kelly Holmes both state that their parents paid for professional coaching in a number of different activities before they found their ultimate sport.

If you think about a family's resources for a moment, they are generally finite. Family resources are often available largely according to family size. For instance, one hypothesis is that those from single parent families might be disadvantaged, since their parents are unlikely to have as many resources and pragmatically, in terms of time alone, one parent can only stretch so far when ferrying children to and from practices. A second scenario concerns large families. Imagine a family with four or more children in which resources, time and money (in particular), are stretched. Or, conversely, a third scenario would be a family with a lone child with all the family's resources directed solely towards them.

Although, these all sound logical and probable scenarios, my research of champions' family stories does not fully support these ideas. It is interesting to note the family situations of some champions and the potential impact on their future successes. This comment about *time* as a resource comes from Steve Redgrave: 'Because I was significantly younger than my sisters [nine and five years younger] … it meant that my mother had considerably more time on her hands to devote to my future.'[8]

For other athletes, divorced or separated parents also feature as having significant impact although the proportion is notably lower in the 21 champions investigated in this book (*c.* 15 per cent) compared to averages in the western world. But in terms of resources, consider the single-parent families that Kelly Holmes, Bradley Wiggins and Michael Phelps (after age nine) came from. Their accounts of the love and support from their main caring parent and extended families suggest this difficulty was overcome. Yet Bradley Wiggins, a lone child for his first seven years, tells, illuminatingly, of how he came by the financial resources to purchase his first competition bike at the age of 13:

... it wasn't long before I had my first bad crash on a bike. Strangely it proved a blessing in disguise ... Mum was incensed at the carelessness of the woman driver [involved] and decided ... to sue her and get some compensation for her poor battered boy. It involved all sorts of tests and X-rays ... and a mountain of correspondence on her part, but eventually – a year later – I was awarded £1700 compensation ... [part of which] I used to buy my first proper racing bike.

In most sports, to step up to higher levels you need the proper equipment, and in this case Wiggins's mother, with very limited resources and making her own good fortune, had found a way to make this happen.

But what can be said of large families and resource scarcity? An extreme example from another era, is that of baseball stars Joe and Dom DiMaggio who were the youngest of *nine* children. Such examples help disprove that big families are necessarily disadvantageous to developing champions. In a more contemporary age, Michael Johnson comes from a larger than average family, and being the youngest of four was evidently not detrimental to his ability to succeed.

We know that resources are important in all sports and it is perhaps not surprising to find that there is inconsistency across many health and well-being measures, favouring those of greater socioeconomic means: this is also reflected in sport participation. Adults of greater socioeconomic means are far more likely to participate in sport than those of lesser means. Resources matter in elite sport: significantly, there is a bias favouring higher socioeconomic groups in those who win Olympic medals too, based on UK data.[9]

Parents as interpreters

Parents influence a child athlete through the beliefs and values they transmit. These values are made implicit for the child, for instance, in the way the parent talks through what's occurred and attributes events which may have the effect of reinforcing feelings of competence and supporting positive learning and development. A good example of this is provided by a study with Olympic-level athletes where the participants' anonymity was protected to encourage them to be candid:

I remember one of my first competitions where I dropped the ball. I started crying my eyes out ... I thought my world was going to cave in, but my dad and I talked afterwards and he said, 'You've got to concentrate and carry on with your performance no matter what happens. You've got to be able to pick yourself up after mistakes.' He drove into me that it was part of development and part of growing up and because I respected him so much, I took everything on board. As a result, I learned to rationalise my thoughts and feelings as I started to realise that how I thought and felt would influence my performance.[10]

You can see how such conversations can be important as long as a parent doesn't try interpreting too often or with too much vigour: it all could get rather earnest. Imagine an over-the-top approach of a parent debriefing their child after every event. Getting the balance right is key.

> My discussions with Kate Peters, educational consultant and mother of two youth champions, captured the skill of interpreting at the appropriate moment.
>
> There is a real art to parents acting as interpreters and I think it may depend on the 'personality fit' between parent and child. But the most important thing is that parents must be sensitive to the needs of the moment in so many ways, saying the right thing in the right place at the right time. For example, delaying comment until the heat is out of a moment. For me, approaching this from a child-led perspective worked best: supply comment when asked, or when a real need is indicated. I adapted as my children matured and progressed. If we as parents are sufficiently attuned, the child will guide us as to their needs – but we have to be able to keep our egos out of it, and this can be one of the hardest challenges! It's the hardest part of parenting – that age-old adage that we can't just pass on all our skills and knowledge, we have to be able to stand back and let them experience it for themselves and then be there to pick up the pieces without even a hint of, 'I told you so'!

A common pattern between Michael Phelps and Ian Thorpe is that both also have mothers who are teachers, and perhaps as educationalists were equipped to play this interpretative role, skilfully drawing on their knowledge of young people and learning. This was particularly important for Phelps and Thorpe, since being world champion and a world record holder is normally something that happens with the benefit of maturity in your 20s or 30s, not as a naive teenager. In their cases there was no easy handbook to help them and their mothers cope with childhood fame, other than parental common-sense and setting the right example.

Parents as role models

Finally, parents as models or exemplars of behaviour: a subtle but powerful influence. Children are always subconsciously learning from their parents, and when parents exhibit behaviours and beliefs consistently and early in the child's life, the child may well automatically adopt these habits as their own.

For example, the values of hard work and always doing one's best, or indeed more negative behaviours (such as complaining about a coach or accepting mediocrity) shape a child's perspective. Take this example to decide what Michael Phelps soaked up from his parents:

> I knew they worked hard, because I remember alarm clocks going off at 4 a.m. so that my dad could drive [my sister] Hilary to practice.

Or listen to this from athlete Michael Johnson about his truck driver dad:

My father didn't just hope that his children would finish their homework or hope that we would take part in family vacations. [He] planned almost every detail of every vacation. He set up guidelines for each of his kids and expected us to live our lives the same way. He constantly told us about the plan and challenged us to have our own when we came to him with things we wanted to do or accomplish ... People marvel at my self confidence, but it is my father's confidence, and it comes from understanding the world around you and knowing that, in your world, things happen according to [a] plan.[11]

This type of learning is a powerful feature of family life. The parent is an unheralded 24/7 tutor. Champions learn lessons about the world, about effort, persistence and a whole lot of other important life lessons from parents. This type of learning works if boundaries and behaviour are consistent. But what happens when a child is faced with inconsistent and erratic parental reactions? Guess what – erratic actions likewise beget similar behaviour in the young and impressionable. One thing is known for certain in sport: that being steady and consistent in preparation and often in competition works.

Final thoughts

I have deliberately avoided too much in the form of prescribed comments about parenting; there is no magic formula. But we do know that early childhood sets the scene for much of personality development.

In particular, the way early interactions and their inherent messages are conveyed, shapes the psychological lives of children and the values they seek to live out. Being mindful of parental motivations and their impact is important if we want to produce top-class athletes who are psychologically robust enough to both enjoy and sustain their sporting careers at the highest levels and go on to lead balanced and fulfilled lives outside sport as they age.

Perhaps it is useful to think in terms of the athlete and his relationship with his sport as a mirror of his relationship with the world, and strive to help make this as secure as possible rather than an anxious relationship as seen with the three football geniuses. The athlete's relationship with the wider world, whether fundamentally positive or negative, will – it seems – surface in top-level sport in the end.[12]

Next we question another common facet of family life: the role siblings play in a sporting champion's early progress. Is it a help or a hindrance to be a younger member of a family? We explore this in the next chapter.

7 Are younger siblings more likely to become champions?

In 1986 David Hemery, the Olympic champion from Mexico City who ran to gold in the 400m, published a groundbreaking book about sporting excellence. He had travelled around the world interviewing sporting icons and came across a question he could not answer: why is there is a disproportionate number of second-born champions?[1]

His puzzle about the influence of birth order and siblings on success can now be unravelled. Michael Phelps is pretty unequivocal about the influence of his elder sister, also a swimmer, on his progress:

> If I hadn't seen her put in all that work, if I hadn't seen all the sacrifices she made and if I hadn't seen first-hand that you can't take success for granted, there is no way I would have been on that Olympic team [his first, to Sydney in 2000].[2]

Table tennis champion and journalist Matthew Syed also describes, in his book *Bounce*, how he also had the good fortune of having an elder sibling, a brother, who loved table tennis as much as he did. 'We would play for hours in the garage after school: duelling, battling, testing each other's reflexes, experimenting with new spins, investigating new paddles'.[3]

Here I combine such personal evidence with recent research, which indicates that the influence of siblings is becoming clearer. Sibling influence in sport is largely about three phenomena. First, the potential impact of siblings as role models, as Michael Phelps described so poignantly. Second, the advantage of having a skilled, motivated training partner 24/7, as with Matthew Syed. And third, the influence of being a younger sibling on goals both in practice and competition.

In 2012, a multinational research team from Canada and Australia announced some fascinating findings in this area of family research. They investigated sibling characteristics of 229 athletes at different performance levels across a range of sports.[4] They divided the athletes into three groups depending on their competition level: senior international, national and all other athletes. They then looked closely at any differences in the proportions of sibling birth order between the different competition levels, categorising those who were only children, first born or later born. The results were striking.

Table 7.1 Sibling relationships of athletes.

	Only child %	First born %	Later born %
National	9	52	39
Senior international	9	24	67
Other	11	46	44

Just over two-thirds (67 per cent) of senior international athletes were later born compared to much lower proportions for national and other athletes. Statistical analysis suggested that this was highly significant: there was only a 1 in 100 likelihood of this finding being due to chance. This is striking, but it is early days yet to suggest that it might be generalised to all champion contexts. It prompted me to look more closely at champions' autobiographies – three-quarters, a huge proportion, are later born.

At one end of the continuum is the experience of Bradley Wiggins and Kelly Holmes, who for their early years were 'only' children.[5] At the other extreme, Andre Agassi and Michael Johnson are both the youngest of four. Sibling influence across champions' autobiographies is almost always talked about very positively as we've already seen with Phelps and Syed. I was cautious of reading too much into this: perhaps few champions cite siblings having a negative effect on their progress due to autobiographical bias. As a champion you are hardly going to highlight dysfunctional aspects of your family relationships so publicly. I needed to look for further illustrative examples

Siblings as role models

Both Victoria Pendleton and Jonny Wilkinson explicitly identify their elder sibling as influencing their taking up the sport and/or supporting their progress. Most strikingly Ian Thorpe and Michael Phelps had international-level swimmers as elder sisters and role models. Their elder sisters clearly demonstrated, in a most vivid way, what was involved in progressing to the top.

Others have also recognised a potential pattern. For instance, the New Zealand netball squad, after chatting to each other independently, identified a similar theory:

> We did a little survey and all of us were younger, like we all had older siblings … I do always remember having to try harder in anything I was doing. Playing netball, doing passes, shooting for goal, sprinting round the back garden, I had to be chasing her, and she was obviously two years older so that much better. So that's my theory that it pays not to be the oldest.[6]

Beyond teammate conversations some researchers in Canada took it a stage further by using recorded interviews to explore families' thoughts on sibling dynamics. By interviewing families with children in serious swimming training and those who had dropped out they sought comparisons and contrasts.[7] They applied due diligence to their interviews and carefully matched interviewees' age, gender, years of experience, ability, family structure and parent education characteristics. Those who had dropped out spoke of 'competition', 'rivalry' and 'jealousy', while the engaged athletes talked of a general positive influence from their siblings, usually, like Phelps, in the form of role modeling. One quote from the interviews is particularly revealing:

> 'That's what they do. That's what I do.' I didn't choose to go into swimming when I was five. I just kind of did what everyone else in the family did. They went to the pool and worked hard – that's what I did. They went to swim meets and tried their best – that's what I did.

This points to siblings having a positive influence on development for those staying in the sport. However, any sample of champion athletes, such as in this book, is more likely to be skewed towards those with support-orientated family environments and, in many instances, supportive siblings.

When siblings become competitors

As a spectator I watched two siblings battling it out against each other for Olympic podium positions in 2012 – one of the Olympic events that was ticketless, and for anyone to watch was the triathlon in Hyde Park, London. I rose early in order to get the best possible position at the feeding station for the bike and run stages. Hundreds of thousands of people had the same idea, and there were huge crowds all around the course. We'd all come, in particular, to watch a British sibling pair in direct competition: the brilliant Brownlee brothers. It was elder brother Alistair (aged 24) versus younger brother Jonathan (aged 22), with the rest of the world trying to upset the pair's dominance. They became the first pair of British brothers in 100 years to stand on the podium together after competing against each other: Alistair won. Later Jonathan said this:

> He is my brother, we compete at everything, we're more competitive over other stuff like Monopoly, table tennis and badminton than we are in triathlon. When it comes to triathlon we kind of realise that we can use each other on the world stage, when we're on the bike leg we can push each other on and in training we can use each other: it's a massive advantage we've got.[8]

The two best athletes in the world rankings, living near to each other, training together, having a laugh, egging each other on and then working together with a third team member in the heat of Olympic competition. You can see how it works – it's a hugely advantageous training and competition scenario perhaps unlike other sporting siblings (e.g. the Williams sisters) due to the teamwork possible in the triathlon.

Such unique inter-sibling situations have also been the subject of in-depth interviews in the USA where 10 same-sex siblings in direct competition were questioned. Here are some of the positive things they said:

[Sibling] competition pushes me harder. Because if someone else is beating me I'm like, 'OK, she's better than me, I can accept that', but if it's my sister? You are like, 'No, I can beat her. Let's go.' I think it pushes you that much harder.[9]

[My sister] kind of just pulled me aside and said, 'Get your head out of your ass! You've got two more events to swim. You've got two events to make your mark … Just go out there and do it.'[10]

There were also negative examples in which rivalry, gloating and trash-talking predominated, illustrating the inconsistent pattern of sibling relationships. Overall though, among *successful* sports people sibling competition was viewed positively.

Competitiveness and rivalry

Competitiveness is often a feature of champions' family environments, but while this characteristic might be a negative feature for some children, potential champions thrive on it. In an anonymous interview a father of a multiple medal winning British Olympic javelin competitor expressed it this way:

If his older brother, nearly two years older than him, if they did press ups, when his older brother did 20, [he] would do 21, you know he was that type of kid and he was a competitor, he wanted to do one better.[11]

We've ended up drifting towards the notion of sibling rivalry – surely it is not as simple as one sibling trying to prove they are better than another?

Psychological studies may offer further insight; notably some researchers in Belgium who specialise in motivation and the type of goals (goal orientation) that people tend to pursue. They proposed that differential parental treatment of siblings within the family due to birth order may be a contributing factor in the emergence of individual differences:[12]

During a brief period, firstborns are the only child within the family. Without siblings, parents have few standards available to evaluate their child's competence. As the firstborn child is the main point of reference, parents may tend to evaluate their firstborn's progress primarily by self-referenced standards (e.g., 'last week my baby could only crawl and now s/he is taking his/her first steps').'

Consequently, we hypothesize that firstborns have developed a preference for mastery goals. In contrast, when evaluating the competence of secondborns, the older sibling is available as a reference. Hence, parents may be more likely to evaluate their secondborn's progress by standards set by the older sibling (e.g., 'my youngest baby takes his/her first steps sooner than his/her brother did'). Hence, we hypothesize that secondborns have developed a preference for performance goals.'

To test this idea they recruited 375 siblings with an average age gap between siblings of 2½ years. The student participants rated the extent to which they agreed or disagreed with a range of statements connected to mastery or performance goals such as:

- mastery goal: 'in my studies, I am striving to understand the content of the courses as thoroughly as possible'.
- performance goal: 'in my studies, my aim is to perform well relative to other students'.

Their results showed that birth order is closely correlated to people's goal preferences. They found that firstborns are 54 per cent more likely to have stronger mastery goals compared to secondborns, whereas secondborns preferred performance goals. They concluded that simple narratives about different sibling upbringings leading to different life characteristics may be right after all. 'Firstborns may be more motivated to learn, whereas secondborns may be more motivated to win.'[13]

These ideas about goals may help explain why people differently define, experience and respond to learning environments and sport. Surely the folk psychology interpretation of sibling rivalry, even if expressed as differences in goals, is rather limited. Overall, a more complete picture seems to be provided by thinking about an interaction between older siblings acting as role models, excellent training partners and a stimulus to constructive competitiveness.

Let's return to Phelps and Thorpe's domain again: swimming. The experience of British double gold winner Rebecca Adlington, may help bring this discussion into focus. She has often spoken about the influence of her two elder sisters (two and fours years older) on her development.

Adlington and her sisters

Much to her annoyance Rebecca was always being compared to her older sisters, Chloe and Laura, by teachers at secondary school.[14] In her own words she was 'crap … absolutely rubbish at other sports' and dreaded doing Physical Education lessons as a result.

But after being dragged along to the local swimming pool by her sisters she felt she had to keep up with them in the water. Adlington refused to wear water-wings, in order to be like her sisters and joined Sherwood Swimming Club at the age of seven, racing for them for the first time at nine.

Laura and Chloe were strong national level swimmers and, at first, Rebecca was very much in their wake, but a competitive streak and a determination not to be outdone by her big sisters spurred her on. She first beat her sisters at the age of 12.

Rebecca Adlington: is there more likelihood of swimmers being later born?

As an adult Adlington also drew motivation from her mum and dad's sacrifices to help her along the way and the inspiration of her sister Laura's battle with illness when she was 17 and nearly died.[15] My interpretation is that when someone close to you fights serious illness, it perhaps gives you more perspective to make use of the opportunities you have, a sort of negative episode by association.

Role models, early training partners, competitiveness and family illness are all in her story along with a determination to try and do something distinctive that would set her apart from her sisters. Notice the reference to finding the academic comparisons with her sisters at school annoying. We can perhaps all relate to trying to define our own distinctiveness in adolescence. It is noticeable how, later in her career, she recognises parental sacrifice and her sister's battle with serious illness as motivating factors. This may have given her broader perspectives on life when her elite training was crowding in too much.

It is fascinating how – without intending to – we have kept coming back to swimming. Perhaps there are many strong examples of sibling effects in other sports ? Or is it the nature of the hard childhood training and early mornings in this sport that makes the influence of total family involvement, including that of elder siblings, more likely?

Final thoughts

For a final view we turn to twins. Identical twins have the same DNA. Scientists love to study those who have come from the same sperm–egg combination, since it means they can investigate to what extent our DNA and other influences determine success. In 2001, a fascinating enquiry in Italy focused on identical twins who had both competed at the Olympics in the 20km race-walking discipline.[16]

The twin brothers had trained together between the ages of 15 and 33 under the same coach and a virtually identical regime, but one became a gold medalist and was more successful. Afterwards in 'retirement' (aged 40) they were extensively tested and, as DNA predicts, their physical abilities were almost identical. Clues to the twins' performance differences were found only in their contrasting personalities and psychological characteristics. They both completed a recognised 'State-Trait Anger Expression Inventory'. The Olympic winner scored almost 100 per cent for reaction to anger and anger control, while his brother scored almost zero for this attribute. The Olympic winner had excessive control over his emotions and behaviour, with his anger rarely being openly expressed. The emotional reactions of his brother were, however, at the opposite extreme: in my household we call it 'venting': getting emotions out.

It seems likely that this, as the only measured difference between the twins, may partly be responsible for their difference in performance. Psychological tools such as emotional self-control add a further layer to champions' accounts of success (see chapter 14). As yet, it is not clear how sibling interaction contributes to these psychological differences.

Siblings as role models, training partners and a stimulus to competitiveness may account for the disproportionate numbers of later-born children who are champions, with elder siblings unknowingly contributing to their success.

8 Selection myths and compromises revealed

Five years as a national selector wrestling with decisions about who should be included in junior squads meant I became used to trying to take into account that athletes were at different stages of adolescent development. It is a hot topic for parents, coaches and young people. Those selected for the next level keep going in their sport but those deselected are at risk of dropping out; many great athletes are potentially lost. Most of the champions discussed in this book made the cut: they were identified and selected to national teams by the age of 18 or 19, and many a lot earlier, but other athletes, as we shall see, had a more rocky experience.

The myth of selection is that the cream always rises to the top, results talk, but here and elsewhere in this book I show that many chance factors are at play. For example, in previous chapters we've examined the circumstantial influence of parental support, resources, sibling influences and touched on the location factor (i.e. where you live).

This chapter is about selection amid the maturation and growth of adolescence. We look at the latest thinking on the influence of ethnicity and birth dates, and this recent research takes us in surprising directions. I also spoke with an expert into selection in junior tennis and then consulted an account from another sport – professional baseball – considering how identifying late adolescent talent can never just be down to data as *Moneyball* suggests.

The rewards and risks amid maturation

Basketball is our starting point, as a sport in which being a coordinated giant is rewarded. Kareem Abdul-Jabbar (born Lew Alcindor) is the NBA all-time leading scorer with 38,387 points over a twenty-year career until 1989. He was off the height scale in terms of early maturation: at the age of 13, he was 2.0m (6ft 7in). Maturing early in many sports confers a size/strength advantage making age-group selection a whole lot more likely. You could only imagine the dominance Lew had at school as he towered over opponents.

This advantage, no doubt combined with considerable skill, continued into adulthood. He became so unusually tall (2.18m, nearly 7ft 2in) for the 1960s that in his early college years what became known as the Lew Alcindor rule was invented to reign in his dominance. *Time* magazine reported in 1967 that college basketball's rule makers decided that players may no longer slam dunk the ball through the hoop, in a move aimed at Alcindor, who was a UCLA sophomore at the time.[1] The banning of the slam dunk lasted until 1976, when it was realised it was an ill-advised reaction.

At the opposite end of the maturation scale, there are two basketball late developers who made it to the top despite growing far later than the norm. Michael Jordan first blossomed at university, and even more spectacularly Dennis Rodman grew nearly a foot in a single year at the age of 19. Rodman had trialled for his high school American football team but was too small. After the growth spurt, his life began to look up, and he started to thrive in basketball making it his profession.[2]

We have all experienced our own, or other people's, different paced versions of the maturation process and seen the rapid progress or otherwise of early bloomers in particular. But it turns out that developing fast and early, like as Abdul-Jabbar, needs to be combined with mental tools and self-awareness. For instance, Abdul-Jabbar recognised that 'your mind is what makes everything else work'.[3]

Without a mature mental approach, young athletes who make it to the top rapidly can often fall as quickly as they have risen when they encounter the almost inevitable hard times ahead. These hard times follow when everyone else catches up with an early developer, and they can no longer rely on stature or strength alone; they may not have learnt the finesse of how to win by other more skilful means, or have established training and learning habits needed to keep improving. Usain Bolt is an example of this, achieving world junior success early, at 15 years of age, and then taking five more years to achieve senior success (see chapter 4).

Professor Craig Sharp, an experienced physiologist, explains the risk of rapid success for early developers:

> Those who enter the growth spurt early often do very well in age-group athletics, so become used to success without training very hard. In their later teens however, when their slower-growing peers catch up, they are unused to being beaten, and often drop out of the sport. Equally, many of the later candidates for the growth spurt may feel hopelessly overpowered from the start, and believe simply that they are 'no good at sport'. Thus both ends of this normal distribution should be spotted and, counseled accordingly.[4]

His description of both ends of the normal distribution (i.e. fast and slow developers) highlights how many people are lost to sport through the difficulties that both early and late maturation bring.

The taboo of ethnicity

There are all sort of ethnic stereotypes, misconceptions and unknowns about so-called 'natural' attributes and racial norms, but my attention was drawn to one key question among all this noise: how does ethnicity influence the timing of maturation and selection?

First, maturation and gender: Marcia Herman-Giddens from the University of North Carolina produced some fascinating results about the timing of the onset of puberty over decades. Puberty among girls is starting around four years earlier than it did in the 1920s. Similar figures exist for boys, with a delay of around a year from girls in the onset of puberty.[5]

Recently she published some even more startling results about ethnicity, which have implications for selection in sport. By collecting measurements on 4131 boys across the United States she found that African American, Hispanic and non-Hispanic white boys differed in their start of maturation by *over a year*. African American boys started sprouting pubic hair at an average age of 10.2 years compared to 11.4 years for Hispanic and white boys.[6] For girls it was 8.8 years for black girls and 9.9 years for white girls.

These differences therefore add to the difficult task of selection decisions, since a black youngster is likely to be better developed than Hispanics and whites in the same squad. Let's consider some extreme examples of sports in which size, speed and power are all-important. Rugby and American football are both benefiting from an influx of skilful and powerful Pacific Islanders (e.g. Fijians, Samoans and Tongans). This influx has stimulated a major forward-thinking selection policy change in one popular city where Pacific Islanders congregate: Auckland, New Zealand. A rugby coach I spoke to put it bluntly: in Auckland

---

Children terrified of tackling giants – a weight group solution?[7]

Coaches have been monitoring the burgeoning numbers of South Pacific players in rugby union in Australia for more than a decade and are alarmed by the fall in numbers of white juniors caused because children are terrified of 'tackling giants'.

Weight restrictions could soon be introduced in schoolboy rugby competitions. The president of New South Wales Schools Rugby Union, Colin Murray, said over the past 12 months there had been more consideration given to the idea of weight categories, particularly for players under 16, to allay fears about the increasing size of some young players and the physical risks associated with collisions on the field.

With over 40 years experience of school-age rugby, he observes that players are more powerful, generally speaking, and the physique of the younger generation has changed.

In Auckland, New Zealand, there are weight categories for club and school rugby union teams for the under-8 to under-13 competitions. Here, there are a lot more players from Pacific Island nations. Auckland under-8s to under-14s have two weight divisions – a restricted weight division and a capped weight division, which is 50 per cent above the restricted weight.

For example, the under-14s have an under 60kg division and an under 90kg division. Any boy above 90kg must move up to the under-15s.

This sounds sensible and is likely to keep more youngsters in the game for longer. I played the sport avidly for school teams and loved it, but now weighing in at about 78kg I'd be nervous of playing under-15 rugby against 89kg players!

they needed to introduce weight groups for rugby to help keep smaller white youngsters in the sport.[8] It may be compounded if there is an early maturation advantage for Pacific Islanders just as there is for black youngsters in the US. Qualitative observation suggests this early maturation advantage exists. A weight group policy is now being discussed in Australia.

A similar debate about weight groups in junior American football is also taking place, and it was fascinating to see five Pacific Islanders play in Superbowl XLVII (2013; Baltimore Ravens vs San Francisco 49ers). The Ravens fielded the largest of them: Tongan defensive linemen Ma'ake Kemoeatu at 1.95m (6ft 5in) and 156 kilos (24st 8lb).[9] An incredible bulk.

The more we know about puberty, the better it is to think of it as a stage rather than an age. Selection amid adolescent growth and ethnicity variables is therefore less even handed than it appears: especially in power-based sports without the use of weight groups.

Continuing the maturation theme: consider selection in adolescence as an attempt to predict future potential. I want to use an example of a supremely gifted white athlete from the autobiographies, with an aptitude for speed, for whom we have the fieldnotes of a coach's first impression of him as he struggled to adapt to hard training.

White men can't jump?

At the time of writing, the Olympic gold medalist triple jumper, Jonathan Edwards, holds the longest enduring world record in male athletics, having risen from his first recorded competition, aged 15, to national junior champion, aged 18. Here are a coach's initial evaluation notes of the 20-year-old Edwards as he started his senior training:

> [Edwards is] slight, naturally quick, reasonably springy, but not greatly so in my estimation – no real experience of athletic training (had so far succeeded on natural talent) thus athletically rather naive … [Edwards] did not give the impression of being prepared to accept hard training … found reasons, usually slight injury, for stopping work or not doing it.
>
> [The coach's plan] – train [Edwards] quietly to each point of stress then back off. The athlete, despite previous indications and reservations, must be allowed to determine [their own] rate of progress …[10]

In other words, the coach might have been direct and said: 'you've got to really *want* to do this, so you need to self-determine how fast you want to progress'. Jonathan Edwards took up his triple jumping at school and it took him two decades to achieve his Olympic Gold, aged 34, five years after shattering the world record by a huge 4 per cent margin. It indicates a few ups and downs along the way and he was a very slow developer. The ups and downs, if you persist through them, teach you things that can be added to the mental toolbox.

The examples of Abdul-Jabbar, Edwards, the Pacific Islanders and others point to the difficulties of judging or selecting potential at a snapshot in time, often in the growth chaos of adolescent hormones. This can be compounded further by the irregularities caused by athletes' birthdates.

Birthdates revisited

It was Malcolm Gladwell, drawing on others' ice hockey (1980s) research in his 2008 book, *Outliers*,[11] who popularised the existence of the Relative Age Effect (RAE). Most people in sport will be familiar with the idea that your month of birth relative to the selection year cut-off point can have a big impact on your chances of sporting success in some sports. Since the RAE is fairly well known we'll keep the explanation swift. A recent twist to ice hockey research, however, suggests Gladwell may have not been entirely correct in his narrative. We'll return to this recent discovery later.

Since the original 1980s research, investigations have been extended to other sports. For example, in 2009, professional English youth soccer academies were grossly over-represented by players with birthdates in a three-month period – 57 per cent of youngsters were born in September, November or December while only 14 per cent celebrated their birthdays in June, July or August. This is not a one off. Likewise in tennis at the 2012 World U14 Team Tennis Finals, of 96 players (48 boys and 48 girls), 78 per cent of boys and 68 per cent of girls were born in the first five months of the academic year.[12]

The RAE is determined by the cut-off date for age-group competition. In English school soccer, children are placed into year groups based on whether they are born before or on 1 September (the academic year's start date). Children born in September have an advantage on children born in August because they have nearly a whole extra year to grow and develop. This is amplified in the growth spurt at puberty, as we have seen, when children can shoot up in a single year. Unfortunately, adults often believe size and coordination advantages translate into better performances. Football and ice hockey coaches, faced with selecting their team often confuse talent with age and, often unknowingly, select a team with larger youngsters that are more likely to win. In tennis, increasingly, power pays.

It takes a brave coach to put long-term child development first with competitive parents on the sidelines. Imagine then, aged 10 years 11 months, you as a relatively older, taller player get selected for your team and identified with 'talent'. Your parents beam with pride and coaches invest more time in your progress; you get more feedback, practice and games to play in. Before long your small chronological age advantage is magnified by this input. Also, you now feel more confident that you are competent, reinforcing your willingness to practice honing your skills.

The smaller, less developed 10-year-old player therefore needs to be resilient to the knock-backs they are likely to experience, not easy for a child. Eventually, if they are not mentally robust to persist, they may get dispirited and leave the sport.

In England the governing body of soccer is acutely aware of the problem and is trying to do something about it by changing the emphasis of the children's game. The chairman of the Football Association at the time, David Bernstein, illustrates a new approach.[13]

Would Lionel Messi have prospered in Bernstein's team

Many years ago Bernstein managed his son's under-12 football team. It was a pretty successful one-year stint of management: they won the league and cup double.

He looked back with hindsight and concluded that his style of selection might not have worked long-term. Like many other coaches and managers of youth teams he followed a traditional formula: put the bigger, more physically developed players up front and get the ball to them quickly; partly since they played on a big pitch with goals the same size as those used at international level.

While his team achieved success, he wondered how a young Lionel Messi would have progressed under his coaching method. 'He probably wouldn't have fitted in with my winning formula.'

He now realises that times have changed. To develop a generation of youngsters who love playing and have the skills, while preventing the adverse effects of being excluded by a largely size-based selection philosophy, then things need to change.

By reducing pitch sizes at critical age groups, the 'kick and rush' style of play, where bigger, faster players prosper over those who are more slight and technically proficient (like Messi), becomes less important.

Lionel Messi: daily growth-hormone injections aged 11–14 years

Here we have a sport adapting the rules of play for younger age groups to reduce the impact of physical development – it will take 5 to 10 years to see if the plan works. What we do now with 12-year-olds takes that long to work through to adult level.

Further insight into Lionel Messi's early life is that his growth was so limited as a nine-year-old boy (he stood 1.27m, 4ft 2in) that after a year of tests he was prescribed growth hormone treatment involving an injection every day for some three years until the age of 14. It is claimed that without this treatment 'he would not have grown to his genetically intended height'[14] of 1.69m (5ft 6in). Messi's late June birthdate may not have helped.

In Canada, relative age processes have been shown to operate in ice hockey for a while. Since it is an even more physical game than football it is no surprise that similar proportions were skewed towards the early months of the year (unfortunately information on ethnicity was not recorded). However, since the hockey selection cut-off date is the calendar year (i.e. 1 January), it is January, February and March that are the heavily favoured birth months.

The implications of the RAE for Olympic sports are more complex. The effect is not found so obviously in combat sports like boxing, wrestling, taekwondo, and judo since weight groupings operate to help group similarly sized athletes together. As an aside, the use of weight classes in the early stages of American football competition is also thought to account for the phenomenon not being evident in that sport.[15]

Nevertheless, some interesting results emerged when some number-crunchers applied themselves to the monumental task of analysing the birth dates of all 18,132 competitors at the 2008 Olympic Games.[16] The cut-off date for international junior competition in Olympic sports is January, and for males and females the following sports showed statistically significant results in that there were more competitors born in the first quarter of the year:

- females: athletics, badminton, basketball, modern pentathlon, rowing and swimming;
- males: athletics, basketball, canoeing, road cycling, football, handball, rowing, swimming and volleyball.

Notice that of the eleven sports mentioned here almost half are team/squad based sports, in which selection is more subjective and often coaches' unconscious bias can creep in.

The sample of champions' birthdates in this book suggests that there are plenty of exceptions to the RAE since there is no noticeable effect, i.e. one quartile of the year is not dominant. This is perhaps not surprising as size and strength is only useful in the early years of *some* of the sports featured in this book.

However, this should not distract from the overall message of the RAE: that children born immediately after the age cut-off point in size/strength related sports have a tendency to be more developed, and therefore are more likely to be picked in their early years, leading to more practice time and a cumulative self-fulfilling effect.

Totally valid selection can only happen as an adult when everyone stops growing physically and the lingering effects of birthdate are more distant.

Superseding Gladwell

New research – not available to Gladwell – is now starting to suggest cases of an actual *reversal* of the RAE at top professional levels of ice hockey. By reversal we mean 'relatively younger' players (born later in the year) eventually do better at the very top of the game. This latest rethink started in 2007. Ice hockey threw up an intriguing question: why are relatively younger Canadian players chosen earlier in the National Hockey League draft?[17]

Let's look at this in more detail. Ice hockey is a fertile place to consider this because not only does it as a team sport use subjective selection decisions, it is also data rich (salaries, appearances, assists, yardage, passes etc) and the draft system selects or ranks those players considered most desirable. European readers not familiar with the draft process may like to read this endnote.[18]

A research team analysed 27 years' worth of National Hockey League (NHL) drafts (1980 to 2006).[19] They suggested the RAE still exists as a legacy of its strong impact in ice hockey's junior game: there were still 36 per cent of NHL draftees with January–March birthdates compared with 15 per cent with October–December birthdates. They also checked that the publicity generated by Gladwell connected to the RAE had not affected recent team recruitment practices by looking at the 2012 draft: scouts and managers recruiting of far fewer relatively younger individuals has not waned.

However, the effectiveness of relatively younger professional players (i.e. born July–December) showed they were roughly *twice* as likely to reach major career milestones, such as 400 games played or 200 points scored (goals plus any assists). This is a remarkably strong finding: they're twice as likely to do well in their career.[20]

Relatively younger players doing well in the long term can be explained by the 'underdog' effect. Younger individuals, because they have faced greater challenges, compensate by developing greater adaptability to different roles or better work habits; these traits then lead to greater long-term achievement.[21] This connects to our earlier observations about how hypothetically a 10-year-old footballer who misses out on selection would need to be robust to keep going. Also consider our early description of a 'rapid success not sustained' path. This explains how larger or very talented young athletes may not learn 'the finesse of how to win by other more skilful means' or 'have established a work ethic habit needed to improve'.

No doubt as this reverse relative age effect in top professional sport is studied further the mechanisms and processes involved will become clearer. But the impact of RAE on junior squad selection still remains, as ice hockey and football show. One question remains – can selection acknowledge junior age-effects in some way?

A selection dilemma

To address this question, imagine you have to select a national under-15 squad for two prestigious events. To keep things straightforward we'll consider selecting individuals rather than a team sport, for instance anything from table tennis to taekwondo in which indicator event(s) produce an overall ranking at a point in time. The ranking list for the top-12 is in Table 8.1 below.

The three right-hand columns show the athlete's age, their years remaining in this age category and their points. For the sake of this example, points equals performances over a number of events (rather like a tennis ranking list) or if the sport performance has been converted to cumulative points (e.g. as in heptathlon).

As a selector you have to identify who you would pick for:

▦ a *World Championships* in which only two athletes can attend, and
▦ a simultaneous *Junior International* to which your federation can send a different squad of five athletes (i.e. the same athletes cannot do both events).

Make a note of who you would select for the *Worlds* (two athletes) and for the simultaneous *Junior International* (five athletes).

Table 8.1 Final result list for indicator or ranking event(s) including age.

Rank	Name	Age (yr/month)	Future years @ U15	Points
1st	Betty Swashbuckle	14/2	none	31
2nd	Sheena Mayday	14/10	none	25
3rd	Laura Kim	12/9	2	24
4th	Lola Shaz	14/5	none	22
5th	Carla Denantz	14/2	none	21.5
6th	Qian Kan	12/4	2	21
7th	Charlie Dubretski	14/11	none	19
8th	Lian Charles	13/8	1	18
9th	Sheila Bobs	14/4	none	15.5
10th	Annette Beeler	11/7	3	15
11th	Mary-Jane Kitu	14/3	none	11
12th	Amy Smith	13/11	1	10

Different sports and even nations have different cultures and underlying beliefs about the purpose and role of age-group selection. Some make selection decisions solely by running down the result list from top to bottom since they believe this is transparent to all, it enhances the prestige/integrity of the indicator events and it represents a meritocracy. In this culture the strongest possible squad is identified and younger athletes who miss out may be advised that 'your time will come round'. In this case the selections to each event would be:

World Championships	Junior International
Betty Swashbuckle	Laura Kim
Sheena Mayday	Lola Shaz
	Carla Denantz
	Qian Kan
	Charlie Dubretski

At the other end of the spectrum are beliefs underpinned by the encouragement of younger developing athletes. This perspective considers that exposing young athletes to international experiences is worthwhile even if this is at the expense of a lower collective performance level of the group selected, at least in the early years. Taking this view to its extreme, backed up with a published selection policy with clear parameters,[22] the following selections would result. The four different selections from the first scenario are marked with an asterisk:*

Neither of these approaches avoid the impact of the Relative Age Effect. You can, however, begin to see how beliefs about squad selection send messages about the recognition or otherwise of age differences in the progress of young athletes and the value of accruing experience.

World Championships	Junior International
Betty Swashbuckle	Sheena Mayday*
Laura Kim*	Lola Shaz
	Qian Kan
	Lian Charles*
	Annette Beeler*

Notice that every selection you make also deselects individuals and in this case Carla Denantz who missed out on selection in the second scenario despite finishing fifth – she may be completely demotivated by the selection experience. It all depends on the way each sport's culture acknowledges such developmental approaches as standard and in peoples' expectations of the purpose of selection. As ever, perceptions of selection practices are very much shaped by how it is communicated to athletes and parents.

A striking finding from champions' autobiographies is the contrast in the international experience accrued between two teenage Olympians at their first Games. Michael Phelps at his first Olympics (Sydney, 2000, result: fifth) at the age of 15 had to get his first ever passport since he had never competed abroad before. By contrast, sailor Ben Ainslie competed at his first Games (Atlanta, 1996, result: second) at the age of 19, having gained international experience on 15+ occasions, starting at the aged 12 in far off Japan.

In sailing, often described as a type of physical chess on water, gaining experience is all-important since you only learn how to make good decisions and deal with alien weather conditions through being exposed to a range of situations.

But this is about different practices between sailing and swimming rather than different junior sport cultures between USA and Europe.

Misunderstandings about selection in junior tennis

Anne Pankhurst, who has worked for GB and US tennis federations, knows a thing or two about selection issues in and before adolescence. First, she was the mother of two tennis players who were themselves part of tennis selection and identification regimes. Second, she used to be in charge of the training of all English tennis coaches. Third, she was recruited to US Tennis and became involved in trying to solve the problem of how few 12-year-olds there were on the radar of US Tennis. It was fascinating talking to her.

In 2006, she set up a US-wide system to identify and select for enhanced training over 100 young girls, aged between eight and nine years. Of that group only two or three now remain near the top of the sport at the age of 16. She is quite sure that selection at a young age is almost pointless in any sport because the children are far too young and the processes can result in early specialisation that is often harmful to the athletes and stressful for families. The US project was abandoned after two years.

Now after years of study she has a doctorate in the subject. It lit a passion in her to research beliefs and perceptions of the selection of juniors. As we've said earlier, people's underlying beliefs about selection influence their perception of its role and purpose. She asked English coaches, parents and federation staff, 75 people in all, to respond on a 1–5 scale about the extent to which they believe statements such as:

- talent can be identified at a young age through a number of standardised physical, technical and tactical tests; and,
- rankings in junior tennis predict adult success.

Guess what? Coaches, parents and federation staff gave very different answers. She concluded that these and other results suggests a lack of coherence between the understanding of Talent Identification and Development processes by those three groups. In many instances people did not realise that, for example, the two above statements are not even supported by research evidence. She confirmed that 'in almost every instance the early selection of young players before puberty is underpinned by false assumptions of coaching/federation staff and subsequently parents.'

This illustrates that there are many misunderstandings about selection and development. The growing scientific evidence points out how difficult it is to predict adult success at least until the growth and maturation chaos of adolescence is over.

Final words

My closing words are about team sport: the role of chance and a mental toolkit in selection. We look at football and baseball.

Being in the 'right place at the right time' can have a notable influence on the selection in teams, perhaps more so than in individual sports. A professional football coach explained:

> Timing is everything … to have the right game at the right time. I think that is so important. Now, people would call that random, call it luck. I think chance is a good word.[23]

Good fortune in making a team is often related to unforeseen events and turning points that can have a positive or negative influence on a player's progress. Examples include a change of coach, performing well when the senior team manager is present and getting an opportunity due to injuries. A study of youth academy coaches at English football clubs illustrates how lucky breaks often shape a players trajectory for the better:

> You could be a left back and suddenly there's two [senior team] left backs injured. The manager says to me 'Who have you got?' He puts him in, he does a great job and now he's in the manager's mind. So you've got to have a little bit of luck.[24]

Team sport selection is often subjective and down to perception of coaches and/or scouts. This combined with the circumstantial influence of parental support, resources and living in a place that has good clubs and coaches means that there is a little more luck involved in making it in team rather than individual sport. Consider the recently released analysis by Arne Güllich of the development of top German professional players in 36 Bundesliga youth academies (see Table 8.2). The annual turn-over and deselection of players is staggering.

A child has a less than one in 10 chance (7 per cent) of making it all the way to the U19 squad if they start at U10, a one in four chance from the U15 category (25 per cent) and even when in the U18 squad, a third (33 per cent) are cut from squads before the U19 category. Again this evidence from 7900 young players suggests that selection before puberty has finished is not accurate at predicting U19 potential. I'd love to know how many who were deselected managed to get back into the system.

The respected econometric analyst, Nate Silver, attempted to reduce the subjectivity and randomness in selection decisions in professional sport. Silver's predictive analysis as a pollster was lauded in the 2012 US presidential election between Barack Obama and Mitt Romney, he correctly predicted the winners of all 50 states. His reputation is sky-high but he largely made his name earlier in US baseball by using data: his Player Empirical Comparison and Optimisation Test Algorithm (PECOTA) was designed to predict performance in Major League Baseball.

When his latest book was published in 2012 and he'd included a chapter about sporting talent, I simply had to read it. In essence one of the main messages of his writing is that we're not far off being able to measure and analyse every movement on a baseball field and in sport generally. 'This new technology will not kill off scouting but it may change its emphasis toward the things that are even harder to quantify ... like player's *mental tools.'* [my emphasis].[25]

Table 8.2 Proportion of U19 football players in German elite club football academy programmes who had also been members of the academy in previous age group categories.

Under 10	7.0
Under 11	8.5
Under 12	11.7
Under 13	14.3
Under 14	18.6
Under 15	25.2
Under 16	37.4
Under 17	45.8
Under 18	67.0

Arne Güllich, European Journal of Sport Science (2013): Selection, deselection and progression in German football talent promotion, European Journal of Sport Science, DOI: 10.1080/17461391.2013.858371.

From speaking to baseball scouts he describes mental tools as being slower to develop than physical ones. A scout he interviewed considered the age of 24 as about the time when the scout will no longer cut a player some slack if he sees signs that their mental tools are not developing: this sounds very generous to me. Silver identified five different components to a player's mental toolbox. Here we list the headings Silver uses and later in the book we devote a whole chapter to this theme (see chapter 14).

Silver claims the abilities that help predict success at the major-league level are:

- preparedness and work ethic;
- concentration and focus;
- competitiveness and self-confidence;
- stress management and humility;
- adaptiveness and learning ability.

These abilities are hard to measure and perhaps only emerge after young athletes have been stress-tested in the heat of competition, season-long training and dealing with setbacks. It is hard for selection decisions amid adolescence to take these abilities into account, which means we normally have to fall back on the evidence of competition results.

The more coaches, parents and young people know about the unavoidable compromises of selection amid adolescent growth the better. Ultimately adolescent sport mirrors one of life's lessons: it is unfair. But awareness of the processes involved has to help slightly dampen its effects.

9 Location, location, location
Revealing the geography of success

Geography, or more precisely the place and size of the town where you grow up, exerts a huge influence on your chances of sporting success. I thrived in a small town 50 metres from the sea – my windsurfing training environment – benefiting from being able to practice immediately after school. There were many other young wannabe racers like me, all desperate to improve and win the next local competition; we'd watch videos of the latest moves and then go out and have a go ourselves. The sport became part of our adolescent lives. Without knowing it we were all pushing each other on. I excitedly went to my first national championships aged 17 and finished fifth; from then I was hooked. Companies started to loan me the very latest equipment and my progress accelerated. It was all about location, a passion and seizing an opportunity. If I had grown up 10 miles inland it would never have happened.

Geography counts. But what is known about this on a national scale? Are there any patterns? The researcher Jean Côté and his colleagues[1] have identified the *size* of a town or city where you are more likely to become a champion as one with between 1000 and 500,000 residents. This equates to very small towns and modest cities (for example Bristol and Edinburgh in the UK have a population close to 500,000).

They realised they were on to something in 2006 when they looked at the birthplaces of 2200 Canadian and American professional athletes. Players from the National Hockey League (NHL), the National Basketball Association (NBA), Major League Baseball (MLB) and the Professional Golf Association (PGA) were sampled. They found that 15 per cent of these professional sportsmen came from towns and small cities, yet towns and small cities were home to only 1 per cent of the entire population. It must have been an eureka moment for them.

Investigating further, they established where *not* to live. Big cities with more than 500,000 residents were particularly poor at producing professional players. Cities of this size accounted for 52 per cent of the US population but significantly lower proportions of professional basketball (29 per cent), baseball (15 per cent), golf (13 per cent) and ice hockey (13 per cent) players. This was another striking finding – you might expect golfers to need wide open spaces, but the other sports are often associated with large urban areas. Think of informal baseball and basketball played in urban backyards and ice rinks often located in large cities.

Similar results were found in Australia, Europe and the Middle East which broadly supported these initial findings, although the optimal city size for producing elite athletes varied.

This phenomenon was quickly dubbed the 'birthplace effect', but perhaps the 'growing up place effect' might have been more accurate, if rather less catchy; what is really important is the quality of early training environments and developmental assets (e.g. clubs, schools, coaches and competitions/leagues) available. Once a finding like this emerges, people inevitably start looking for a cause or explanation, although scientifically proving precise cause and effect can be problematic. Let's look at the possible processes involved in making geography so important.

Big fish, small pond?

In your early years in any activity, achieving success and developing confidence in your abilities motivates you to keep going and, with more practice, improvement follows. One educational theory, the 'big fish small pond effect' is useful here. 'Is it better to be a relatively large fish in a small pond even if you don't learn to swim as well?' asks the paper which originally proposed this effect.[2] The answer is 'yes' – being a big fish probably has advantages.

Athletes in smaller communities are more likely to gain both the devoted coaching attention and the confidence to progress. A small fish in a very large, competitive pond (e.g. a junior in London or New York) will, the theory suggests, find it harder to develop their confidence and abilities as effectively.

Well that's one angle. But researchers involved with the original US study consider it is the overall environment and facilities in towns that are important. They identified that athletes in towns or smaller cities go to better schools, receive more attention from their PE teachers and have more access to open spaces, facilities and coaching.

The researchers concluded that these small communities 'may facilitate the achievement of elite sport performance by providing a more supportive and facilitative psychosocial environment for early development'.[3]

It seems that sport programmes in smaller communities may offer more opportunities for helpful relationships with coaches, parents and peers, a sense of belonging and relatedness and effective integration of the sports programme to the community.[4] These all help young athletes develop.

Andy Murray is one example that springs to mind. He grew up in the small Scottish town of Dunblane, population 8000. An understanding tennis coach mum, Judy, helped too. Judy has spoken about a significant event that enhanced their small town facilities, without which Andy would very likely have taken a different sporting path: the building of the first indoor courts in Scotland five miles down the road at Stirling University in 1994, when Andy was just seven years old.[5] It enabled year-round practice from a young age. From Judy's small district under-10 training squad, three world top-30 ranked players emerged: Andy (singles), his brother Jamie (doubles player) and Colin Fleming (top doubles player).

However, aged 15, Murray had to up and leave to go to Spain in order to further his training. This was his autonomous choice. He and his mother visited three European tennis academies; she favoured one due to its coaching but Andy preferred another. She let him make the final choice saying, 'You have to let them [young people] make their own decisions'.

So at what point in development does the need to *change* your environment arrive? At some stage a previously useful, but no longer helpful environment needs to be enhanced to challenge and extend developing athletes. It is almost inevitable that the competition and coaching at a local club is not enough and young athletes either have to travel a lot or relocate.

Rethinking place of birth

I was still puzzled: is your place of birth (i.e. what is on your birth certificate), really an accurate proxy for where you spend your developmental years as an athlete? You might be born in one place, grow up somewhere else and spend most of your primary or secondary school time in yet another location, commuting to school every day. I started searching for evidence that took some of this into consideration. I did not have to look far.

After it was announced in 2005 that London would host the Olympics, Britain assembled a team of sports scientists to help sports expand their pool of athletes with elite potential. As part of their work they surveyed just over 1000 top athletes and asked where they were born, but also where they went to school.[6] Comparing this to census data, two startling findings emerged that support the idea of smaller town environments being favourable. Compared to the general population, elite *team* sport athletes were almost 10 times more likely to spend their developmental years in very small villages (<2000 residents) while athletes from *individual* sports where 10 times more likely to spend developmental years in small towns (<5000 residents). Remember the US study found the difference to the general population census data to be a factor of 15, so these findings are also in the same ballpark and again point to small towns being important but this time looks beyond a birth certificate, is in another country, the UK, and is in different Olympic sports. Therefore, we can start to be convinced there's something in this.

While youngsters in cities can and do succeed, as Londoner Bradley Wiggins and other champions clearly illustrate, it is just statistically less likely, pointing towards location, facilities, early coaching encouragement and the overall environment as being very important.

Champions' examples

Looking at champions' autobiographies, there are clear examples of running, football and swimming being easily accessible in cities. What about sports using specialised equipment and facilities such as rowing, sailing or cycling? Remember it is British success in these specialised sports that Australians use to taunt the British, saying: 'you are only any good at these *seated* sports'.

Steve Redgrave is the all-time most decorated rower, with five gold medals in five successive Olympic Games (1984–2000). Would he have started on this path had he not lived in a town on the banks of the River Thames? I suspect not. He had the good fortune to be at a state school with a certain English teacher and rower called Francis Smith:

> Francis thought [Redgrave] had the ideal physique for rowing, according to his fairly crude, yet effective selection procedure. [Francis] would go round and look at pupils' hands and feet. If they were bigger than average, he'd ask them to row because the chances were that they would grow into tall, powerful specimens … His enthusiasm was infectious. Often [Francis] would meet [the rowers] by his car, drive [them] to the rowing club and take [them] home. Without his patience and enthusiasm, [Redgrave's] future would have been very different. If there was one person – other than [his] parents [Redgrave had] to thank for planting that original seed of interest and then proceeding to encourage [his] burgeoning talent, it was [Francis].[7]

Location helped Redgrave again, since in the same town lived an international rowing coach, Mike Spracklen, who was to mentor him in his first six years as a senior international oarsman. He set up an elite training group in the town, a mini hub of excellence within which Redgrave went to the next level.

Consider other all-time Olympic greats in sailing (Ben Ainslie, four golds, one silver) and track cycling (Chris Hoy, six golds, one silver). They also grew up virtually next to places where they could express their early passion: next to the ocean (Ainslie, in Falmouth) and near to a velodrome (Hoy, in Edinburgh). For all three of these British greats, plus Andy Murray, their local club and enthusiastic coaching support allowed them to play and practise their sport, getting better and better; training becomes a lot easier when you live just down the road.

The importance of environment is highlighted by a recent trend in sport's organisations acknowledging the location factor and attempting to exploit it by pooling their talented athletes and best available assets (coaches, staff, facilities etc.) in special training hubs or academies. Within this model, those with the necessary attributes are identified and encouraged to move to the hub location, where everything is in place to help them develop into champions.

Take, for example, Joanna Rowsell, the British Olympic gold medal winning cyclist (see chapter 2). After doing well, aged 15, in a cycling test run at her school, she was encouraged, when she finished her school education, to relocate to Manchester to join a specialised development programme at the British Cycling academy. Here she was immersed in full-time training, conditioning, nutrition, psychology, strategy, cooking for herself and competing overseas and gradually learnt how to become an elite athlete.

The need to move location to further a career is nothing new but it perhaps applies more in sport since the resources and competition are focused on a limited number of places. As we will see later in the book, parents and athletes make some big decisions about relocating in search of optimal environments.

This logic of bringing people and resources together partly explains why having a large talent pool alone (i.e. pyramid thinking – see chapter 3) is not enough. It is possible to succeed without investing in widespread grassroots facilities (which might level the playing field) when it's much easier and probably more effective at producing champions to identify those with potential after puberty and take them to a hub location.

Kenya and some 'what if?' examples

I want to change the scale on which we are examining this from the population sizes of towns to a whole country perspective. Using some examples of unique champions from Kenya, I consider the influence of national culture on shaping athletes' opportunities. In a moment I will try and respond to an outlandish question: 'what if Usain Bolt grew up in Kenya?' But first, let's consider the extent to which being from Kenya shaped the success of three athletes: their national football captain Victor Wanyama, their 800m Olympic gold medallist and world record holder David Rudisha and their Tour de France winner Chris Froome (now riding for Great Britain).

A country's national sporting culture contributes to which sports talented athletes migrate towards. In Kenya, the two national sporting passions are running and football, and the choice of sports available at the highest level is far more limited than, for example, in Canada or Australia.

The Kenyan football captain, Victor Wanyama

Kenyan football has traditionally had few international role models but now they have a rising star – a man who made the Celtic football club fan Rod Stewart cry when he scored against Barcelona in 2012. Wanyama's contribution helped Celtic to a famous win against the multiple European champions, and helped secure his own future; in July 2013 he transferred to the English Premier League club Southampton, making him the most expensive player ever to be sold by a Scottish club.

Wanyama started early. The third child in a family of eight, his early success was stimulated by Kenya's football culture and role models in his family. His father played for Kenya and his elder brother was so successful that he left for European football clubs. He has said that playing football against his brothers, who were bigger and older was where he learned his competitiveness.[8]

Wanyama grew up in the large capital city Nairobi (population 3 million), so his case suggests, along with many other football examples, that football development may not be so affected by city size as other sports.

Indeed family background, hard work, the right mental tools and moving on to new club locations in Nairbobi and then Sweden probably account for his rapid progress. By the age of seven he was representing Nairobi and, astonishingly, Wanyama made his senior debut for the Kenyan national side aged just 15. Clearly he was an early developer, with eight years of rapid development (from 7 to 15) leading to a place in the national team. He is now 1.88m (6ft 2in) and 76 kilos (12st). His physique was overlaid with further finesse and skill development when he joined his brother in a Swedish football academy aged just 17.

Travelling so far away from home, so young, to a new culture and managing to progress suggests a steely mental resilience. His good fortune in scoring that high profile goal against Barcelona propelled him further. Now Wanyama is the captain of Kenya's national side and his move to Southampton almost instantly made the club one of the most supported overseas teams back in Kenya.

In summary his path can partly be attributed to national culture (football), learning from the challenge of relocation but also role models in his family.

What if David Rudisha grew up elsewhere?
Kenyan 800m Olympic champion and world record holder David Rudisha is from Kilgoris, 200 miles east of Nairobi. What if he had been born a few hundred miles away in another African country or on the coastal plain, rather than adjacent to the Kenyan Rift Valley where distance running has high cultural importance? Would his story be different now? Probably 'yes' – here is why.

There was no indication that distance running was a national passion in Kenya until their first Olympic success at the 1968 Mexico City games. Some sport historians even claim that distance track running is a tradition 'invented' after independence from Britain in 1963 which helped define the identity of a very ethnically diverse new nation.[9] From 1968 onwards the Kenyan distance running tradition has taken hold, particularly in the Rift Valley, and even more particularly in the Nandi district.

David Rudisha: astonishingly broke the world record without a pacemaker

Good runners can turn semi-professional at a younger age in Kenya than most other countries due to the importance placed on running and the opportunities available. The history of running since 1968 and a number of successful athletes as role models make it the main path to international sporting success. Those with potential often use running to enhance their education, securing sports scholarships to US universities. Rudisha, however, did not follow this route since his ability was so great that Olympic gold and world record achievement already beckoned.

Had he lived in the lowlands or a neighbouring country his story may well have been different; being athletic alone does not propel you to the top. The surrounding culture and environment act by a sort of osmosis and heighten an individual's and their coach's expectations, the available opportunities changing their aspirations. Living away from the Rift Valley running hub would have been a huge handicap to Rudisha's development.

What if Chris Froome had grown up outside Africa?

The 2013 Tour de France champion was born in Kenya and lived there until he was 14, when he moved to South Africa for his secondary school and university education (although he later gave up his economics degree up to pursue professional cycling). Before considering the 'what if?' question of his living elsewhere we need to appreciate his unusual multinational journey to the top.

Froome was the youngest of three brothers. While they went to school in England he lived with his single mother, a physiotherapist, in a modest apartment on the edge of Nairobi. When he was 12 years old his mother approached the Kenyan national cycling champion David Kinjah, 13 years Froome's senior, to help direct her son's interest in the sport. He thrived on the freedom of an outdoor lifestyle and long rides with Kinjah, who became his mentor and lit the spark for his interest in competitive racing.

In the school holidays his mother asked if Chris could stay with Kinjah for those weeks; often staying in spartan conditions he was enlivened by the adventure of long rides and camping in the bush. Training with someone so much older meant he often pushed himself to exhaustion and sometimes collapse, such was his inner determination.

This drive to progress continued when he had more cycling opportunities while attending school in South Africa. With Kinjah he continued to find ingenious ways of competing abroad. But according to Kinjah he had to fight the Kenyan authorities, who were reluctant to support a South Africa-based athlete at the 2006 Commonwealth Games – the cycling team threatened to go on strike before he was eventually included.[10] He went on to complete two-thirds of an economics degree in South Africa before taking the opportunity of cycling in Europe with a professional team. He rode his first Tour de France burdened with grief shortly after his mother died in 2008.

Then he kept getting sick and eventually discovered he was affected by an undetected strain of bilharzia – a parasitic disease often found in Africa which affects your red blood cells and oxygen-carrying potential, the worst condition for an endurance athlete.[11] Eventually, fully fit in 2011 he rode the Tour again with Team Sky and started to realise his true potential with a fully funded team, underpinned by sports science and Olympic expertise.

The opportunity to roam and the outdoor lifestyle he enjoyed in Africa certainly shaped him, and we can only wonder if he would have found cycling living elsewhere, perhaps in Europe. It would depend on two big 'ifs': would he have come across the sport and also found a suitable mentor or coach to encourage him? It seems unlikely had he followed his brothers' English private school education; such schools are not renowned for offering cycling on their curriculum, preferring team sports like rugby, football or cricket. Perhaps we'll be better able to answer this question when his unique story is fully told – it will no doubt make a fine autobiography with its twists and turns!

What if Usain Bolt grew up in Kenya?

Usain Bolt needs no introduction. If he had grown up in Kenya, the likelihood is that, like the small village of his childhood, Sherwood Content in Jamaica, he too would find the wild bush a natural playground. 'I only had to step out of my front door to find something physical to do. There was always something to play, always somewhere to run and always something to climb. The woods delivered an exercise programme …'[12] Like Chris Froome's enjoyment of similar freedom outside in Kenya, Bolt would still have been able to play wild.

But what about school? Compare Jamaica where, at the age of 11 he had to decide between the two sports winking at him through the lens of Jamaican national culture: sprinting and cricket. He talks of a conscious decision guided by his father:

> … school didn't want me to play cricket any more … I was hoping to go to PE lessons, pick up my pads and bat and continue my dream of becoming a Test sensation. The teachers had others ideas, though. They wanted me to focus on my running … I was turned away [from cricket].[13]

His father counselled him on the benefit of the individual sport of athletics offering more chances of being in control of his own destiny rather than the vagaries of team selection in cricket: Bolt chose his running. Were he in Kenya, football would compete with his running such is the attraction of soccer in Kenya – who knows which sport he might have chosen – it would depend on his parents' advice.

Once fully matured aged 15, at 1.95m (6ft 5in) and 95kg (14st 13lb), what direction might he have gone in as a tall runner in Kenya? Such is the place long distance running holds in the Kenyan identity, I suspect he would have been encouraged to try other longer disciplines beyond sprinting. In Jamaica he tried 800m, 1,500m and even cross country once, but in his words, 'it was clear I didn't have the lungs or will-power to run anything longer [than 400m]'.[14]

It is probably a whole further book to discuss if and how willpower and work ethic might differ between countries but it is pretty clear genetically he had plenty of fast-twitch muscle fibres for him to excel at sprinting. But we might wonder if the coaching expertise for sprinting exists in Kenya to take him to the levels he has subsequently reached, or whether Bolt might have been encouraged to take on the one lap (400m) or two lap (800m) distances in which Kenya has had previous Olympic success?

Maybe the lure of American University scholarships and specialist sprint/power-based conditioning expertise would have tempted him away? He had turned down such offers in Jamaica, since he was wary of being burned out by a gruelling intercollege competitive schedule and he didn't want to move away from his mother – he was her only child. Instead he moved to a specialised High Performance hub in Kingston.

Sprinting expertise does exist in Kenya, but a dedicated coach would have to raise their knowledge levels and access the medical expertise Bolt needed to identify, and then manage his scoliosis. In Bolt's real life story this medical input was eventually sourced by visiting a German doctor.

National culture and location exercises such a strong influence on sporting practice and family aspirations that Bolt's path would probably have been different. We cannot be sure what shape it would have taken, but in Bolt's case his parents' advice was key.

Final thoughts

This tour through location influences at two different scales – the town and the nation – suggests that geography is a compelling influence. Well it is, but it does not stand alone since the local and national environment is the context in which athletes, coaches and parents live and work. It is very difficult to filter out the discrete influence of location on champions' paths since national culture and smaller scale motivational climates seep in everywhere. We often can't see their influence. That is why I used some thought experiments, contrasting 'what if?' situations, which help to illustrate the possible impacts. But one intriguing separated twins story recently emerged that illuminated this debate further. Mo Farah's (Olympic and World Championships double gold in 5000m and 10,000m) separation from his identical twin Hassan in Somalia, aged 8 and his subsequent life and athletic success in London, England and now Oregon, USA, vividly demonstrates how two youngsters with identical genes are influenced by where they grow up, with geography largely determining their opportunities.

When viewing what shapes sporting champions it is often rather difficult to grasp what we mean by a social perspective. This chapter's focus on location and context makes the case that the social world within which people develop profoundly shapes us all. In the next couple of chapters we turn our attention away from looking at immediate surroundings to consider what it means to gradually adopt the identity of, and become, a genuine athlete, sometimes with an epiphany moment.

10 Fitness and recovery epiphanies

Michael Johnson hated doing weights; he avoided them. It sounds odd doesn't it? He was one of the supreme athletes of his generation, world record holder, an athlete whose body showed that he worked out a fair bit. OK, this is disingenuous; his dislike of weight workouts was in his early years of serious training at Baylor University. In each of three years at university he picked up injuries and these stunted his progress. Finally, he had an epiphany of sorts: the purpose of the conditioning and weight programme he had been asked to do was as much about decreasing the likelihood of injury as it was performance. He picked up the phone to his coach, 'I know I'm not doing as much as I should on the stretching front and in my strength-training sessions, I'll do whatever it takes' to minimise the risk of injury.[1] A commitment was being made to change from being a talented sportsman to becoming a genuine athlete.

For him, like other champions, it was a key turning point in realising what it takes to progress. He moved his gym sessions to the morning to help avoid any skimping and, with his coach's help, started using a strength and conditioning specialist coach to refine his conditioning. With video analysis of the final 100m of the 400m race they identified how his running technique broke down under fatigue. They developed a conditioning regime to develop the shoulder, chest, bicep, triceps, deltoid and trapezoid muscle groups (arm, shoulder, neck). The following season his performances dramatically improved.

My point is that, for many athletes, the transformation from sportsman or woman to podium-level athlete is achieved through getting stuck into some serious, structured, sustained conditioning – often, but not always, gym work. It is not an overnight fitness fix: it takes a while for the body to respond, in between the demands of the competitive season. Michael Johnson's private epiphany was matched by Usain Bolt's more public one: it took being overtaken off the bend of the 200m World Championship final in 2007 for him to step up his conditioning to champion levels: it worked, he shattered three world records the following year. Success, as we know, comes with much hidden work behind the lines.

Tennis is tough

Five-set tennis matches are brutal tests of conditioning: not just conditioning but the ability to recover during tournament play from playing multiple matches in the earlier rounds. Remember just one match often takes over 4–5 hours (men),

3–4 hours (women) often in stifling heat. Roger Federer's conditioning coach outlined the problem he faced with his 19-year-old client, ranked 29th in the world back in 2000:

> [Federer's] problem was that his enormous talent allowed him to cover up his athletic shortcomings … I had a timetable of three years to bring him up to the best physical condition.[2]

We all know which direction his game and ranking went in after that.

Likewise for Andre Agassi. But listen as he recounts one of his first conversations, also at the age of 19, with Gil Reyes, his influential conditioning coach. He'd unsuccessfully worked with two other trainers.

> Reyes: How much do you run every day?
> Agassi: Five miles.
> Why?
> I don't know.
> Have you ever run five miles in a match?
> No.
> How often in a match do you run more than five steps in one direction before stopping?
> Not very.
> … The way I see it, your sport isn't about running, it's about starting and stopping. You need to focus on building the muscles necessary for starting and stopping.[3]

The following year, aged 20, he made his first grand slam final and went up the world rankings from seventh to fourth. By the US Open he comments that

> under Gil's care and close supervision I pack on 10 pounds of muscle … I feel lean and rangy and dangerous. I punch and scratch my way to the [final] … and still have plenty of rocket fuel in my tank.[4]

If you have watched the rise of Andy Murray towards the top of the rankings you may remember he also desperately needed better conditioning early in his career when he would often run out of gas in long matches, sometimes accompanied with leg cramps. Now with specialist work he is one of the fittest players. All of these athletes were 18–20 years of age when they saw the light and realised what was required.

Conditioning as science

Conditioning coaches' influence on champions' careers often goes unrecognised, but they teach training and body awareness that helps sportsmen become authentic athletes and often lifts them to the next level. Modern conditioning coaches have a degree in sports science and additional training that allows them

Andre Agassi: felt lean, rangy and dangerous when he finally reached elite tennis

to analyse human movement of any sport and translate the physical demands of an activity into specific training programmes. What Johnson and Agassi described so well in their accounts is the specificity and intensity of the training involved in their sport that is key to improved performances.

Conditioning commonly has strength and/or endurance purposes along with others such as flexibility, weight gain (e.g. Ben Ainslie) and/or injury prevention. But there is also the use of conditioning to improve stability or balance of a complex biomechanical system. As Seb Coe describes:

> The foot alone has 26 bones, 33 joints, 107 ligaments, 19 muscles and 19 tendons. And while on one level the body is extremely strong, it is also extremely fragile, and the difference between the two is often related to balance. If your left side is stronger than your right … [it suggests] that you're running asymmetrically.[5]

Champion athletes spend considerable time behind closed doors working on stability and balance. In the popular parlance 'core stability' focuses mostly on the trunk, but the shoulder and hip also have a crucial role to play through the serape effect. The serape effect is based on the concept that the core muscles act as a diagonal connector between opposing hips and shoulders. If you have ever had a dislocated shoulder, knee or ankle injury you will also appreciate the complex range of muscle groups that stabilise these joints. If the muscles that support these joints are appropriately developed they help prevent injuries. Stability and balance of the shoulder, hip, knee and ankle is something that triple jump tests to the limit.

Jonathan Edwards and others find that repeatedly belting down the runway and hopping, skipping and jumping (the triple jump) is not particularly good for the body. Like many sports too much repetition of one movement bearing high loads can lead to injury. Edwards is a good example of someone who spent considerable time with his conditioning coach lifting weights and refining his stability and balance. He even experimented in balance by wearing roller blades in the gym, not to help him get around, but to provide an unstable platform to refine his stability! Something not for the fainthearted: stability balls are the more common balance aid these days.

Stress, adaption and the lactic myth

Just as psychological challenge and stress leads champions to adapt and grow, so does physical stress. The difference is physical progress can easily be measured. Under the right level of stimulus, body systems respond to increased demands by developing to cope. Some of the main body systems that respond to training stimulus are the skeletal, muscular, cardiovrespiratory and nervous systems. The skill of the conditioning coach is to set the training at the right level: am I setting the training too hard or not hard enough?

You might think all training changes are muscular or related to the heart/lungs but some of the most significant changes occur in the nervous system's ability to make the muscles do what is needed. Mark Jarvis[6] neatly summarises three main aspects of adaption through training:

- The signals to our muscles to move comes in rapid pulses. When we train these pulses are speeded up (the 'rate coding' is increased) and this results in more force or speed being produced.
- Each nerve controls a certain number of muscle fibres and what training does is increase the proportion of a muscle that is recruited for use. Surprisingly, the average person uses only 30–40 per cent of their muscle – with training this proportion is increased.
- Coordination of nerve signals both within a single muscle and between muscles is developed – for example, the precise pattern of contraction and relaxation is refined making movement more efficient.

There also a surprising amount of bone development going on. For instance, even among young adolescents who play sport a few times a week, the bones are getting stronger compared to those not in training. Bone is a living tissue; it is in a constant state of change. It is made of a calcium mineral, embedded in a protein mesh, which makes bone slightly flexible. A study of female gymnasts, both young girls and middle-aged women, found that not only are prepubertal gymnasts likely to have a much better bone mineral density, but that later in life, women who had trained as gymnasts also had much denser bones than non-gymnasts.[7] Also, boys who did the most vigorous daily activity had 12 per cent more bone strength than less active boys.[8] Bones as well as muscles become stronger to cope with increased demands.

In addition, weight-bearing exercise strengthens ligaments and tendons, thus making joints more stable. Prolonged training therefore lays down the foundation for increased efficiency and withstanding some of the incredible stresses placed on the limbs and joints in elite sport – think of triple jump or rugby or American football.

But what of lactic acid? It has been blamed for everything: the burning sensation in muscles, fatigue and the muscle soreness afterwards. The bad press that lactic acid receives is ill-informed. Most athletes believe that lactate is a byproduct of anaerobic exercise that causes muscle fatigue by increasing the acidity of the tissues causing them to no longer function effectively. New discoveries in 2001[9] and 2006[10] provide a more nuanced view and show that lactate provides a link between anaerobic and aerobic metabolisms. In fact it serves as both a direct and indirect fuel for muscle contraction. Lactate delays fatigue in a two different ways.

First, lactate production in muscles supports the rapid pulses that trigger muscle contraction (related to the polarisation of sodium and potassium molecules) and without it you would fatigue sooner. Second, the big discovery was that when lactate is released into the bloodstream and pumped around the body it is used as an energy source by essential organs such as the heart, lungs, brain and liver. Not only is it reused in these important places but the more you train the more muscle cells adapt, and it can be used again *within* the working muscle thereby sparing the use of key glycogen energy resources. This lactic reuse provides a more detailed explanation of how training improves the efficiency of the body systems.

Recovery is training

If you have ever done a hard training session you'll know that the physiological stress induced by intense exercise is associated with energy depletion and mechanical muscle damage; this is the real cause of muscle soreness, and nervous system fatigue along with possible inflammation. Put someone in a performance laboratory after hard training days and they won't function well: they will experience decreased muscle function, disturbed muscle position sense and reaction time as well as increased stiffness that can last for several days.[11] It is a wonder that athletes can go again the next day when in training, tournaments (tennis, athletics) or the ultimate grind, the Tour de France. The only reason they can is that they have learnt to approach recovery.

Chrissie Wellington explains why she thinks recovery is training:

> I realise it is not the actual sessions of swim bike and run that make you fitter, it is the periods you spend recovering in between, during which your body adapts and regenerates. That's why I say I train 24/7 – recovery is training. It is the most important part of it, in fact … spending the day shopping or gardening doesn't count as rest. It has to involve sitting down preferably on a sofa.[12]

Perhaps the logic of Victoria Pendleton being asked to have an afternoon nap at her Swiss training camp (see chapter 12) makes sense – but how easy would you find it to switch off and rest in a large group room?

We'll come back to sleep in a moment. In the last decade there has been a plethora of suggestions of aids to recovery. For example, ice-baths, compression garments and anti-inflammatory drugs. Research has shown that after hard, intense sessions such as repeated sprinting, measurements of performance disruption and muscle damage were partly mitigated by such aids. Steve Ingham, from the English Institute of Sport, explains that there is an application of research into training aids to situations when:

> … recovery in a short time frame is of paramount performance, such as between matches in football say Wednesday to Saturday, or in competition scenarios where an athlete could have a round in the morning and semi-final the following evening. The sights and sounds (ooh aargh, grit teeth) of ice baths is now not just inherently familiar … but it is also worn as a badge of just how 'hard' athletes are! [13]

He reports something international runner Hayley Tullet said:

> I didn't do ice baths, this year I did. Now I am doing 10 per cent more mileage, I am feeling fresher after my hard sessions and more able to go harder the next day. But if I look at my training diary for the last four months and compare it to last years comparable sessions I am not going any faster. So am I just doing more to get the same effect?

The message emerging is that inadequate recovery is caused by not getting the basics (sleep, eat and rest) right and using poorly scheduled training programmes. The more sexy, explicit recovery tools such as ice baths 'should be regarded as icing on the cake'[14] and getting the basics right is the main focus of athletes and coaches. While I was at a workshop with the strength and conditioning team of Leicester rugby club they confirmed that they didn't go in for 'all the fancy stuff' but concentrated on delivering prompt food for their team and then getting them home for a good sleep.

How do champions describe their experience of training and recovery? First, Chris Hoy on how his attitude changed:

> … my attitude was: if I'm not going well [performance wise], then I should train harder. Instead of resting, I thought I should put in more effort; that I should just try harder. I can say without hesitation or reservation that a big turning point for me – and the reason for later improvements – was that I learnt that less can be more.[15]

And, Bradley Wiggins, perhaps not coincidentally his teammate with the same professional back up personnel, expresses similar ideas using the lexicon of recovery-speak:

He [coach Shane Sutton] is great at knowing when to make an athlete stop and rest. He's always saying, 'You need to recruit now.' By which he means letting the work soak in. His argument is: you need to do all this training but you also need to take the time off to let your body recover and adapt. Not a lot of athletes do this, but you need to recruit all the effort and repair all the muscle damage for the training to have any effect. If you don't rest you don't recruit.[16]

But not every team can afford such detailed one-to-one support from experienced experts who can manage an athlete's daily schedule and supply top facilities and easy access to food/sleep.

What happens when you are an emerging athlete and have just started strength and conditioning and pushing for Olympic qualification as a full time athlete? UK high jumper Matt Roberts was in that position in 2012 and he identified a number of challenges in making the step up in level.[17] He describes becoming physically a lot stronger very quickly, but his training technique did not keep pace. He also 'trained himself to death' at the start of his conditioning but gradually listened to coaches and his body and learnt how to organise himself and recover.

The trouble was, he says, 'until the age of 18 I had cooked one hot meal before I moved away'. He recognised that part of recovery is eating but he was not really able to manage mealtimes well at the start – especially hard when as an athlete you have to eat every 3–4 hours. At first he resorted to nuts and cottage cheese. This is a glimpse of the hard lonely road that exists for those with limited coaching back up. His personal best remains at an impressive 2.26m (7ft 4in) and we may yet see him at the Olympic Games. In 2012 the medals were won with heights of 2.38m (7ft 9in) for gold and 2.29m (7ft 5in) for Bronze: only 3cm (1.2in) above his personal best. A tangible target and motivation if ever it were needed.

A strength and conditioning coach comments:[18]

I tend to think of the people like Matt getting into conditioning as making the transition from exercising to training. The two can be very similar and are differentiated by one word: planning. You can exercise very hard every day using work which looks just the same as the training athlete. The critical factor comes from the key constructs of a training process, namely progression, planning, specificity and overload. Many people pay lip service to these but their training remains static, meaning they are not optimizing all their effort.

In emerging athletes such as Matt the question is: how can the warning signs of overtraining without enough recovery be spotted?

An intriguing investigation of 94 young Dutch soccer players, aged 15–18, recently looked into what is known as the stress–recovery balance.[19] An established stress-recovery questionnaire (The RESTQ-Sport) was used each month over two competitive seasons along with an interval shuttle-run test. Seven players with declining shuttle run results of at least a month were classified as 'overreaching' in their training – a sort of amber traffic light that their physical performance was stagnating.

An unfavourable questionnaire score appeared two months *before* the overreaching signalled by declining shuttle run tests. What were most interesting were the areas that the questionnaire identified most strongly with the overreaching athletes compared with the healthy group. These were: emotional stress, physical recovery, general well-being and sleep quality. Physical recovery then also has emotional and sleep-related elements. The implication is that there are potentially ways of monitoring overreaching in its early stages.

Commercial tools using these types of ideas are evident in web-based applications such as *Restwise*, whose snappy tag line of 'superior performance through intelligent recovery' encapsulates the wise use of rest. It uses 11 physical and psychological markers to help athletes and coaches monitor their stress–recovery balance, including appropriate sleep quality.

Athletes and sleep: a paradox

The paradox with sleep and elite athletes lies in the fact that exercise is often prescribed as a treatment for those with insomnia yet it appears athletes aren't great sleepers compared to the general population.

While most champions understandably talk of poor sleep often before a major day of competition, adrenaline normally does its job in making athletes alert, sharp and able to perform to their optimum often with minimal sleep. It is often a part of the anxiety of championship life: new surroundings, shared living with teammates, unfamiliar noises and so on. The effect of limited sleep on performance has also been trialled scientifically – imagine the grumpiness of eight swimmers who were tested for the effects of only 2.5 hours sleep per night over 4 nights. All that effort and there was no effect, yes none, of sleep loss observed when strength, lung and swimming performance tests were completed.[20]

But when poor sleep continues day after day, as parents of young children will know, the overall effect can be draining. Ask singlehanded round the world sailors. They don't like to sleep too much: they might bump into something or adverse weather might bump into them while they are snoozing. They get by with 2–5 hours of sleep a day for the 95-odd days that their race takes.[21] Some even train themselves before the event by taking 20 minutes of sleep every four hours in the weeks beforehand with the aim of developing a quick and effective deep sleep pattern. Physical and mental tasks are still possible with such little sleep.

However, this is in an extreme environment. The sleep habits of elite athletes in training have only recently been uncovered. Forty-seven elite athletes from Olympic sports wore a wrist device which detects movement (actigraphy) over a four-day period, and a matched group of non-sports people did the same.[22] The athletes group took longer to fall asleep (18.2 vs 5.0 min) and had lower measures of sleep quality and time asleep. Also, male athletes' sleep markers were poorer than female athletes. It is not clear why athletes aren't great sleepers, since intuitively one would expect training tiredness to take effect. Since sleep is such an important component of recovery it is likely that we'll be hearing more about this in years to come as further research is done.

Perhaps two of the most amazing feats of planned recovery in recent years were these:

▪ the way Michael Phelps kept his body and mind together while winning eight gold medals over nine days of swimming at the 2008 Beijing Olympics and
▪ Mo Farah's polished recovery routine in winning both 10,000- and 5000-metre titles at the 2012 Olympic Games and again at the World Championships a year later.

Final thoughts

The transformation from sports person to podium athlete does not happen overnight but I can see a pattern among champions that signals the start of their move to world beating performance. Once they begin to engage fully with strength and conditioning and also learn how to recover from their extra training load it often signals the beginning of a new phase in their progress to the top. The expertise and skills needed to achieve this smoothly cannot be taken for granted, as Matt Roberts's frank observations highlight.

Consider, though, if you are an athlete, how you and your coach need to keep the engagement and interest going in stressing and overloading your body thereby ensuring the necessary adaptations are maintained or improved. You can't keep on doing the same routine; somehow you need to devise ways of maintaining interest through variety, changed training locations, partners, equipment and even coaching personnel. How easy must it be to maintain this for a decade or, in the case of Steve Redgrave, almost two decades? It does point to the unique mindset of serial champions.

11 From passion to persistence, perfection and obsession
How does personality shape champions' paths?

Now let's explore in more detail two personality characteristics and their contribution to champions' development. First, *perfectionism* is often venerated as a positive attribute in elite sport but does it carry dangerous obsessive risks? A leading Olympic funding organisation, UK Sport, actively encourages athletes to develop 'an obsessive drive to be the best and maintain it'[1] but how good is this advice? Second, *persistence* as an attribute is key to many athletes' irregular paths to the top (examples include Mo Farah and Michael Jordan). Professor Angela Duckworth has made persistence and its contribution to achievement her metier, colonising the word 'grit' to describe 'effort and interest over years despite failure, adversity and plateaus in progress'. In this chapter you'll see that all champions need Duckworth's *grit* but not necessarily *perfectionism*. On the way we'll also discover how passion and obsession contribute to these two personality characteristics. For me, passion helps to explain how and why people follow their sport with such vigour in the first place. Passion then is not part of personality, but a motivational process.

Lighting the rocket: Passion

Ideally, after sampling a range of sports, most young people eventually start to show preference for some, especially those that they find enjoyable (see chapter 5). Of these a limited few may be perceived as particularly meaningful and start to have some resonance with youngsters, affecting how they see themselves. A special bond has thus been created between the youngster and the activity; they become passionate about the sport.[2]

Take this unusual story of how a scout leader changed Olympic canoe slalom gold medalist Etienne Stott's life:

> One of my early memories in canoeing was when we were going on a scout camp and they let us go down this little gravelly rapid. My scout leader Tim said 'Wow man you were brilliant out there, you must be a natural there must be something in your Canadian blood. You really know which way to

paddle'. I am actually half Canadian and something got into my mind sort of 'yeah I did actually go down that rapid, I can do this, I could be really good and he thinks I'm good' and that sort of flicked a switch in my mind and it kind of encouraged me and I suppose it inspired me really and that moment changed my life.[3]

The inspiration of a scout trip and his scout leader's reference to his heritage sparked Etienne Stott's passion. It was something Scott cherished and he also thought others would value his new interest. This early encouragement from someone outside the family potentially opens opportunities for far more young people because they are not fixed by their family's interests and aspirations. The early coach/teacher therefore plays a crucial yet often unrecognised role. Passion is deeper than excitement. A bond is formed, a link between the activity and the person's view of themselves.

There are also champions who are influenced by a parent's passion. For instance, Bradley Wiggins's mother encouraged him to watch Chris Boardman winning the individual pursuit final at the Barcelona Olympics on TV. His father's past cycling exploits were part of his fractured family's history, even though his distant father left him in their Belgium 'cycling home' when Bradley was two years old. This TV moment sparked his interest in the sport and by engaging with the activity he – like other young people – was constructing his identity.

It is more than a spark or an inspiration then, it is a process of becoming. For instance, a passionate boxer does not simply box, he or she *is* a boxer. Boxing is part of his or her personality. The activity is part of one's life and a regular expression of who they really think they are. Enjoying boxing occasionally would not be considered a passion. To become passionate about boxing, one would need to greatly enjoy it regularly and read about it, watch it live or online, discuss it with friends, find it meaningful and so to perceive oneself as a boxer.[4] This helps fuel motivation for relentless practice and, if the passion continues, to persist in long-term training. In turn, such determined sustained effort helps propel an athlete to ever-higher levels.

An educational psychologist commented on this description of passion:

> Both of the examples are quite mythical: the Canadian blood of Etienne Stott and the distant but talented cycling father of Bradley Wiggins. There is a personal mythology at work here. The passion that arises makes the person part of something bigger than themselves – passion has a narrative and this narrative begins somewhere, with the episode that lights the fuse.[5]

It is interesting, that we often construct our own narratives of our lives which partly reflect something rooted in our past family or community history.

However, something you love can be positive and harmful at the same time. Staying with the example of boxing, an unbridled passion could cause problems both within the sport and in everyday life. One or more of the following might disrupt someone realising their boxing dreams: overt aggression, overtraining and related illnesses, exercise addiction, disordered dieting due to trying to make weight and gambling on results. This might be called a sort of compulsive passion and a lay audience might say it was bordering on obsession. Passion can become compulsive when conditions are attached to the sport such as participation being fundamental to bolstering feelings of self-worth, or because the buzz from the sport is constantly sought and cannot be controlled. Athletes can thus experience 'an uncontrollable urge to partake in the activity they view as enjoyable. They cannot help but engage in the passionate activity, as the passion comes to control them'.[6] It's who they are, it's what they do. So passion has its risks.

The perfect performance

Can you distinguish between a champion athlete who is striving for excellence and one who is striving for perfection? I can now spot the difference, but before my research I'd fall back on stereotypes, such as perfectionists being 'never quite satisfied' or having 'high standards'. By interpreting what champions say and do, you can start to understand perfectionist patterns in how they think, feel and act. Their pattern of thinking is a multidimensional personality trait. Take a look at these comments by Chrissie Wellington with my emphasis in italics:

> Mentally it is hard trying to be the best the whole time. And I don't know who I'm trying to *prove myself* to. There is something inside me – not a voice exactly, but a deep seated *compulsion* – that strives for perfection … That can lead to *unnatural and excessive pressure* … I *constantly worry*, am I making the most of this … instead of just accepting and enjoying what is.[7]

The clues to part of her personality lie in the *italicised* parts of her description: *prove myself, compulsion, unnatural and excessive pressure, constant worry.* Perfectionism has many ingredients, some of which Wellington alludes to here. While someone striving for excellence would pursue high standards without strings attached, perfectionists display certain attributes and set themselves conditions. Here are six characteristic conditions used by perfectionists that interact with one another:

1. Use of inflexible and excessively stringent criteria in their commitment to flawlessness.
2. A harsh self-critical evaluation, pressure and sort of hyper-vigilance with little, if any, scope for error. This makes them profoundly sensitive to evaluation from others.
3. Even success can be problematic because they simply become more demanding until they inevitably experience failure.
4. As a result, perceived failure is commonplace and they condemn themselves as inadequate, which only generates further subsequent distress.
5. Self-worth is tied to accomplishments.

6. Thus, in order to compensate for these perceived inadequacies and reduce their distress, striving to achieve or train becomes compulsive: they have to do it to dampen negative evaluations.[8]

Consider this perfectionist's view of sport in which the boundary between success and failure is rigid, producing irrational thoughts such as: 'I'm worthless when I fail to achieve my targets'; 'anything less than a flawless training session is not good enough'; 'when I don't make my standards, it is complete failure'; 'everything I do on the field that is less than perfect will be criticised by others' or 'when I make mistakes, people will think negatively of me'.[9]

I am arguing that some elite athletes are perfectionists and that this carries a risk. However, is it actually necessary to be a perfectionist to succeed? In my opinion, it is naive to assume that promoting perfectionism in sport is positive. Many champions succeed without being perfectionists; their passionate drive for excellence is what propels them (e.g. Michael Phelps, Matthew Pinsent, Lionel Messi, Tanni Grey-Thompson, Jessica Ennis). They thrive on the project of working to be the best that they can, realising that losing and not being perfect is all part of the process of identifying errors and improving.

By contrast, the perils associated with a perfectionist's way of thinking can lead to vulnerability. It is true that early in an athlete's career this pattern of motivation can frequently achieve world-beating performances but without the compulsive aspects of perfectionism being managed, sustained success is unlikely; as some athletes have described, it can lead to burn-out, turmoil or path to purgatory.[10] Describing a period in which he was falling into a state of depression, Jonny Wilkinson relates how his perfectionist thoughts had both helpful and unhelpful elements:

> My fiercely obsessive mind, which has always given me the upper-hand on the pitch, has latched on to this negativity and turned on me in a bad way ... My obsessiveness, has become my undoing.[11]

Earlier in his life Wilkinson's perfectionism was the motivational prism through which he viewed his sport. He relentlessly practised two things he could control and that could be measured: his kicking of penalties and his fitness compared to teammates. For instance, once the regular team practices had finished Wilkinson would often spend hours refining his kicking, but his own harsh and inflexible rules often meant he stayed out until darkness and beyond:

> I always like to finish on a set of six perfect kicks, and that if I mess up the sixth, I'll start again... if I'm hitting a set of twenty drop goals and the last two aren't absolutely perfect, I'm going to say sod this I'm doing twenty more'.[12] Three hour kicking sessions were sometimes the result of this compulsion. This appears to be bordering on obsessive behaviour.

Wilkinson also describes the way in which his own self-imposed standards were supplemented by how he thought others were evaluating him, a characteristic known as 'social prescribed perfectionism'. Striving to reach standards *perceived* rather than imposed by others, in comparison to standards applied by oneself leaves athletes more vulnerable. In a study of 167 junior male soccer players in academies and centres of excellence attached to English professional clubs it was found that up to 25 per cent of the boys reported sometimes experiencing symptoms of burnout (being exhausted physically and mentally, resulting in loss of interest and poorer performances). Those who reported perceived pressures from others, a fear of making mistakes and other external pressures were at the most risk from burnout. Non-perfectionists and players who displayed perfectionism driven by their *own* high standards were significantly less vulnerable.[13]

Fear of failure is a strange thing to be motivated by because effectively you are driven to avoid something. However, it is more likely when you think others are imposing standards on you. The rower Martin Cross felt this fear of failure vividly and it was what drove him to win Olympic Gold with Steve Redgrave and other crewmates in 1980. Thirty or so years later, speaking in an interview with Sky Sports, Cross reveals his negative mindset at the time going into that Olympic final as world record holders and favourites:

> What my mind did was to sort of say I mustn't lose it – and that mindset, negative away-from motivation is very strongly fear based motivation, so you create a fear and you want to get away from it as quickly as possible. So the fear in my mind was of losing the race. And so, you know, it's not great if you spend your life using negative motivation since you just get good at creating fears to move away from.[14]

This was spoken with a wry smile, as eventually Cross's brand of obsessive perfectionism would lead to severe depression 17 years after that podium moment. Through a fear of giving up the sport, Cross obsessively continued in his sport, resulting in burnout and eventually a mental breakdown. So perfectionism is something of a paradox: it appears to energise a motivational pattern of striving for the top while 'contributing to a plethora of debilitating processes. These may ultimately diminish the quality of both motivation and performance and lead to psychological distress'.[15]

But does perfectionism in sport spill over into other areas of life, as you would expect of any consistent personality feature? For Chrissie Wellington it did – she recognises that her life has been dominated by 'an obsessive lust for control and self-improvement'.[16] Her obsessions, which she sometimes calls 'addictions' were first with body image, leading to anorexia, academic achievement (first-class degrees, twice), work in 'international development', running marathons and, finally, ironman. She seems to have been able to live with her perfectionism, but not without considerable distress or being close to burnout at times.

However, research suggests that Wellington is the exception rather than the rule, as striving for perfectionism is usually constrained to the specific activity that the person really cares about. Sport is, therefore, often the place in which perfectionism is ripe to surface, because it provides opportunities to establish a meaningful identity, validate self-worth or gain recognition through accomplishments.[17]

Chrissie Wellington: writes candidly and movingly about her lust for control, self-improvement and addiction

To help absorb more of how perfectionists are motivated you might want to consider yourself against this checklist for the more risky aspects of perfectionism. It is framed from a lighthearted perspective by Professor Gordon Frett.[18]

Top 10 signs your a perfectionist

1. You cannot stop thinking about a mistake you made.
2. You are intensely competitive and can't stand doing worse than others.
3. You either want to do something 'just right' or not at all.
4. You demand perfection from other people.
5. You will not ask for help if asking can be perceived as a flaw or weakness.
6. You will persist at a task long after other people have quit.
7. You are a fault-finder who must correct other people when they are wrong.
8. You are highly aware of other people's demands and expectations.
9. You are very self-conscious about making mistakes in front of other people.
10. You noticed the error in the title of this list.

With the lists and attributes mentioned above, hopefully it is easier to begin to understand the world of the perfectionist. However, it is such a complex multidimensional phenomenon that there is a danger that it seems more structured than it actual is. It is nevertheless helpful for coaches, athletes and parents to appreciate these signature attributes which shape how perfectionists think, feel and act compared to the more standard personality attribute of striving for excellence. It helps interpret champions' development.

Obsession misunderstood?

We've already glimpsed elements of obsession, addiction and compulsions in the experiences of athletes such as Chrissie Wellington and Jonny Wilkinson. The trouble with a word like *obsession*, however, is that it is rolled up with distorted public misunderstandings. On the one hand there are conditions like Obsessive Compulsive Disorder (OCD) and on the other sensationalist claims confusing competition rituals and routines with obsession. For instance, Rafa Nadal's superstitions of carefully placing water bottles on the ground near the umpire's chair and not stepping on court lines supposedly demonstrate an obsession – the internet is awash with talk of his behaviour – but in my opinion this is not the case. They are a type of pre-competition routine linked to controlling nerves and anxiety (see chapter 17).

Obsession in sport is the compulsive element of both passion and perfectionism. The link is in the avoidant nature of some training behaviours: a particular behaviour is driven by *preventing* an obsessive thought or anxiety from occurring. It's a bit like the obsession (thought) is an itch and the compulsion (behaviour) is to scratch it – you need to do something to relieve a sensation. Jonny Wilkinson provides a good example in his compulsive kicking practice. He simply has to do it (the compulsion) to help subdue the fear of failure and anxiety that builds within

---

Lesley Paterson: Selfishness, focus or obsession?

I have friends who are concerned about me. 'We're worried about you,' said one. I could have become angry, or defensive, since it felt like they didn't understand my elite sport world – don't they know what it takes to get there and then stay at the top? However, deep down I knew elements of what they were saying were right. I had become pretty grumpy, I was always tired and every workout had a real focus and intensity. I was deliberately pushing the limits and extremes beyond what most thought were healthy.

These are the demons I face as a professional athlete on a day to day basis. Who am I doing this for? How much is too much? Why am I doing this? How can I be so selfish? I think of the countless birthday parties I have missed or nights out I have sidestepped, ruining family occasions ... the list is endless. It boils down to this: I was born with an incredible amount of drive and determination which I know is largely what helps me succeed. I have always lived my life to extremes. Call it unhealthy, maybe a touch perfectionist if you want, but that is the way I roll no matter what it is I'm applying myself to.

Can this become obsessive? Absolutely. But if your dream is to stay on the podium, you had better be obsessive about your sport. It is certainly not a balanced way to live and it is certainly not normal but then those words are generally not used for anyone who is striving to be exceptional.

And so I now realise this lifestyle is going to come with judgement from others. People who will say you are crazy or that your passion has become too obsessive. Every top athlete is living in their own driven little bubble, with its own selfishness and beyond most norms.

him when things don't go exactly to plan (the obsession) '… the only solution is to stay out practicing until [he has] literally kicked the feeling away'.[19] His obsession with flawless kicking led to a string of injuries to his back, groin and leg largely due to the high volume of kicking repetitions in his long practice sessions.

A feature of obsession from the medical perspective is that obsession interrupts normal daily functioning. Obsessive Compulsive Disorder is an anxiety-related condition in which people worry excessively about particular issues. This usually includes both obsessions and compulsions with obsessions being described as a persistent disturbing and intrusive thought. Obsessions will usually have an associated compulsion. This compulsion is a repetitive behaviour that a person feels driven to carry out. It can be performed to reduce anxiety or guilt, or in a belief that it will prevent something harmful happening.[20]

This can be seen in Jonny Wilkinson's kicking practice; the inability to bring rational thought to the decision to stop practising in that session. So how does elite sport training impact on daily functioning? Many people outside sport can't believe the dedication needed to become a champion, and indeed champions are often amazed at their own sacrifices when they languish over weekends in the normalcy of retirement. Opposite, you can see the daily compromises that Lesley Paterson, XTERRA Triathlon World Champion, explained to me. She herself wonders if she is obsessional.

She is right, champions do not lead a normal life, but when they feel obliged to train and start saying 'I ought to …' or 'I should do …' it starts to sound like the sport is controlling them and a compulsive drive to satisfy an obsession is taking hold. Some writers have talked of 'exercise dependence' in which people feel compelled to train, experiencing anxiety when prevented from training, and continually pushing to achieve greater personal goals. Perhaps one of the markers of having an impact on daily functioning (i.e. obsession) is when extreme passion or perfectionism starts to affect relationships with colleagues, family and/or friends as Lesley Paterson's concerned friend suggests.

Obsession can harm relationships and, so too, major championship preparation. The period in the build-up to an Olympic Games is often one of intense training and attention to detail such as weight, fitness, equipment, performance, clothing, sleep, potential illness or injury. It is an unusual, often closed, world, which from the outside appears obsessive, and no doubt a proportion of those involved are obsessed and can lose perspective, but it does subside, often to athletes' cost after the event. They are often left in a void without structure or daily goals. Post-championship blues are common, even with a few gold medals around your neck.

Elite sport can undoubtedly lead to obsessive thoughts sometimes leading to compulsive behaviours as champions are both attracted by a profound desire to succeed and a wish to avoid the consequences of failure. Although it is harder said than done, the ideal is to try to keep self-worth and performance well apart.

Personality and sporting champions

It is tempting to look for other personality characteristics of successful athletes beyond perfectionism, since finding neat patterns of personality traits of champions would help explain what shapes champions. Thinking about different people having different personalities: what does this actually mean?

Your own life experience no doubt reveals that different people respond in remarkably different ways even when faced with roughly the same circumstances. Anna might be happy to live and train alone in a quiet and orderly apartment, and stay at the same club for twenty years, while Bob thrives on travelling through sport and needs to be surrounded by vivacious friends and loud music. Sid continues training through a string of relationships that seemed solid, while Deborah stays in one for most of her life despite it seeming unsuitable to friends.

In all of these cases, we feel that it cannot be just the situation that is producing the differences in behaviour. Something about the way the person's 'psychological signature' seems to work, determining how people react to situations, and – more than that – the kind of situations they get themselves into in the first place. This is why personality seems to become stronger as we get older; when we are young, our situation often reflects external factors such as the social and family environment we were born into. As we grow older, we reap the consequences of our own choices more and more, living in places we chose, doing sports that we were drawn to, surrounded by people like us whom we have sought out. Thus, personality differences that might have been very slight at birth become dramatic in later adulthood.

Personality is a set of enduring and stable dispositions (traits) that characterise a person. These dispositions come partly from the expression of inherent features of the nervous system, and partly from social and cultural learning.[21] There are many different theories used to explain personality and I employ one of the most widely used here. This uses five main personality traits recognised as a means of describing the different aspects of human personality – they're known as the 'Big Five'.[22] These traits are: *openness* to experience, *extroversion*, *agreeableness*, *conscientiousness* and *emotional stability*. The terms don't quite mean what you think they do, but our main focus will be on the last two since they have a lot to do with passion, perfectionism (including obsession) and persistence in sport.

Everyone exhibits these five traits to a greater or lesser degree, allowing psychologists to build up a sort of 'personality signature' that can be used as a point of comparison between individuals. Various aspects of perfectionism have been shown to be associated with *conscientiousness* (the degree of organisation, persistence and motivation in goal-directed behaviour)[23] and *emotional stability*. But the more destructive side of perfectionism, while benefiting from conscientiousness is complicated by emotional *in*stability (worry, doubt, self-consciousness and vulnerability). Emotional stability and the ability to control emotions is a key attribute for champions – think about tennis grand slam finals and Roger Federer's and Andy Murray's different histories of controlling their temperament (see chapter 17).

So perfectionism can be viewed as a personality characteristic, but we've also discussed how often it is not a helpful attribute in the long term. Persistence, however, is a helpful quality, and is increasingly viewed as an antecedent to success.

Gritty behaviour

Professor Angela Duckworth has assembled mounting evidence for this persistence personality trait and called it 'grit'. Grit (in terms of the personality 'Big Five') is closely related to conscientiousness and, if identified in an individual, predicts success in many different situations. Duckworth takes up the story:

> It may be obvious that effort and stamina are required to accomplish anything worthwhile in life. Who among us presses on even as we are passed by those stronger, faster, and/or smarter? Who among us stays the course, running the race we committed to rather than choosing a different, new pursuit, after stumbling and losing ground? Who lives life as if it were a marathon, not a sprint?
>
> ... individuals differ dramatically in their stamina for long-term goals. *Gritty* individuals are distinguished by their propensity to maintain effort and interest over years despite failure, adversity and plateaus in progress. Less gritty individuals are, in contrast, more easily discouraged, prone to take 'naps' mid-course, and frequently led off track by new passions.[24]

Duckworth measures grit by asking people to rate the extent to which they agree or disagree with statements such as:

1. I often set a goal but later choose to pursue a different one.
2. I have been obsessed with a certain idea or project for a short time but later lost interest.
3. I have difficulty maintaining my focus on projects that take more than a few months to complete.
4. New ideas and projects sometimes distract me from previous ones.
5. I finish whatever I begin.
6. Setbacks don't discourage me.[25]

One of Duckworth's important initial findings using this type of questionnaire was among West Point military cadets entering training, a major, tough physical and mental transition. Cadets' responses showed 'grittier' recruits were less likely to drop out. Her simple questionnaire predicted dropout better than the army's 'Whole Candidate Score': a combination of SAT (Scholastic Assessment Test) scores, class rank, leadership ability and physical aptitude. The army's tests notably don't ask about (not) dropping out. Her 12-statement questionnaire was more accurate than what the army thought were comprehensive predictive rankings.

A second major enquiry explored the link between grit and deliberate practice among finalists in the Scripps National Spelling Bee. The finalists performing best in this major spelling contest were found to be grittier and consequently had practised hardest, particularly in the most severe, least pleasurable type of practice. Those that can keep themselves going through hard practices and setbacks are more likely to succeed. When deliberate practice is mentioned we can quickly and easily see how it applies to sport.

Duckworth's findings suggest that grit is very important and that it increases through adulthood. Importantly, however, she observes that 'talented people are, on average, less gritty individuals', suggesting that talented individuals, for whom learning and progress come easily, have fewer opportunities to develop a resilient approach to failure and setbacks. This idea, occurs throughout this book, but the challenge for researchers will be to prove this over a long period and a significant number of individuals.

The relationship between grit and the capacity to delay gratification has also been investigated, with the hypothesis being that grit relates to the ability to forgo immediate pleasure for the sake of greater deferred benefit. So, for example, being patient and gradually progressing through teenage training years in sport may eventually yield success. Good examples of this are perhaps in the athletic experiences of Chris Hoy and Chrissie Wellington, both relatively late developers and 'slow cooked' champions. Duckworth evokes a fable, which works well to illustrate the point:

> The metaphor of achievement as a race recalls Aesop's fable of the tortoise and the hare. This oft-told story, which many of us heard as children in one form or another, preaches the value of plodding on, no matter how slow or uneven our progress toward goals that at times seem impossibly far away.[26]

The classic study of preschool children in the 'Stanford Marshmallow' experiment demonstrates the value of delayed gratification and self-control attributes. Children were offered a marshmallow to eat but instructed that if they waited they'd get more marshmallows. In this and further studies children who delayed gratification, tended to grow up to be more successful, competent adolescents and adults – further evidence that grit, delayed gratification and self-control all contribute to success.

Final thoughts

This journey from the rocket fuel of passion, through to perfection, obsession and grit reflects the intersection of nature and nurture. We can't tell, at the moment, to what extent these attributes are learned behaviours layered on to young developing personalities. Perfectionism and grit in particular have been identified as heavily studied personality characteristics that impact on champions' paths in both positive (grit) and mixed (perfectionism) ways. If you are interested in perfectionism, I strongly recommend you also consider the links with depression (see chapter 22).

Knowing more about passion, perfection, obsession and grit helps us better interpret young athlete's progress.

Part III

Turning points and mental tools

12 How do critical episodes shape champions?

When Roger Federer's parents describe one of the greatest of lessons in their adolescent son's life we should stop and take note. Federer always looks so calm but his young life was shaken up by a move away to train at a Swiss national centre at Ecublens, near Lausanne, three hours from home, aged 14. The lesson he learnt was: 'that things don't always go your own way, and that you don't get anywhere in life with talent alone. You have to work at things,' his mother said.[1] It was tough for Roger there but those struggles were good for him since, his mother claims, overcoming the highs and lows was a challenge that helped him to develop as a person.

For Federer it was almost like being in another country since he hardly spoke Swiss French, having come from the German speaking part of Switzerland. His mother describes how Roger took the decision at a very early age that he wanted to play tennis away from home; he made a lot of important choices himself as a youngster and 'that was key to his success because he had to learn how to do things for himself. He learned to be very independent'.[2]

Federer struggled with his broken French, he was the youngest and worst in the programme, struggled at school and recalled that '[he] found it difficult to get motivated and … was sad quite often'. He was housed with a local family who were supportive, and he made daily hour-long calls home to his parents.[3] He struggled over five months but quickly matured.

In this chapter we consider how the process of being shaken up or jolted, while an unpleasant experience at the time, can build resilience and coping strategies. Negative episodes in life and sport play an important role in learning independence, personal responsibility and coping with hostile and stressful environments. We'll cover the sporting obstacles first since they are fairly common and are often predictable, then we will consider negative episodes in champions' childhood which may severely dent their self-worth but, rather than breaking them, can fuel a hunger to break records instead. Understanding the impact of both types of obstacle is central to what shapes champions' paths.

Sporting challenges

A pattern emerges in sporting autobiographies. The typical sequence goes something like this: champions describe their family circumstances, growing up, starting their sport, first competitions, serious training and then the challenge of living and training away from home, often alone as Roger Federer did. Outgrowing the expertise and competition available in their local area means developing athletes often have to move on to move up. In one survey 60 per cent of top athletes identified relocating as one of the biggest career challenges they faced.[4]

We explore different champions' experiences of relocation as a common example of athletes facing an early but major challenge. The idea that athletes can gain an unusual type of learning from navigating obstacles and overcoming challenges is one of the themes of this book.

And the family come too

Let's start with four relocation success stories: Ellie Simmonds (swimming), Lionel Messi (football), Wayne Gretzky (ice hockey) and Ben Ainslie (sailing).

Ellie Simmonds is a British swimmer who, so far, has accumulated four Paralympic gold medals. Her success is largely down to a bold relocation at the age of 11. In her first Beijing final at the age of 13, with 25 metres to go she was looking to be out of contention, but she surprised herself and a roaring crowd with an incredible final surge to take gold. Disorientated and in tears after the race she told reporters 'I had a dream about the race last night, but in my dream I got silver.'[5]

Ellies's relocation, aged 11, split her family in two in order to support her progress. Val Simmonds, Ellies's mum explains:

> Our pool in Birmingham was closing down for refurbishment. [Ellie] had been down to Swansea for weekend training and a few camps. She gelled really well with the coach, the pool facilities were very good and she really wanted to train there … We work for ourselves so we had the flexibility to move. In the longer term she would need to make that step up in training and support. So we thought why not make the change now [aged 11] rather than later [aged 15].[6]

During the week, Ellie, went to school in Swansea. Her training load involved two hours of pool sessions before and after school, plus four hours on Saturday morning. She then, with her mum, went home to near Birmingham to be with the rest of the family (dad, brother and three sisters) for the weekend.

Ellie's relocation only worked because of the physical presence and organisation of her mother and regular family contact. Ellie's mother planned the move well in advance with coaches and schoolteachers. Her coach Billy Pye said, 'It takes guts to up sticks like that. I've got nothing but admiration for Ellie's parents for moving down here to let [Ellie] follow her dream.'[7]

A family move in support of an athlete also features in the accounts of three all-time greats in their sports: Messi, Gretzky and Ainslie. But they moved for different reasons, all of which are equally illuminating.

Lionel Messi moved to Barcelona, aged 13, to join their academy and progress his football but also, it is sometimes claimed, to help fund his growth hormone treatment. His whole family came too but after only five months the family was split in two with father and son staying in Spain and mother, with Lionel's three siblings, back in Argentina.

> It was not easy. Messi says: 'In order to make it you have to work hard and make a lot of sacrifices. And you have to go through some very tough times, like when I decided to stay in Barcelona … It was my decision. No one forced me to make it … I wanted to stay in the youth academy because I knew that was my chance to be a footballer.'[8]

He made his senior team debut in a friendly at the age of 16.

Ice hockey legend, Wayne Getzky, was also a child prodigy. By the age of 10, Gretzky had scored 378 goals in just one season with his local Brantford (Ontario) ice hockey team. Gretzky's play started to attract media attention but his extraordinary skills were 'overshadowed by jealousy. Other hockey parents called him a "puck hog" and older boys threatened him. Gretzky sometimes went home from a game in tears.'[9] He was often booed. This cannot have been good for his self-worth. When Gretzky was 14, his family relocated to Toronto, partly to avoid the uncomfortable pressure he faced in his hometown. With hindsight, it was a great call.

Ainslie's career, like Gretzky's, was also showing considerable promise, with Junior World and European Championship titles. A year older than Gretzky at the time of moving, his family also relocated from the far west of the country (Cornwall, England) mainly to be nearer the centre of gravity of the sport in Hampshire. He was also bullied at his previous school which he said had a profound effect on how he developed. We'll come back to this bullying since – like Gretsky's 'puck hog' taunts – it can sometimes be a very significant type of childhood episode.

All these cases demonstrate parental commitment, flexibility and resources to move: Ellie aged 11, Lionel aged 13, Wayne aged 14 and Ben aged 15. In overcoming initial anxieties at a young age they all learnt important mental skills in adapting to a new environment. They were all carefully planned *family* moves, and the challenges involved were modest compared to many later career events. But what is it like when athletes move independent from their family support network? In three words: a lot harder.

Away alone

The stories of the cyclist Victoria Pendleton's move to Switzerland, Francine's (a French fencing champion; Francine is not her real name) move to Paris and Andre Agassi's Florida tennis academy experience show how threatening transitions to training hubs can be.

There is ongoing debate about whether central sports training hubs for young people are appropriate. Unless you live nearby, it represents a major upheaval and challenge especially if any of the four self-determination nutrients of autonomy, relatedness, competence and intrinsic motivation (see chapter 4) are compromised. My own visits to Chinese, Spanish and French residential high-performance centres influenced me. Initially my visits made me think that bringing developing young athletes together supported by coaches and other specialists along with applied sports science was the most effective way to create champions. But now after this research, I'm not so sure: shorter stays of between four and eight weeks at such centres may work better.

Examples of training academies in developed countries include gleaming national flagships: publicly funded venues such as the Australian Institute of Sport or the French equivalent in Paris, l'Institut National du Sport, de l'Expertise et de la Performance (INSEP). In addition, some National Olympic organisations run their own flagship academies, for example, the US Olympic Committee runs three large, independently funded complexes at Colorado Springs, Chula Vista and Lake Placid. These institutes or academies are usually multisport, seeking to create a culture of excellence that involves competition and the sharing of information with fantastic facilities. Then there are private enterprises, for example the IMG Bollettieri Academy in Florida, which previously taught solely tennis, but is now multisport. There are other facilities run by world sports governing bodies to make training opportunities available to all nations such as the Union Cycliste Internationale (UCI) track academy in Switzerland. Income from the Olympics is distributed to each sport and it is sometimes used to subsidise such ventures to help grow the sport.

The allure of central training hubs, academies or institutes is that they do produce results by bringing expertise together. But this approach does not suit every sport, every nation and certainly not every individual. The examples of Victoria Pendleton (cycling), Francine (fencing) and Andre Agassi (tennis) represent the full range of world governing body, public and private academy ownership respectively. They are three different and personal stories.

To make sense of these stories we need a reference point: something to make comparisons against. Aine MacNamara, again working with Dave Collins, has investigated these type of re-location transitions among 18–19-year-olds[10] since these ages are so important in an athlete's development. Six international track athletes were interviewed before, during and after their relocation, with additional meetings with the athletes' parents and coaches.[11] The seven challenge themes that emerged show typically what relocating athletes have to deal with.[12] They fall under three headings.

The athletic transition
- Moving to a new training group;
- higher standards of training and coaching;
- changing coach.

The psychological and social transition
- Changing relationships with parents;
- changing and loss of home friendships;
- social support from other athletes.

Unpredictable challenges

- Injury;
- Illness;*
- Bereavement.*

* My additions

The *athletic transition* items are rather like the experience of starting out at a new more demanding school or job as the culture, expectations and mentoring style change, and physical training demands are raised. The pressure is on: both self-inflicted and from others. Athletic progress is perceived as the *raison d'être*. And because competitive sport can be so tangibly measured, progress – or lack of it – is seen by all in every training session.

The *psychological and social transition* items connect to something we can all relate to: moving away from home into a completely new group where new friendships and social support will hopefully develop. Often parents become rather more distant at this stage. *Unpredictable challenges* were experienced by half of those interviewed. Injury can be a key event throughout an athlete's career (see chapter 13) but in MacNamara and Collins's interviews it was particularly poignant. Athletes spoke about how their injury was frustrating since they didn't really feel part of the training group, instead feeling like a bit of an outsider.[13]

So how do these reference points of transitional challenge compare with the experiences of three champion athletes away alone?

Victoria Pendleton: Cyclist

Aged 22, Pendleton was a relatively new member of the GB national team. She set out on an 18-month visit and, to use her words, 'life-changing adventure' to Switzerland. British Cycling coaches were determined to push her to higher levels and she accepted their plan to relocate to the UCI sprint academy in Aigle, paid for by the GB team. It was a cosmopolitan environment with, at different times, 12–15 top riders from China, Holland, Canada, Cuba, Japan, Korea, Malaysia, Russia and South Africa in residence: potentially exciting, but also threatening.

MacNamara and Collins' research was right: she immediately experienced a tough athletic transition. A combination of *moving to a new training group,* facing *higher standards of training and coaching* and adapting to *a change of coach.* Her new coach was Frenchman, Fred Magne; he used a fairly autocratic approach, which was regimented with early starts and time-bound rituals. We know that sleep and rest is important for recovery but it sounds rather odd hearing how, after lunch everyday, athletes went to a 'Salle de Repose' to take a communal sleep in a large room in which mattresses were laid on the floor in the style of a Japanese dormitory. Pendleton put her head down and got on with her new life but found the going tough.

> [her] body was not accustomed to such intense training... [she] had never seen such big black bags under [her] eyes ...[14]

[she] was motivated by a need to try and keep up with the other women. Every time [they] went out on the track [their] individual times would be logged in the book, and compared by the whole group the same day. There were no secrets ... [she] was always at the back of the battlers, clinging on for dear life ... It felt as if they were miles ahead of [her] ... [Her] lack of confidence was apparent.[15]

Gradually, her times on the track quickened. She kept on working. At the 2003 World Championships she took a huge step forward, finishing fourth. Many were astonished by her sudden leap into the top four in the world. Pendleton describes her delight at being seen to be making progress and being included in newspaper articles, which suggested she had a bright future ahead. A profile from the *Guardian* in December 2003 was headlined:

Young gifted and on track to make headlines in the coming year: Coaches and experts from 12 sports name their top tips to make a breakthrough in 2004.

British readers may recognise some of the prospects: Alastair Cook (England cricket captain), Beth Tweddle (former world champion and Olympic medalist in gymnastics) and Lewis Hamilton (former Formula 1 world champion). Esteemed company indeed for the then 23-year-old being billed as the next bright young star.

Pendleton identified the start of her problems as being connected to her relationship with her new coach, Magne, and her own wish for some autonomy in her training.

Victoria Pendleton: Switzerland was a life-changing episode – 'lost in the mountains'

It seemed to [her] that … [she lacked] core strength. [She] had studied core stability at university and thought [she'd] include some additional abdominal exercises in the gym … [Her colleagues] dobbed [her] in … Fred called [her] into his office. 'What's the matter with the programme I give you?' He asked angrily.[16]

Feeling increasingly isolated from the group she describes how her relationship with Fred deteriorated. She spent many hours in her room, alone, feeling like an outcast. It got worse. She started self-harming, using a Swiss army knife to cut her arm (Kelly Holmes describes a similar sorry situation away at a training camp in South Africa, see chapter 13). I'd be disingenuous to attempt any analysis of the complexities of this for both athletes; it must have represented a terrible low point, alone, far away and without support.

She maintained the facade of normalcy by wearing long-sleeved garments and saying she was 'OK' to those around her, and on the phone to her worried mother. The *psychological and social transition* challenges from MacNamara's research resonate here.

Pendleton continued competing. Later in April she won her first World Cup in Manchester. Then in May her mood dipped as she finished fourth in the World Championships in Melbourne. Pendleton's fourth was made more negative by a snide comment made by a competitor, 15 years her senior, who had just beaten her to take bronze, 'You will always be a princess – but you will never be the queen'.

After 18 months of training under Fred [she] did not seem to be making progress [she] should have done. In [her] depressed mood [she] considered fourth place at the Worlds a failure – as it repeated the same finish from the previous year in Stuttgart[17] … [She] felt stuck – and emotionally blocked[18]
… 'So here [she was], once more, post-Melbourne, reaching for the same Swiss Army knife.'[19]

Eventually, Steve Peters, British Cycling's psychiatrist came to meet her. She broke down in tears the first time they met when he said he was there to help her. Pendleton's account of this difficult period is aptly titled 'Lost in the mountains' and she finishes it by recounting the words of Steve Peters, now a close confidant. He reported back about her situation to her UK coaches, 'There's no quick fix. This girl has serious issues.'

The challenge and pressure of relocation and in particular, changing coach and a lack of social support probably triggered the expression of underlying difficulties. Victoria Pendleton, by her own admission, at the time, had personality traits related to perfectionism (see chapter 11).

Francine: Fencing

It is a brave person who allows the public to look into their inner world beyond an autobiography. French fencing champion, 'Francine' agreed to allow notes from psychological counselling interviews to be combined with her own account over a 14-year period: hence the use of the pseudonym. It was published in a psychology journal in 2012 and, as you can imagine, it makes interesting reading.[20] We'll look at her initial entry to an elite academy and any similarities with Pendleton's experience.

Francine's rapid fencing progress as a child meant that at the age of 20 she was invited to join the senior elite foil-training centre at INSEP. She was apprehensive at living 900km (560mi) away from her family but she soon realised that she had to go there if she wanted to continue on an elite sport path.

Three months after joining, Francine described how she overcame competition stress, but things changed for the worse, with misunderstandings, conflicts and disagreements about the organisation of training. Francine chose not to discuss this with the psychologist, saying 'I was not ready for that. I was really turned in on myself.'

Like Pendleton, isolation took hold but was made worse by injuries. Francine decided to leave the elite centre to go back home aged 22. Francine said: 'I was weary of the high level training system. I no longer enjoyed myself when fencing. I no longer wanted to fight in competitions.'

Fortunately, she partly fulfilled her potential on returning to the national academy and eventually won a gold medal at the European Championships, aged 26, and competed in the Olympic Games (finishing 13th). The comparison with Pendleton's experience of 'relationship difficulties', 'training', 'distress' and 'withdrawing in on herself' are eerily similar. There is a pattern here of young adults struggling with relocation and moving up to higher levels with limited support networks close by.

Andre Agassi: Tennis

Did the well-known Bollettieri Academy support Andre Agassi as a young adolescent, aged 13, to any greater effect than Francine and Pendleton as young adults?

Agassi's account of his experiences, written with the help of a Pulitzer Prize-winning author are intriguing. He was sent to the Bollettieri Academy, then independent of IMG, by his domineering father. Here is a glimpse of how he saw his move to Florida – it might have been written colourfully to sell more books but it makes an interesting read:

> People like to call the Bollettieri Academy a boot camp, but it's really a glorified prison camp. And not all that glorified. [They] eat gruel – beige meats and gelatinous stews and gray slop poured over rice – and sleep in rickety bunks that line the plywood walls of [their] military-style barracks. [They] rise at dawn and go to bed soon after dinner. [They] rarely leave, and ... have scant contact with the outside world. Like most prisoners [they] do nothing but sleep and work, and [their] main rock pile is drills. Serve drills, net drills, backhand drills, forehand drills, with occasional match play to establish the pecking order, strong to weak

... The constant pressure, the cut-throat competition, the total lack of adult supervision – it slowly turns [them] into animals. A kind of jungle law prevails. Its *Karate Kid* with rackets, *Lord of the Flies* with forehands.

... [he] started to rebel ...What more [could he] do? – no one seems to notice [his] antics anymore. .[21]

These antics include: mutilating his hair, freakish nails, pierced body parts, broken rules, busted curfews, fistfights, tantrums, missed school classes, tobacco chewed, weed soaked in whisky. He asks: 'What new sin can I commit to show the world I am unhappy and want to go home?'

To top it all there is an incident with the academy owner in which Agassi has something to trade: a giant teddy bear, something which Nick Bollettieri, the proprietor, dearly wants for his daughter. Agassi trades the teddy bear and in return is able to quit school at the age of 14 and play in more tournaments – an unusual arrangement. Andre starts training with the academy coaches on even more of a full-time basis while the other youngsters go to school. Another form of isolation.

You might view Agassi's case as one of 'sink or swim' in which, like Federer a few years later, he became more independent and picked up important mental coping skills in a hostile competitive environment, while also doing a huge amount of practice. Perhaps his prior experience of exposure to bullying behaviours at home may have partly 'inoculated' him? But Agassi claims, for the first part of his career, he hated playing tennis: not a great start to a profession and evidence that success is possible without all the self-determining nutrients.

His path is unusual; there must be better ways of preparing young children for challenge and adversity.

Challenging sporting lessons

Simmonds, Messi, Pendleton, Francine, Agassi and Federer's responses vary, partly due to slightly different challenges. MacNamara and Collins's suggestion is that 'talent needs trauma', in that being able to anticipate and negotiate transitions and challenges is important for the training of athletes as coping strategies and mental resilience are developed. They urge that being able to overcome challenges by prior preparation and specialised support, 'would seem to hold considerably more promise ... than trying to address these issues mid-crisis, or even using the transition as some implicit "survival of the fittest" additional test'. In other words, training for, and careful coaching through, challenges, thereby gradually building athletes' mental toolkits helps prepare them for their uncertain and stressful sporting path.

For Pendleton, Francine and Federer it was a case of managing mid-crisis, which can be worked through provided the right people are there to talk to. Agassi survived a sort of Darwinian test at a very tender age.

So far we've just explored one type of sporting career challenge that often occurs early in a champions' path. But there are a whole lot more challenges and obstacles that athletes need to negotiate; each time learning something from the experience provided they have a reasonably positive, optimistic mindset ... and are open to seeking appropriate support. The most important learning is to develop overall adaptability and resilience to the pressures and unique situations they are put in. Those that practise using and refining their mental tools are more likely to become serial champions (see chapter 14).

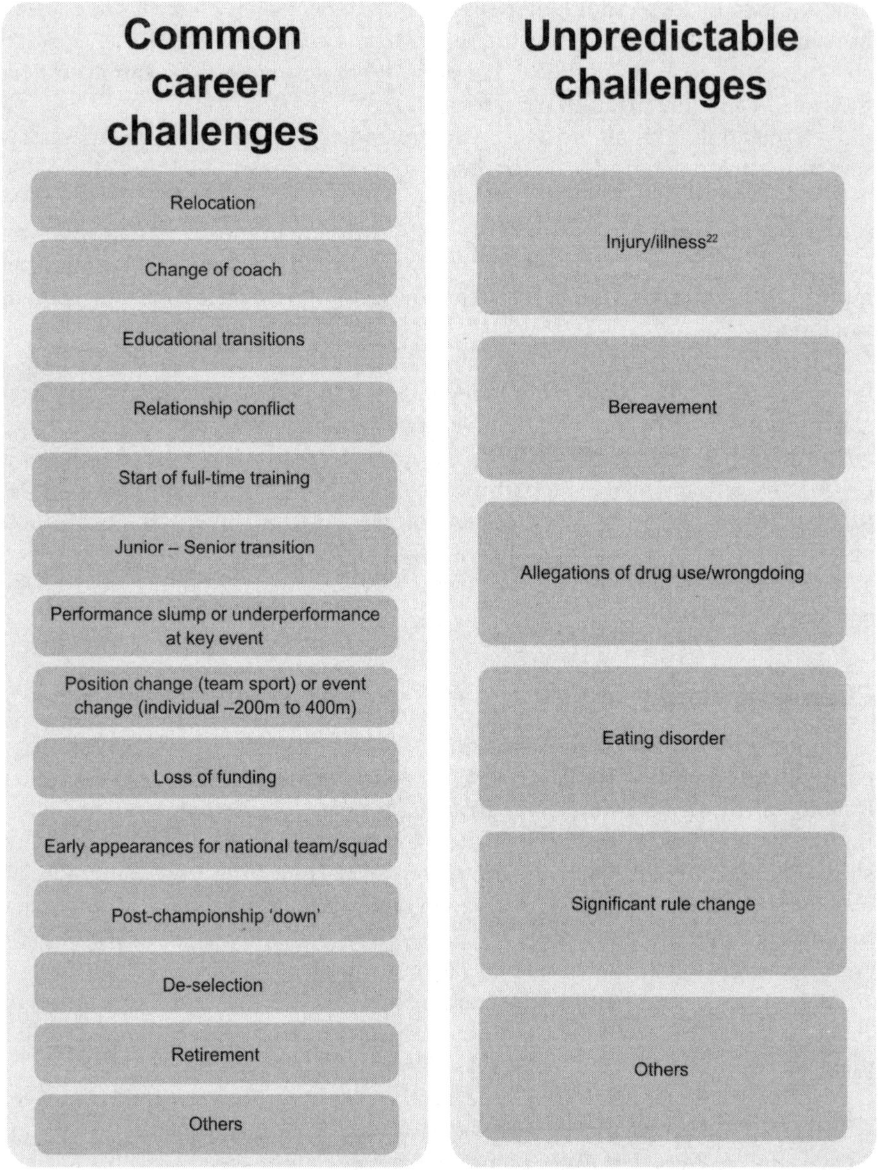

Common career challenges	**Unpredictable challenges**
Relocation	Injury/illness[22]
Change of coach	
Educational transitions	Bereavement
Relationship conflict	
Start of full-time training	
Junior – Senior transition	Allegations of drug use/wrongdoing
Performance slump or underperformance at key event	
Position change (team sport) or event change (individual –200m to 400m)	Eating disorder
Loss of funding	
Early appearances for national team/squad	
Post-championship 'down'	Significant rule change
De-selection	
Retirement	Others
Others	

Figure 12.1 Categorisation of possible critical episodes that may be faced in champions' careers.

Researching champions from so many different sports leads to a realisation that it would valuable to identify and list the range of sporting challenges that athletes are likely to face. In Figure 12.1 you'll see two distinct categorisations of critical episodes. Champions are likely to face only some of these episodes and it is the way they interpret and respond to them that shapes their future path.

You'll see some of these critical episodes addressed in different parts of this book. There are individual chapters devoted to injury/illness (see chapter 13) and retirement (see chapter 23).

Negative life episodes

Now we turn to life episodes. How can the response of young developing athletes to negative life events that dent or shatter their self-worth have an impact in shaping their future motivation? Negative episodes are varied, perhaps a child struggling with bullying or maybe the childhood loss of a sibling or parent. Both episodes may in some cases lead to a deep-seated need to achieve, especially if they are already competent at a sport and are able to immerse themselves in their childhood play or training to help overcome feelings of inadequacy. A deep-seated need, plus appropriate physical attributes (i.e. genes) for a sport, plus good coaching and a little good fortune may produce special athletes with a unique record-breaking hunger.

In chapter 6 we examined how football geniuses Diego Maradona, George Best and Paul Gascoigne compensated for negative childhood experiences and limited secure attachments to their carers by overdeveloping their physical skills in football because it meant they could start to feel successful at something and express themselves, thereby helping suppress anxieties and low self-esteem. This fuelled their endless practice and a deep connection to their passion.

Identifying negative childhood episodes is subjective: one young person's challenge, such as bullying, might not register much with one individual but may have far more impact with another. Individuals react in very different ways, or as some psychologists have framed it:

> Stressors may be considered as adversity for athletes if they are 'potentially challenging to their success as an athlete, to their athletic identity and *to their broader sense of self-confidence*' [my emphasis]. Adversity can vary … based on individuals' subjective appraisal of and meaning attached to a particular event. Although some events (e.g. death of a teammate) are often appraised as more severe than others (e.g. injury), it is not the event per se that dictates the severity of adversity but rather individuals' appraisal of the event.[23]

It is the threat to athletes' broader sense of self-confidence that defines the type of stressors we hope to tentatively identify. Here, we extend Gogarty and Williamson's argument[24] that adversity is the unconscious driving force behind some athletes in overcoming the unprocessed losses and humiliations of childhood, and a way of helping rebuild self-worth.

The sometimes angry drive that can propel athletes to achieve can, if it is guided by a coach and a strong internal moral compass, lead them to become serial champions but equally may end up with them in jail. For example, Mike Tyson had a troubled childhood followed by skilled mentoring which led to him being lauded as the supreme boxer of his generation. Later, with the loss of his mentor, his anger and mental health problems led to a rape conviction. Or consider Lance Armstrong who took a drug-fuelled 'win at all costs' approach but was obsessively driven. Speaking in 2003 he discussed what may have driven him: '[he had] the suspicion that it's the old secrets in [him], the cheats and slights of childhood, all melted down into one purpose, that [made him] turn the wheels'.[25] Athletes don't tend to talk about the influence of their childhood adversities readily – we get only occasional glimpses in what they say or write, as on the whole it is suppressed. It is, as Gogarty and Williamson say an 'unconscious driving force' and in my opinion particularly relevant in shaping their early careers.

While there is much written about how adversity and trauma in childhood predicts later problems, sometimes evident in lower academic achievement, dropping out from work or education and mental health difficulties, it seems that sport, music or the performing arts can sometimes provide an alternative path. The activity needs to be accessible, and preferably the young person already shows some promise.

When you start to consider the range of negative episodes which have the potential to seriously undermine self-worth and then start to research how such episodes are fairly common among champions it becomes, at least at the surface level, fairly striking. Take Ben Ainslie and his being bullied at school: it was hidden away in a few lines when describing his childhood. Ainslie said bullying had a profound effect on how he developed: 'It made [him] ferociously determined to be good at something to prove to [himself] that [he] could be a success and that there was more to life than school and being picked on'.[26] This pattern repeated itself with World Champion boxer Joe Calzaghe – he was severely bullied at school and withdrew to his boxing club training, wiping memories of his tormentors away and helping recover some self-worth. Both were already of a good club standard in their sport but the need to prove something to themselves lit the fuse.

Below, we identify some one-third of the champions who are referred to in this book and the various negative episodes and conditions that *possibly* harmed their self-worth and stimulated their inner drive to achieve.

- Bullying/abuse: Ben Ainslie (sailing), Wayne Gretsky (ice hockey), Joe Calzaghe (boxing), Andre Agassi (tennis), Kayla Harrison (judo).
- Medical conditions: hair-loss disorder alopecia areata, Joanna Rowsell (cycling)
- Absent parents or separation: Kelly Holmes (athletics), Bradley Wiggins (cycling), Chris Froome (cycling), Mike Tyson (boxing), Lance Armstrong (cycling).
- Dsyfunctional unhappy childhoods: Diego Maradona (football), George Best (football), Paul Gascoigne (football).

▨ Loss or separation: Mo Farah (running; separation from identical twin and family), Cathy Freeman (running; loss of sister).

There is also a difficulty with the way the education system is orientated which makes some people's early education challenging. One of the most common specific learning difficulties is dyslexia, which, if undetected, may give rise to untrained observers concluding that a student is 'lazy' or 'not trying hard enough', particularly with reading and writing tasks. This often has an impact on self-worth. The following champions mentioned in this book live with dyslexia: Muhammad Ali (boxing), Steve Redgrave (rowing), Magic Johnson (basketball), Chris Boardman (cycling), Mo Farah (athletics); in addition, Michael Phelps (swimming) had the specific learning difficulty of ADHD.

We don't know the impacts of these different events or conditions without a detailed discussion with the athletes concerned and their parents. This small sample might not be statistically significant (that is, representative of all athletes) but it does involve a high proportion of champions featured in this book. I hesitated before committing some of the names to this list since for some, like Chris Froome, we only know parts of his early life story (see chapter 9).

There are two questions that I would like to ask Chris Froome and all fifty or so champions once I had established some rapport with them over a few hours or days. It is unlikely champions would open up to a stranger:

▨ Thinking back to your childhood and adolescence tell us about any examples when your self-confidence or general self-worth took a severe knock?
▨ Did you feel there were there any safe havens, places, people or activities where you felt you could re-establish who you were and what you were good at?

Ideally, interviews with their parents would help corroborate responses and behaviour amid these, perhaps uncomfortable, childhood experiences, but this is a subject that probably deserves a book in itself.

These potentially new insights into what may lie behind *some* champions' hunger to succeed could transform the way we interpret champions' autobiographies and accounts of their development. Throughout this book we have introduced three different accounts of champions' possible motivational processes; we don't yet know to what extent champions may exhibit i) *self-determined characteristics* and/or ii) *perfectionist characteristics* and/or iii) *deep-seated needs* from childhood episodes or conditions. There is a lot more still to discover about what drives champions.

Final thoughts

Nico van Yperen from Goningen, Holland, is a very patient man; he measured the psychological attributes of young Dutch football players when they were teenagers and then he tracked them down 15 years later to how far they had progressed.[27] The teenagers were part of professional Dutch club academy training programmes and for van Yperen 'making it' at adult level was indicated by whether they had played for a premier league soccer team in a European competition for 10 of the subsequent 15 years – this is certainly a high level of achievement.

His findings are stark. Three psychological attributes predicted if teenage academy players 'made it' as adults:

- the extent to which the teenagers diligently committed themselves to goals – this sounds fairly intuitive since athletes who are determined and focused towards success (you might say persistent) are more likely to achieve;
- how they coped with problems; this is largely what we have been discussing in terms of being proactive in responding to critical episodes, and;
- their willingness to seek out support from others: as we have seen isolation and lack of connection with others is one the main difficulties for athletes struggling, and those who seek support are more likely to make it.

The proportion of adolescent youth players who, using these three characteristics, were classified correctly as having 'made it' or not was 72 per cent: pretty impressive – imagine being able to predict almost three-quarters of the adolescents who will succeed, in any field.

It was also noticeable that those that made it had a family background with three times the divorce rate of peers who failed to reach the highest level. Divorces can be harmonious or messy so it is difficult to suggest that this was a negative episode, which may have triggered an insatiable desire to succeed: we'd need to talk in detail to the youngsters involved. But Van Yperen used this presidential quote to suggest a link to resilience among some children with absent parents. Barack Obama said:

> my strength actually comes, in my case, from the absence of a father. At some level I had to raise myself … I have been able to navigate some pretty tricky situations in my life, it has to do with the fact that I had to learn to trust my own judgment; I had to learn to fight for what I wanted … maybe having an absent father meant also that … you have to grow up faster … you need to take responsibility and make sure that you're able to solve problems.[28]

Here, then, is some confirmation that a robust mental toolbox is significant in shaping some achievers' career paths and important in predicting success. I look forward to more researchers like Van Yperen exploring the topic of negative life episodes further in sport since this is currently probably best assessed on an individual case by case basis.

By looking at a series of individual cases in the chapters that follow I want to answer two related questions: what can we learn from understanding the lived experience of tough injury and rehabilitation periods that almost all champions face? And how can we describe what is actually in a champion's mental toolbox? We are getting to the centre of what shapes sporting champions.

13 Broken bodies, broken minds?

'You'll never get to play at the level you were at before'. Helen Richardson, Olympic hockey medallist, found these words from a doctor very painful.

I also have vivid memories of broken athletes that haunted my early Olympic coaching experience. One was a young boy with great potential who was trying to cope with a severe eating disorder. Two others were athletes facing a potential career-ending condition of the forearm known as compartment syndrome. This is when pain occurs when pressure within the muscles builds and hampers blood flow making it impossible to grip. Both athletes pursued private surgery but this left them with a 10-inch Frankenstein-like scar on their arms. I felt like I'd failed them.

I'm keen to discover how champions whose bodies break down cope. Virtually every athlete has an injury story, with the worst being the absolute nadir of their sporting careers. Career low points are often triggered by injury or ill health and then followed by the subsequent struggle through rehabilitation. This challenges the patience of finely tuned athletes who up until then have relied on their bodies. Frustrated like caged animals crashing around, they try desperately to find answers to the complex problems facing them. Richardson's injury story was my starting point:

> At the Sydney Olympics [at the age of 18] I looked at the women on the podium and our manager at the time turned to me and said 'that will be you one day' and I thought yeah, that is what I want to do – and two years after that moment I got injured and one surgeon said to me after three operations on my ankle, 'you'll never play at your previous high level'. To hear those words was really, really painful, I didn't have much else at the time. Sport is my passion, I love playing sport and it took a lot of hard work, dedication and determination in rehab. In that time I learnt a lot about myself, I learnt how to train properly. I'm technically good at lots of sports but physically I'm not an athlete, well I wasn't, but now I can say I am an athlete. I set myself small goals to get back, I lost about 8 or 10kgs (17–20lb), so in hindsight that really crappy time in my life has propelled me to where I am now [a medallist in 2012] and has made me a much stronger person and athlete.[1]

Injuries are absolute make-or-break moments for athletes. In Richardson's case she was convinced that the injury and rehabilitation made her a stronger and fitter person and it helped redefine her identity as a genuine athlete but as she recalled 'when you're "in it" you genuinely think it's the end of the world'. Hungry for more detailed stories of long-term injury struggles that affected an athlete mentally, I didn't have to look far.

Sir Steve Redgrave's story is a great example of an athlete overcoming illness while Kelly Holmes's 12-year progress as an adult to double Olympic gold in 2004 is largely about injuries. Both journeys opened up a new world of medical rehabilitation and injury prevention. They also led me to the discovery of a medic's story: someone who has treated numerous medalists, including Kelly Holmes, and has some interesting observations as a result. These three perspectives can give us some insight into the athlete's world.

A giant's 10-year illness battle

Let's start by looking beneath the surface of rower Sir Steve Redgrave's career. Redgrave is a man of enormous stature and taciturn glare and is known for his invincibility, achieving a record-breaking five golden Olympic Games victories. But, hidden from view, there is a different story of his 10-year battle to overcome not one but two serious conditions which almost caused the sport to give up on him while he struggled to find the answers. As you may already know he has type 2 diabetes, but his struggle is about far more than that.

Have you or a member of your family ever waited nervously for medical tests to reveal exactly what is wrong with your body after a mystery illness? Your mind will often go into overdrive imagining all sorts of doom-laden 'what if?' scenarios. If you are waiting over Christmas and New Year in that grey, timeless, mid-winter period, it can make it even worse. This was the situation in which Steve Redgrave found himself during Christmas 1997 and it was the lowest point of his career. He had cause to be worried because of signs of trouble a month earlier.

Already with four gold medals in the bag, here he was as a 35-year-old at a training camp in South Africa having been diagnosed with *diabetes mellitus* a few months before. It seemed as though time was catching up with him. The difficulties were most apparent on the extended endurance bike rides in which he often lagged half an hour behind his colleagues. He wasn't performing and thought it was just a problem with getting his blood sugar levels right with his diabetes. No other elite rower had ever attempted to train full bore and manage their insulin levels; he was in uncharted territory. Having had conversations with a psychologist specialising in injury,[2] it was clear to me that, whether it is due to illness or injury, these experiences are largely about dealing with the unknown and how people respond to the huge uncertainty this creates.

Near Christmas, gut and digestive problems seemed to indicate a reappearance of *ulcerative colitis,* something Steve thought he'd shaken off in 1992. He went for tests to see if it was anything more, but these were inconclusive. Further investigation was needed to see if it was the more serious Crohn's disease or worse still.

Eighteen months previously, Redgrave had seemingly announced his retirement on live TV but then rescinded it in full media glare to push on for a record five gold medals. His wife, Ann, was concerned about this decision for a number of reasons: his young family's needs, his well-being, and planning for his future beyond the sport. It may have created tension between them,[3] but this was probably far from his mind as he lay on the surgeon's table while 12 samples were taken from his intestines, '… a thoroughly unpleasant experience'. Driving back from London, he stopped on the M4 motorway, in his own personal emergency, to throw up.

It got worse. Dejected and suffering from chronic symptoms, Redgrave decided to go AWOL, skipping training for the first time ever. He went with his family to a ski resort without telling his coach or colleagues. Psychologists would consider this to be 'a very common response to illness/injury – a type of avoidance approach – this is an effective coping strategy but only in the short term.'[4]

During this trip Redgrave and his wife listened intently to hear the latest test results by phone. It was partly good news, confirming the return of colitis, a condition at least known to him. However, the condition is still a very serious inflammatory condition of the gut, which can sometimes lead to removal of the intestines and the use of a colostomy bag, but fortunately the doctor was able to rule out these extreme measures and Crohn's disease. However, Redgrave was still left with two serious obstacles to his sporting future – the challenge of managing diabetes and colitis while in full-time training – but at least treatment for his two conditions could now start. One informed observer, Martin Cross, who had rowed with Redgrave to gold in 1984, claimed that it bought him and his wife closer together as they overcame these challenges:

> It seems crazy to think that diabetes and colitis could have actually helped Steven towards his fifth gold. But through the revitalisation of his relationship, this was just what happened.[5]

Having a lot on your plate is something hungry rowers are used to, but now he also had a whole heap of challenges to face. Days were now complicated by having to monitor his diabetes closely, with up to 10 injections a day. He was also having to work out with the doctors how his colitis could be treated alongside the diabetes as at first the drugs for one compromised the other. The trouble was that there was no established medical approach for someone eating 6000+ calories a day and then doing tough Olympic training. So this champion athlete rewrote and overturned accepted medical opinion of what was possible: he represented a unique case, different to anything they had seen before, not just physically, but mentally.

Redgrave stated: 'It took a great deal of balancing and slowly I was able to return to a consistent [power] output.'[6] Losing 14lb (6kg) of muscle bulk that winter had been a blow and he had felt vulnerable, no longer being the top dog in the crew physically. Exasperated, Redgrave, rather than developing as an athlete, was now spending more time battling with other things; he was different to his colleagues, becoming set apart in his daily regime.

One of other things I learnt from this story, aside from the importance of mental strength, is that there is a common feeling of isolation among injured athletes and those recovering from illness. Quite remarkably, later in the year following that miserable Christmas, he won his 12th World Championship gold, surely ranking as one of the greatest unheralded comeback stories in sport. This is a testament to his mental tools in overcoming physical and psychological lows. But let's not forget the benefit of experience: Redgrave had 'previous' – if you've faced down a similar problem before, it helps to be able to recall that in your darkest moments.

In 1990, Redgrave had been hospitalised with an unknown intestinal problem for three days and placed on a drip, but it wasn't until 1992 that it was finally diagnosed as colitis. It cleared up, but amazingly his 1992 competitive season was blighted with the same problem with familiar symptoms. There was only a two-month window when he wasn't affected by the condition; a window in which he performed in the Barcelona Olympics and his greatest race ever with Matthew Pinsent. 'Either side of that window [he] was a very sick person'.[7] What is it that allows someone to pull through that and perform so well? A mixture of experience, conditioning, good management by the coach and a well-developed mental toolbox.

The underlying cause of his colitis was unclear. Was it stress-related or diet? Redgrave concluded stress. He seemed a fairly calm person even in the heat of championship media interviews. But that was exactly the root cause: the underlying expectations and pressure. '[He] came to the conclusion that being in a must-win situation nearly every time you go out and race must be stressful … made worse by the fact that during most of [his] rowing career [until 1992] [he'd] had financial problems.'[8] With hindsight, the onset of diabetes had been so stressful that it had triggered the return of the colitis.

So beneath the invincible aura of Redgrave was a person whose commitment and persistence enabled him to solve some pretty big, stress-related health issues. He also benefited from some patient management from his coach and the very good fortune to have his wife Ann as the rowing team doctor. Medical teams don't win medals, but in this case they deserved one.

The secret to Kelly Holmes's success

American coach Dan Pfaff (who worked with gold medallists Donovan Bailey, Greg Rutherford and Jonnie Peacock) said this about training:

> I think there is a tendency for athletes to do more than they should. They think if *two* was good let me do *four*, well *four* was pretty good let me do *six*; well there is a breaking point and more is not better. I'm actually the opposite, every year I write training [plans] I'm looking what can I get rid of, you know, how few of things can we do?[9]

Straight away it made me think about Kelly Holmes. After meeting Kelly at an Open University degree ceremony, I was drawn to her story because her double gold in Athens helped to break down a few barriers for women's sport in the UK. But actually much of her story is about overtraining and injury with various syndromes. What could we learn about how she navigated through her injuries towards double gold?

Table 13.1 Kelly Holmes's descriptions of injury episodes.

Age	Kelly's description of her injury episode	Condition
25	Just as I got back into training, I pulled a hamstring … putting my progress in jeopardy again. Had I rushed things too soon?	Torn hamstring
26	Now I understand more about the intricacies of footwear and how careful one has to be breaking in a new pair of shoes … I should have been much more careful, but at that stage I didn't know much about injury prevention.	Stress fracture to tibia
30	Overcompensating for my injured leg … I [put] too much stress on my lower limbs. When eventually [after rest] I tried to run on the calf it went altogether.	Calf muscle tear
31	I constantly felt very tired and so lethargic in training.	Chronic fatigue syndrome
33	Every time I ran the pain in my knee was excruciating … I struggled through it but, me being me, decided that … I would travel to Scotland to run in a mile road race … regardless. I won the race but was in agony. I didn't let anyone there know about my leg and I refused to admit it to myself that I was injured. Returning to South Africa the pain during training was so bad that … I had to stop. I had started to overcompensate, damaging my right calf.	Iliotibial band friction syndrome and unspecified calf injury
33	I felt I was punishing myself but at the same time I felt a sense of release that drove me to do it again … I had began to feel like an outsider … I reached rock bottom.	Short period of self-harm to arms

Source: pages 135, 139, 170, 208, 211 from Holmes, K., *Black, White and Gold: My Autobiography* (Virgin Books, 2008).

Let's start by considering her chronological injuries: not just a list of them, but the words and interpretations she used (see Table 13.1, above). It is rather an uncomfortable series of events culminating in serious mental pain and self-doubt. As you read towards the bottom of her sequence of injury episodes you'll see she has something in common with cyclist Victoria Pendleton.

Holmes and Pendleton both expressed frustration and feelings of separation and being an outsider and in both instances this lead to self-harming. Injury largely led to Holmes's feelings of despair.

Holmes's story is a sorry but brutally honest tale of the problems caused by overtraining and overeagerness to return to training following injury; an echo of Pfaff's words, 'if two was good let me do four'. But her story is also about fragmented and inconsistent medical supervision. Holmes had two main weaknesses: injuries and lack of confidence. These foibles became entwined, as with a lack of training an athlete can lose confidence in their ability but also with limited confidence an athlete needs to be patient and take training gradually. More and more is being written about the psychological aspect of injury, and Holmes's experience is a poignant example of how she was eventually able to overcome this cycle and remain injury-free in her preparation for Athens. We know that preparation is a key source of confidence (see chapter 16).

One person set up the infrastructure to help improve things for Kelly Holmes: a UK Athletics employee, Zara Hyde-Peters. She had been an international distance runner herself, giving her instant credibility. Her first act was to get a good doctor, Bryan English, and a physiotherapist, Alison Rose, to stick to Kelly like glue, and to hustle her into committing to regular check-ups. This was backed up with regular blood tests to pre-empt problems such as low haemoglobin, low ferritin (iron stores needed for blood cell formation) levels or low magnesium counts. Soon they realised that six-monthly epidural injections also helped overcome Kelly's career-long stomach problems and other ailments.

The next act was to sort out a local doctor and physiotherapist for training in South Africa, and to ensure that there was close liaison between them, Zara, Bryan and Alison. Eventually, Holmes begun to practise what was being preached and responded to the slightest niggle by seeing both experts immediately, once even flying back to the UK from Madrid for urgent checks. Her confidence flooded back with a period of uninterrupted preparation for Athens. Physio Alison Rose said:

> Behind the scenes, seeing the confidence come back to her as she realised that she was remaining injury free was key. Free from injury, she was able to remain more consistent in training and therefore become fitter and therefore more able to achieve the results she did ... the change in confidence levels as she became more resistant to injury ... was rewarding to be a part of.[10]

The lesson from this? Close-knit support team relationships – where each person knows their precise role and there is excellent communication between everyone involved, even if they are on another continent – are incredibly important. In this case, Holmes also needed to change her behaviour towards training and her body. Looking from the outside, we assume that athletes have sustained periods of training yet, as we can see, it took quite a vigorous intervention with excellent support to bring Holmes to fruition. For Holmes, sustained training had been the exception – it hardly ever happened until Zara stepped in.

A further lesson is that in elite sport, trust, reputation and credibility of support staff matter. Not so much in how eminent a medic or physiotherapist someone is, but more in how people conduct themselves and are able to make a connection and rebuild rapport with athletes: it is hard won and worth its weight in gold. Talking about treating runners generally, Alison Rose describes a sort of placebo effect when your credibility is so esteemed:

Being a runner helps, as runners believe in you anyway. But having Kelly be so generous in her public thanks to me has brought a lot of people to me … It sort of becomes self-fulfilling to some extent: the more an athlete believes in a physio, the more they'll do their exercises and the more likely the athlete is to get better.[11]

It is therefore no surprise that Rose went on to establish productive long-term relationships with two other Olympic Champions. Those from the 2012 Games include home Games poster-girl, heptathlete Jessica Ennis and Alistair Brownlee, the dominant triathlete of his era.

The mechanics

Listening to Alison Rose talk about her work I learnt a new word: prehab. Taking triathlon as an example of injury-free training across three disciplines (swimming, cycling and running) she has some interesting observations.[12] In particular, the importance of running technique drills. She considers that these drills hone an athlete's nervous system's movement patterning (i.e. coordination) to make them more biomechanically efficient and resistant to injury. Alistair Brownlee is not going to make improvements in his VO_2 max, so any performance improvement will be through improving his running economy; minimising the energy used in each stride. Since the run is the final triathlon discipline, athletes are fatigued and their technique often becomes ragged, making them far less efficient. So, potentially, this is where big race gains can be made. But the problem is that running also accounts for most injuries (about 65 per cent) in triathlon, as Brownlee was to discover with an Achilles tear six months before the 2012 Games.

Another particular problem in triathlon is when athletes come off the bike on to the run; their upper body has been taut and stiff, which, if this persists through all their running training, can cause all sorts of leg problems.

We see that in 95 per cent of runners that come [into Alison Rose's clinic], they are very stiff in their upper back and their arms are quite fixed and they're not using their shoulder as a joint … the minute you lock up that [upper body] rotation through the spine you end up having to rotate elsewhere [i.e. foot on the ground, the knee, the hip] … and it adds an enormous rotational stress to those joints.[13]

Stiff upper backs and shoulders are often associated with lower limb overloading problems, so when Brownlee came back from his Achilles injury months before the Olympics the medical team looked closely at his technique. They noticed that he was locking up his arms slightly which was causing twinges in his delicate Achilles. He was quickly able to adjust to the team's feedback due to his previous experience of running technique drills. Maintaining his smooth, loose rotating-upper-body running technique under duress is one of the secrets of his success. This is an excellent example of the importance of attention to detail in gaining small incremental gains in elite sport.

Balance, flexibility, coordination and proprioception (a sense of the interaction between individual body parts) awareness training are all aspects of prehab that Alison Rose swears by. This is also reinforced by the approaches of leading athletics coaches such as Alberto Salazar and Dan Pfaff. They would typically place technique and efficiency training above an extra conditioning session.

The mind

Put yourself in Jessica Ennis's shoes, months before the 2008 Olympics when she heard she had stress fractures of the navicular and a metatarsal of the right foot. Disbelief, anger, frustration, disappointment: life isn't fair, she'd been favoured for gold. It took her a year before she competed again, during which time to protect her right foot she learnt how to long jump off her left foot – quite a feat.

Alison Rose was there throughout Ennis's recovery as a physio but perhaps equally importantly as a confidante. Listen to what Ennis says about their relationship, '[Alison] rang me every day … Another string to her bow was her capacity to listen … It was somewhere I found I could go to clear my head.'[14]

It is starting to be more widely recognised that how an athlete reacts to the initial injury, the rehabilitation and the return to the sport is a psychological journey full of strong emotions and roadblocks. Athletes need extraordinary support such as the medical teams I've described. Ennis even compared injury to grief:

> I know it sounds dramatic, but to devote your life to something and then have it snatched away is a bit like suffering a bereavement. You've lost something that's part of you.
>
> I think the hardest thing was just not being able to do what you normally do … because normally when you train and you're competing and stuff you're always pushing yourself and, you know, you're always in the gym and on the track doing the stuff, and when you're injured you just have to take a real step back and just sit there and virtually do nothing really. So that was really hard. And then the process back into full training as well is so slow, really cautious, really careful, just kind of slowly progressing into each stage is really, really frustrating.[15]

Being patient and coping with injury can be viewed as a measure of the mental strength of an athlete. Research has shown that those who cope best with injury have a positive and proactive attitude towards injury, have realistic expectations, and high levels of self-confidence and belief in their ability to recover.

Ironman champion Chrissie Wellington also puts her finger on another buffer to injury stress: a balanced identity:

> Seeing them [family and friends] was a reminder that there is more to me than being an athlete. If that were all I saw myself as my emotional and physical well-being would be determined only by my sporting performance, with debilitating consequences should that facility be taken way by injury or

illness. But to see myself as a daughter, girlfriend, Scrabble champion and *Masterchef* addict, as well as an athlete, is to leave me with other roles so that my happiness and self-esteem can be maintained when the day job is compromised.[16]

So the interpretation of injury and rehabilitation, mental attitude/beliefs and an identity that is not too reliant on being a winning athlete all help champions overcome some of the severe incidents I have looked at. Perhaps the trick is in finding the right people to help support this approach and enhance these attitudes with athletes.

Final thoughts

It is not surprising that illness and injury often cause feelings of isolation and despair, and the very best thing is to have strong social support around you. Having people with the right mindset around the athlete and a medical budget to support this work is probably key for recovering champions. Luckily the UK National Lottery, and subsequent funding, came around just in time to help make this happen for Sir Steven Redgrave and Kelly Holmes. Now it is commonplace, as the more recent stories of Jessica Ennis and Alistair Brownlee demonstrate.

One curious thing though is that a recent book on the psychology of sport injury and rehabilitation highlighted the paucity of psychology training that sports medicine professionals receive.[17] Perhaps by having more open discussions of the injury struggles of top athletes we'll all start to understand more about rehabilitation and the process of athletes returning to sport. I shudder to think of the ratio of these champions compared to those who have not come through injury and had to retire prematurely.

But let's not get too gloomy. While living through illness or injury is tough, once athletes have come through it they often look back on their rehabilitation and time out as an opportunity that helped shape their progress and mental strength. As Jess Ennis has said about her injury, 'it definitely made [her] stronger'.[18]

Career low points triggered by injury, far from breaking minds, can actually build an athlete's determination and their response to the setback often represents one of the most significant aspects that shapes a champion's career path.

14 What is in a champion's mental toolbox?

I want to identify exactly what is in a champion's mental toolbox that supports their chances of becoming a champion. My search was made easier by the fact that psychologists have already spent considerable energy identifying champions' key mental attributes. Two notable pieces of work were an investigation with US Olympic champions in 2002[1] and almost a decade later one with top UK international performers.[2]

The language that is used among psychologists has unfortunately been varied and somewhat contradictory. One expert might talk about 'resilience', another about 'mental toughness', and a third about 'hardiness': it is like each researcher has created their own terms to 'brand' their work and make it distinctive. In this chapter I want to open some champions' mental toolboxes and rummage around in order to break down and explain these psychological elements by using champions' own descriptions of the tools they use.

My exploration of champions' mental toolboxes is aided by a team lead by Aine Macnamara. Her team's work[3] reveals a number of different tools. The top performers they interviewed are interesting. Take this example:

> You need to be able to deal with the ups and downs because there are a lot of people who struggle with not playing well or when things go badly and unless you can tough out those times you will never succeed. So that is what I did and I came back even stronger from that disappointment.[4]

It sounds like a sports team member, but in fact it is a top musician. Their investigations are appealing since they suggest that identical mental tools are used at different times by elite musicians, dancers and sportspeople. Mental tools – or in MacNamara's words – 'characteristics' refer to strategies such as coping with pressure, but also tools that represent the attitudes, emotions, and desires that developing athletes need to successfully realise their potential. They need these tools increasingly through their careers as the pressures and challenges they face get more intense the further they progress.

Without these tools, developing athletes can be vulnerable to failing to negotiate the challenging episodes that they will face as they go up the slippery slope to the top. Developing athletes can often be knocked back by these critical episodes, be they sporting examples, as above, or life's adversities (e.g. bereavement). Getting back on track if these knockbacks are persistent can be hard and may eventually contribute to dropping out or severe isolation (see chapters 12 and 13).

Here are seven mental tools that MacNamara's team identified but enhanced by the examples from champions' autobiographies and other accounts.

Coping with pressure

Why would Michael Phelps's coach, Bob Bowman, deliberately ask their driver to show up late? Then, at the same swimming meet in Australia, knowing the swimmer was particular about his food routine, a reflection of Phelps's childhood ADHD tendencies,[5] fix Phelps's meals so what he ordered wasn't right? He wasn't trying to prove a point to Phelps. Instead, with meticulous planning months ahead of his dominant 2004 Olympic performance, Phelps explained the rationale: 'Bob wanted to put me through some stress'.[6] The idea of deliberately putting developing athletes through unusual situations, seeing how they cope with and adapt to pressure and then reflecting with them afterwards helps them build their ability to cope.

Another swimming coach, Bill Sweetenham, described a similar approach, that of:

> Providing exposure to a variety of positive and negative experiences in a wide range of countries including poor swimming environments; and, deliberately creating adversity in training and competition in order to create challenge and a sense of achievement.[7]

Coping with pressure is something all champions have largely mastered in their own way over time.

Some of the other tools that athletes pick up in handling manufactured or general life/sport pressures relate to how they adapt to unusual situations, organise their priorities and plan ahead. Adaptability was what swimming coaches Bob and Bill were thinking of – when you compete or train abroad under pressure, flexing to new situations is key. However odd or poor the stadium or half finished event facility was, I always used to remind my squads, 'there will still be a result list with your name on it at the end of the competition, don't let this strange situation get to you'. Athletes have to learn get on with it, whatever new scenarios are thrown at them.

Chris Hoy tells the story of the one of the most intense pressure situations he faced, minutes before he won his first Olympic gold, aged 28:

> For me, the biggest challenge I ever overcame and I always draw on it now was the Athens Olympics. I was doing the 1,000 metres time trial … The three guys before me, the last three guys, had all broken the world record right before I went up there [to start].
>
> You're sitting there about five minutes to go and all of a sudden the goalposts are moved. Then the next guy's gone and they've moved again … Being able to not start thinking, 'Oh my God, I'm not even going to get a

medal here. Four years of training and everything's all changed.' Not panicking.

It was about being able to say, right, none of that is in your control; you have to focus on what you can control, and that is your performance ... I got the gold medal.

... So now it's something I draw upon and something that helps me mentally. The more you show your mental strength, the more it builds ...[8]

World records being broken in the minutes before you perform is pretty unusual and difficult to prepare for. But if you have done it once, as Hoy remembers seven years after the event, it means facing it again is a whole lot easier.

Returning to the meticulous Bob Bowman: again he illustrates what detailed preparation can entail. He deliberately prepared Phelps for distractions. Remember, a slight pause or hesitation in a close swimming race is worth half a metre or more. Bowman deliberately stepped on Phelps's goggles and cracked them without him knowing. Phelps was forced to swim in training with his goggles filling with water in order to prepare him if it occurred in a race. It did: during the last two lengths of the butterfly final in the 2008 Olympics.[9] Phelps said he couldn't see a thing and had reverted to counting his strokes, as he had done in training. He didn't flinch and won the gold.

Distraction and focus control

Colin Jackson is a former double world champion and world record holder in the 110m hurdles. In his post-athletics life he has become a very fluent broadcaster. Two of his BBC programmes show in a very compelling way the mental skill of distraction and focus control among champions. 'The Making of Me'[10] programme investigated physical, childhood and psychological factors that contributed to his athletic success. The producers tried to simulate a high pressure, stressful situation for a television audience. No doubt some bright spark suggested, 'I know let's get him to jump out of a plane' and the die was cast, he did his first skydive: it made great TV.

Moments before he stepped into the small plane that would take him 2½ miles up for his jump a psychologist got him to perform an intense concentration and focus test on her laptop. Remember, there might not have been a much better simulation of a pressure moment since his life depended partly on how he was going to react minutes later as he jumped. Minutes later he jumped with an instructor and landed successfully, buzzing with adrenaline from the experience. He is then given time to calm down and in the quiet of an office he performs the same focus test again.

The results are compared and his performance in both tests puts him in the very top few per cent of the population – he showed excellent focus. Moreover, his test under pre-jump duress i.e. measuring concentration under extreme circumstances, was actually better than his more relaxed test. Adrenaline and some anxiety, if you are used to it, can help you perform better. This ability to totally shut out external distractions and focus is something all champions become very good at over time. They are not born with it; they unknowingly learn and refine it, time and time again as they compete from a young age.

Jackson was also part of a second popular programme – 'Strictly Come Dancing' (the US version is known as 'Dancing with the Stars'). He finished second in 2005. This programme involves highly pressurised live performances in front of millions of people. His dance partner revealed why she thought Colin and perhaps other sporting champions do so well on these shows, other than the obvious physical abilities and a learning orientation:

> The physical side in dancing is the easy side; I think the mental side is tougher, if you can't take it mentally you might as well quit. Your mental attitude [addressing Colin] was far superior to any one else I've danced with on the series … before we went out and danced you did something very interesting. You would go off to the side somewhere and people would walk past you and you wouldn't notice. Every time, 3 or 4 minutes before the call to the floor, you would go off and stand there and go into this kind of 'focus' thing. Did you realise you did that?[11]

Jackson was unaware of this. For me, it clearly shows how sports people often become very good at this compartmentalisation of their attention. They can switch into 'compete' mode, but they find different ways to do this: listening to music, pre-competition routines or in Jackson's case taking himself away to quietly prepare for action. See chapter 17 for more on the role of pre-competition routines when under pressure.

Sportsmen and women have excelled on these dance shows on both sides of the Atlantic partly due to their positive orientation towards learning and using feedback; dancing being a physical skill requiring hard training and knowing how to cope with pressure and maintain focus.

American researchers confirmed the various ways champions' achieve their focus. US Olympic champions described several components of focus including 'abilities to narrow one's attention, block out distractions, attend to what one can control, and automatise one's responses.'[12] These four components of focus are all slightly different but together can make a huge difference to performance. They reminded us of Chris Hoy's description of his focus moment under pressure minutes before racing at the 2004 Olympics.

Realistic performance evaluations

The next mental tool we explore is again articulated well by Chris Hoy in the year before his Athens success. In 2003, he suffered a severe performance slump, a common critical episode that at some time or other effects most champions:

> Up to then I'd been on a steadily rising curve of improvement, which is like winning: it's easy to deal with. I hadn't yet peaked; I hadn't even plateaued. I had just kept getting better – the challenge for any athlete always comes when you stop improving – and in 2003 I seemed to stop improving …

> Looking back at that year now through the long lens I can see what went wrong.[13]

He describes overtraining, cramps, poor sleep, a relationship breakup with his first serious girlfriend and a last-minute change to his race plan seconds before going on to the track in the 2003 World Championships final. For him, finishing fourth at the Worlds was a calamity. Worse was to come a few weeks later when he only managed third at the national championships:

> To say [he] was devastated would be an understatement. [He] was really shattered, and [he] felt [his] confidence evaporate.
> With hindsight … if [he] had not bombed so abysmally – it's possible [he] might not have gone on to win the gold medal in Athens … as it was, [he] went back to basics, and reassessed everything'.[14]

Hoy and other champions all display an important skill: realistic performance evaluations. He went back to the drawing board to analyse his performance that year and how he could change it. You can already tell that, with hindsight, his evaluation was pretty detailed and managed to highlight a combination of circumstances.

At the time he also sought out extra input from former Olympic medalist Chris Boardman, who suggested that Hoy take ownership of his own training plan so that the creation of a new plan became an exciting project. Remember how I explained 'autonomy' as a key part of Self-Determination Theory in chapter 5? This is an example of an athlete taking responsibility and making his own choices and decisions with the help of others. He also consulted the team's psychiatrist, Steve Peters, who helped him place the performance slump into a broader perspective. Hoy's example is one of successfully evaluating and learning from a six-month slump but an equally important skill is to respond and evaluate performance *during* a championship.

At the 1980 Olympics, Seb Coe was world record holder at 800m and hot favourite to win, but he only managed silver. Evaluating his performance and bouncing back in 48 hours to contest the 1500m heats was a huge challenge. He identified the cardinal rules of 800m running that he had broken and rationalised that: first, the statistical chance of running that badly again were low; second, he got to a point where 'I genuinely did not care whether I won, I lost or I was second, third, fourth or fifth'.[15] It was clear in his mind that he would never again leave a track with the feeling of such an underperformance. As the saying goes he recognised that 'you don't become a bad athlete overnight.'

Exactly a week after his 800m defeat he took gold in the 1500m. There is a lot mixed up in this example of Coe's two contrasting performances including response to pressure (800m – 'the truth is I froze'), regulating his emotions (1500m heats), and – importantly – a realistic performance evaluation that was able to identify a strategy to win his first Olympic 1500m gold medal after a calamitous earlier performance. At the time phrases like 'resilience' and 'mental toughness' had not emerged into popular use. So when the BBC asked that typically inane question 'how do you feel?' after he left the track victorious, he exhaled, 'Christ!' – the Bishop of Durham complained to the BBC of his blasphemy.

Coe described his overriding emotion (in common with many athletes under pressure) as overwhelming relief along with ecstasy, elation, euphoria and vindication. He'd successfully bounced back by accurately evaluating his previous final.

Effective use of goals

ADHD not only made Michael Phelps rather tricky to coach as a youngster with his inattentive and impulsive behaviour, it also meant he was prescribed the medication Ritalin to help control the condition. He had to take it three times a day, which meant a daily visit to the school nurse at noon. Later at the age of 13 his decision to come off the drug was for him, a big challenge. Phelps describes it in terms of goal setting:

> We [he and his mum] spoke to Dr. Wax about it and he gradually started weaning me off the medication, first eliminating the afternoon dose so I wouldn't have to take it during school, then the frequency of the other doses, and by next year, all of it. The crutch was gone, and I had learned what it was like to set a goal that was difficult to achieve – and to win[16]

Effective use of goals sounds rather simple and trite when written on the page. Nevertheless all champions are excellent at this skill and, as Phelps demonstrates, it is something that gradually becomes embedded into their lives over time. In fact, a life without goals can be difficult to adjust to when they retire or are injured. Their strong dive, 'their rocket fuel', needs the direction that weekly, seasonal and annual goals gives.

One of the anonymous athletes MacNamara and her team interviewed explained it best:

> So the long term goal is the Olympics but obviously there are other championships before that so they are my goals as well, so it is just having something every six or seven weeks to aim for, and then re-evaluating where you are and setting more goals for the next stage and it helps to map out your progress like that.[17]

As champions develop beyond childhood some are able to exercise more autonomy and start to take more responsibility for their own progress – setting and monitoring their own goals is a key process for this. The voice of another athlete featured in MacNamara's research describes this self-motivation:

> Once you get older you have to be very self-motivating and set out where you wanted to get to and I used to do that … once I started getting selected for international teams I knew I just wanted to get better … get more of that! So I used to set myself targets … goals that I wanted to achieve in a training

session or for a season, and I used to have a sort of self administered reward and penalty system to get myself together and if things weren't going to plan, I would sit down and think what I had to do differently ... what else did I need to aim for ...[18]

It sounds simple but champions' ability to regulate themselves and seek constant improvement through well-framed goals takes time to develop. It helps if you have absolute clarity of the bigger picture or vision.

A vision of what it takes to succeed

'Having a vision' is something you often hear about in business or leadership-speak. The visionary leader who knows exactly what their organisation is striving for and perhaps more importantly how they're going to get there and can articulate it clearly.

For me, while many of the other mental tools are gradually polished over time through experience, this one is vital and rather different. In fact, the next chapter is devoted to a similar theme: learning from defeat – rhetoric or reality? (see chapter 15).

Typically, by the end of their adolescence or into their early 20s champion athletes are gradually learning what it takes to succeed at the very highest levels. Coaches and support staff help convey an overall vision or plan of what is required, but it often needs a jolt or catalyst for athletes to wake up and realise what it really takes to succeed.

Steve Redgrave describes it rather poignantly as a key moment when he was 21 years old. Winning was fairly inevitable as a teenager with physical prowess:

> [He] figured 'all I've got to do is follow what the coaches are telling me and Olympic success will happen'. It wasn't until the 1983 worlds when ... [he] didn't make the top 12, it suddenly dawned on [him] ... it's about how hard and how well you prepare. That was the turning point in [his] career'.[19]

Consider how the runner Mo Farah, a double Olympic gold medallist (5000m and 10,000m) took a while to develop a clear vision of what it takes to succeed. After a number of years without success, he realised if you can't beat the East Africans, join them. He spent long periods living and training in Kenya with the top athletes in his event. Then to help make the final breakthrough he relocated to Oregon, USA, to work with coach Alberto Salazar in 2011. At the 2011 World Championships in South Korea he took a silver and a gold. Significantly, after finishing second in the 10,000m, he identified his need for a faster final lap time of 51 or 52 seconds to claim gold. He went away worked on it and won. It sounds simple, but miles and years of work occurred before his vision emerged with the help of others.

Michael Johnson's view of the development of the vision of what it takes to succeed is a sort of moment of clarity, when everything comes together and it becomes clear what needs to be done. He says that most Olympic champions have experienced a moment when desire to be the best, the realisation of what is needed and the willingness to put in the work all combine.

There are a lot of examples of how this vision emerges. In the chapter that follows one striking reoccurring narrative is the description of a fierce duel to overcome one particular rival early in international careers. This shaped the progress of people like Bradley Wiggins and Ben Ainslie in their first Olympics. Later in 2012, as he'd conquered the pinnacle of cycle road racing, Bradley Wiggins said:

> In spite of the gold medals … I'd say it was only in 2011 that I completely understood how much you need to work to get to the very top, what hard training is, and how much of a lifestyle change is involved.[20]

So even when you get to the top with multiple Olympic medals like Wiggins, staying there and aspiring to win the three-week battle of the Tour de France required considerable adjustment to his vision of what it takes.

Visualisation or imagery

We all daydream and imagine situations in our head. However, champions use vivid positive images of successful performance and skilfully use this visualisation or imagery for three main purposes:[21]

1. For simulating competition situations
   This is the most common reference to visualisation among champions. This is typically used just before competition to help develop clarity about executing a strategy, controlling anxiety or imagining what to do in unusual situations such as Phelps's flooded goggles.
2. For help evaluating performance
   Particularly useful when individual decision-making can be reviewed by visualising part of a performance – imagery of the situation perhaps has a more vivid perspective compared to the one-dimensional analysis offered by coach on a white board.
3. For skill development
   To help rehearse new moves and capture the kinesthetic feeling, cues, sound and timing of new movement(s). Inevitably this use of visualisation tends to be a feature of early career episodes and is often spontaneously learnt without specialist input. Divers or gymnasts are often still using it later in their careers as they learn complex high scoring new moves.

Athletes all use the term 'visualisation' but many psychologists would prefer to talk of 'imagery' since it implies all the senses can be used (sound, sight, touch, smell) to bring scenarios to life in your head. Here are three differing uses of visualisation. The first is from Steve Redgrave who describes being formally introduced to visualisation by a psychologist at the 1988 Olympic Games. He says that he had been developing visualisation ideas naturally over the years and had been teaching himself without really knowing about it. But in 1988 he and his crew would sit down and talk through each race. They then went through a relaxation routine in which their coach would often join in but would often fall asleep!

When relaxed, the psychologist talked about what to expect and what they aimed for in the race. Things like concentration during the warm-up, awareness when sitting at the start, certain points in the race, after 15 strokes, the stride, rhythm and tactics. Which he says 'became ingrained deeply into the mind'. He also went on to use it in the build up to Sydney his fifth and final gold, constantly visualising what was going to happen at these Games where his record-breaking attempt brought unusually high pressures.

Next is Chrissie Wellington who uses it for simulating competition and thinking through possible 'what if' scenarios. When your event is eight or nine hours in duration, as in the ironman, and there are three different disciplines to master there are plenty of potential problems. Wellington, offering advice about preparation, says:

> I find I do some of my most valuable work on the sofa. Visualisation is a hugely important tool, one that requires little more than some peace and quite. Close your eyes, relax, and then go through each stage of the race in your mind. Picture yourself performing at your peak. Then imagine all the things that could go wrong, and picture yourself dealing with them. What will I do if my goggles are knocked off? What will I do if I suffer a puncture, or cramps?[22]

Finally, Michael Johnson uses visualisation to help his concentration in the tense, anxious minutes leading up to an Olympic final. He uses it as a tool in one of the most intimidating places: the athletics call room. These rooms (often deep within stadiums) are used to hold athletes prior to their race before they are released into the stadium at the correct time, rather like gladiators entering for their contest. A call room full of pumped up sprinters must be tough: eye contact may be avoided or sought, while some may be trying to remain lighthearted – each athlete responds differently. Johnson kept it deadly serious and kept himself separate in his own world:

> In situations where the pressure was on, I had a distinct advantage because I could revert to my natural tendency to go inside my mind. Instead of being distracted by exterior people or events, I focused on running a perfect race in my head.[23]

A study conducted for the United States Olympic Training Centre[24] indicated that 90 per cent of Olympic athletes use some form of imagery with a similar proportion of coaches using it within their training sessions. It is widely used then but champions describe it in different ways and for different purposes.

Commitment to excelling

It seems rather obvious after some of the accounts of success already told in this book to talk about commitment, drive, dedication, work ethic, persistence, sacrifice or hunger. Can words really do enough to explain the deep-seated mental resource of commitment to excelling? I'll try. Here are two examples that attempt to capture champions' commitment to excelling.

First, Michael Johnson's pithy description of 10 years of 200m sprint training in 1996, which resulted in his new world record at the time of 19.32 seconds.

> Ten years ago, I had run the same distance in 21 seconds, good for a high school athlete but well short of world class. A decade of tireless work and complete dedication had earned me little more than 1.5 seconds. A second and a half [improvement]! That was the difference between being mediocre and being the fastest in the world ... Perfection. In the end, I suppose that's why I run ...[25]

It captures the constant striving for a perfect performance and improvements measured in hundredths of a second. One of the things that champions do is to constantly ask questions. A healthy curiosity and a constant quest for answers provides a lot of drive.

Next, cyclist Bradley Wiggins's description of a tiny bit of his training connected with me since I too ride a bike (though to nowhere near his standard!). The intensity of training done by the track pursuit team that went on to break the world record in a time 3 minutes 53.31 seconds in Beijing (2008) starts to make you realise what is involved. Here is part of how they prepared for just under 4 minutes of perfection during a winter training camp in Majorca with repeated blocks of three days training.

Day one consisted of a straightforward five-hour ride on the island's testing roads at very nearly racing speed. Day two was 'a complete swine'. The two-hour individual morning ride was at high intensity but not quite flat out, followed by an afternoon of torture on a short sharp hill with four separate efforts. Each was at 100 per cent maximum effort for exactly five minutes to see how far up the hill they got before coming close to collapsing; once completed they came back down to go again. Day three they were back to clocking up the mileage over six hours on Majorca's mountain roads. After a day off – with 'just a light spin' they would repeat the three-day cycle again.[26]

All this as part of the endurance component of their preparation, day after day, for a four-minute Olympic performance. Of course rowers, athletes, swimmers and triathletes, among others, go through similar, perhaps harder regimes. If you have ever ridden a bike up a hill it gives a glimpse of the sustained effort, pain and commitment required in addition to all the other adjectives I listed above. Later in the book (see chapter 21) I ask whether endurance sport champions think differently about pain to the rest of us?

To sustain this intensity of training over the years means your commitment needs to be absolute. I struggle to find the words to do it justice but you have to really, really want to do it and almost have a psychological need to train hard and prepare all aspects to the highest standards. This drive might be self-determined, connected to perfectionism or deep-seated needs from negative childhood episodes or conditions or a combination of some or all these factors.

Final thoughts

Imagine you are Andy Murray serving for the championship, 77 years after the last British man won Wimbledon. I think you'd agree that such a tense situation would require some other mental tools that would address confidence, coping with nerves and control of temperament: how could he have won without these three tools? Of course they are possibly the most crucial. Indeed, MacNamara's research also recognised them, but I give them such weight that I cover them separately (see chapters 16 and 17).

The mental tools from this chapter, and the tools you'd need when serving for Wimbledon and in other crunch situations shape champions' success and progress. Many people working with champions acknowledge that these ten mental tools are essential for reaching one's potential in sport. Without these tools being tested and enhanced by their use in critical episodes champions can face problems. Collins even goes as far to suggest that without these tools: early promise often collapses under pressure; those with great physical potential won't improve and an overly smooth progression path towards the top is often symptomatic of later potential problems.[27]

I said earlier in the book that I was wary of the misunderstandings that can arise in calling athletes 'talented'. Now I'd happily use the term if only talented could also convey having a well-equipped and tested mental toolbox. An athlete with talent and mental tools is far more likely to reach his or her potential.

15 Learning from defeat
Rhetoric or reality?

You often hear coaches and players doing banal interviews after getting beaten, saying things like 'we'll take the positives from that'. This more often than not sounds like a cliché. But it's worth exploring how much of this learning from defeat is just rhetoric and how much is reality. Looking closely at athletes' stories I wondered if champions respond to defeat and learn from it in a subtlety different way to others. The catalyst was something Seb Coe said: 'Winning is predicated on a pretty healthy, robust diet of defeat. You've got to learn how to deal with that, and smart people know how to build out of it and what they need to do to address those issues.'[1]

Looking at first at team sport, the focus is on field hockey, in which sport both Britain and Australia's Olympic teams have had a rollercoaster ride in recent years. We then move on to consider sustained rivalries between emerging individual athletes and how this moulds champions.

Teams: Bouncing back from defeat

What happened in Australian and British field hockey teams and how failure was converted into podium positions over different four-year Olympic cycles (1996 and 2012) is fascinating. New national team coaches have their own vision of how to mix ingredients and resources to try to achieve success. But what if, instead of initial success at the top level, the teams fail? How much can they truly change their vision or paradigm for their second 'campaign'? Two insightful stories from each camp can help us answer these questions.

Team psychologist Corine Reid[2] worked with the Australian women's team as they reconciled to a disappointing Olympic campaign in 1992, finishing fifth despite being pre-tournament favourites. Following this loss, they then went on to win gold at two consecutive Olympiads. According to Reid, when they started preparing for the 1996 Games their loss was still relatively raw for many players, with failure attributed by some to coaching staff, other players or officials, while others blamed themselves. Newcomers to the squad felt like outsiders to those from the previous 1992 team; hardly a strong cohesive starting point.

The team leadership's approach was to set up opportunities for the group to articulate what had happened and what they were going to do about it. This partly involved group discussions that focused on cognitive reappraisal – reappraising and interpreting the disappointment. One proposal that emerged was the abolition of the starting line-up and the associated change to the 'revolving bench' system (new then but now commonplace in hockey to allow fresh legs to work hard in creating space). This challenge to the traditional approach was uncomfortable for some due to the uncertainty it created.

Over time the team's increased confidence to communicate honestly meant players began to advocate the revolving bench when challenged by others. A further change was the group's willingness to create and train under high pressure and high intensity situations, so their learning became more deeply ingrained: 'their active participation [in this] fostered their sense of control over their own development', despite these often unpopular [high pressure] training techniques'.

The coach and psychologist stimulated squad conversations about likely challenging events they would face as a group in the coming years and how they would respond to events, such as non-selection (as inevitably the squad is reduced nearer the Olympics), being injured or experiencing performance slumps. These conversations formed a core part of their preparation for the Olympics, and in 2000, the Australian team extended these conversations to include partners and significant others[3]

Things started coming together as they melded into a resilient team. The players were aware of the ever-present threat of non-selection or injury, but this did not undermine their collective strength. Their two consecutive gold medals in the next two Olympics suggest their enhanced team culture served them well.

A few years later, meanwhile, the British women's hockey squad found itself in the midst of a barren spell with no medals for 16 years. Non-qualification in 2004 was followed by a slightly improved, but still disappointing, sixth place in 2008. These defeats prompted a similar period of re-evaluation. The lead coach started implementing his revised vision of what it would take to succeed. The huge changes will profoundly affect the lives of team members and is still an ongoing project. The team's leading international goal scorer Alex Danson when asked to identify one critical moment in her whole career spoke with feeling:

> My one critical moment was really positive and it completely changed how I thought, not just about sport, but actually about everything. It was in 2008 after the Olympics in a room at our Bisham Abbey training base ... for us this was the biggest decision that completely changed my life in so many ways and the path that I took and how I felt and thought. In this room with 30 of my team mates we sat there four years out from London 2012 and we made a very simple promise to ourselves collectively: we said we were desperate, more than anything in the world to win a gold medal in London.[4]
>
> In that room a part of me thought 'but we haven't won an Olympic medal for 20 years, and never in history have we won a World Cup medal, who are we to think we can win gold?' then someone said, 'who are we not to dream, who are we not to set ourselves the highest standards to try and medal in London'. So that commitment to be part of an amazing group of individuals and support staff to live every day to be gold in our behaviours, gold in our

training, gold in our effort and attention to detail. I'll remember that moment for ever.

Danson had to relocate to live closer to the training base, change her university course and set to work with her colleagues over the next four years. Team GB achieved an Olympic bronze medal in London and England took silver at the 2013 European Championships, but one senses the team is building for future gold. Coach Danny Kerry's perspective on the same period perhaps explains why Danson finds it so very memorable. His experience in Beijing was tough, having been 'put through the mill, you name it everything happened'.

After some reflection he came back and developed a 'Golden Thread' strategy, to which he wanted everyone to commit. The Golden Thread defined the values, culture and behaviours that all the team, coaches and support staff had to buy into. As with Australia's strategy, this was essential in developing the self-awareness and open communication that enabled the team to be honest with each other. Slowly an environment of trust was built, not just among the players, but also among the 17 support staff (medics, analysts, trainers and coaches).

However, the single biggest change that Kerry strove for and eventually achieved was the centralisation of the programme at Bisham Abbey:

> In every other Olympic cycle to date, athletes had been distributed all around the country. The fact is that we are judged on our ability to play in a team. And yet the performance practice environment was nothing like that. It was small clusters of people distributed all around the country. Fundamentally we weren't doing stuff as a team, so our level of team understanding on all sorts of levels wasn't where it needed to be in order to win medals.
>
> So I immersed myself in literature, workshops and spoke to experts about change! Armed with that I took a two-prong approach. Firstly, I 'drip-fed' the seed of the idea very early on in 2006 so that people could 'smell it coming'. I got the need to centralise into people's conversations and on to the agenda, so people knew it was coming. I was well aware that it would take time. The initial point was to get them to come round to the idea: what it would mean for them and what it would mean for performance. But on a really, really subtle level.[5]

Then, when he thought that the time was right, he promoted the idea that would have huge implications for people in changing their living arrangements. His approach:

> to appeal to the athletes on an aspirational level, of what I believed could be achieved through change. What use is it aspiring just to be an Olympian? We're funded to win medals. You aspire to medals! Look at the sports that win medals, look at cycling, look at rowing, look at sailing – they all have centralised programmes. And we're a team sport, think of what we could achieve if we were together![6]

Centralisation of the programme and the Golden Thread started to produce results in London and the meeting in which they committed to these changes had a profound personal impact on the players. Kerry's credibility as a visionary leader has meant he has now been promoted to oversee the whole GB Olympic hockey programme, men and women, and it will be fascinating to watch both teams' future progress.

These two accounts of changes in team culture in international-level hockey were stimulated by failure, and both had a further two things in common: leadership groups with a clear plan or vision; and processes set up within the group to create clear communication with each other, including clear goals shared by all.

Individual duels

Now let's see how transformative examples stimulated by defeat in individual sport compare. Champions' breakthrough performances come from a hunger to chase and fulfil goals but also come from an understanding of how to get there. Some of the best examples of transformation come from one-on-one duels for supremacy that developed over a few years – a sort of fight to the death that raises performance levels ever higher. At the end of the duel the blueprint vision for success has been road-tested and refined through the heat of sustained competition.

These duels to overcome a top rival that continue over a number of years are made even more powerful if the person the athlete is chasing is a respected role model whose behaviour and attributes you admire. Admiration can turn into something much more useful: first helping an athlete to model what the opposition are doing and then improve on it.

An Australian and a Brazilian are respectively to thank for shaping the high standards that Sir Bradley Wiggins and Ben Ainslie reached.

Wiggins explains that: 'without the harsh lessons Brad McGee has taught [him] in 2002 ... and without him to chase, [he] would never had won an Olympic title. Of that [he was] absolutely sure'.[7] The same pattern of thought emerges from Ben Ainslie's quest for gold. Ainsley was 'convinced that without Robert [Scheidt's] presence, [he] wouldn't have developed in the way [he] did.'[8]

Bradley Wiggins

The harsh lessons that Wiggins learned had their genesis in a crushing defeat during a Commonwealth Games individual pursuit, in which he 'choked horribly ... [he] went into the race feeling totally inferior to McGee both as a person and as a racer. The race was lost before it even started'. It was a massive anticlimax and a humiliation for Wiggins in front of a Manchester home crowd and a live TV audience. It partly stemmed from him being in the same professional road team as McGee in which he was treated as and felt to be the servant in support of the leader (McGee).

A summit meeting was called at British Cycling, in which it was decided that Chris Boardman should be appointed as his mentor. Importantly, Boardman the

1992 Olympic gold medallist, had inspired a young Wiggins to dream of Olympic success when he watched him as a 12-year-old on TV. He respected his role model. Boardman set to work and didn't hold back. First, he ensured that Wiggins took more responsibility for his training, including written minutes of meetings and multiple redrafts of training plans to ensure that everything they had agreed on was recorded and followed through. Second, using his contacts Boardman also helped Wiggins exit from one road team to another. Third, he also ensured Wiggins's feet were firmly on the ground even after his first big win, the World Championships, by reminding him that his rival McGee was not there and there was still work to be done to overhaul him.

Wiggins recalls:

> Although [Chris Boardman] had been incredibly hard and critical, he was also always consistent and fair. He was always objective, analytical and realistic. He told the story exactly as it was, even when I didn't want to hear it. He just looked at the facts, the figures and what he saw me doing on the track and compared them with the figures he knew would be required to beat McGee and win an Olympic gold medal. He was remorseless in the way he never deviated from what needed to be examined; he never went down unnecessary avenues.[9]

Wiggins left it very late indeed to show the progress that was needed to realise Boardman's vision of how to beat McGee. In the final 11 weeks of training before the 2004 Olympic Games Wiggins's times gradually improved according to target. He went on to win the gold, admitting to McGee on the podium that McGee didn't know how much he had inspired him and pushed him on. McGee never beat him again.

In elite sport it is drummed into you that it can be dangerous to focus on one competitor too much. It can become too personalised and there is often other opponent to look out for, but it is pretty clear from this cycling example how important one duel was in the development of this Olympic and Tour de France champion.

Ben Ainslie

In sailing, a sport I know very well, the inspiration that Ben Ainslie admitted to of his rival, Robert Scheidt, was equally full of praise but slightly different:

> If he'd been talented but, not to put too fine a point on it, a pisshead who wasn't one hundred per cent committed but whose talent saw him through, then I could have been persuaded that you could get away with being like that too. But I knew I had to beat this guy who was not only an awesome sailor but also a magnificent athlete … He's still the fittest guy I've ever met on the water. Robert was the complete professional …[10]

Ben Ainslie: modelling himself on Scheidt eventually led to his famous contribution to clawing back an 8–1 deficit in the America's Cup for Oracle Team USA

> I was galvanised in everything I did by my desire to beat Robert … It was a stark, ever present reminder that I still had another level to ascend to if I was to reach the zenith of Olympic achievement.[11]

I'd first met Ainslie at a US roadside diner after he'd dominated a storm force race in Miami as a youngster. He was buzzing. A few years later at Savannah, Georgia, in 1996 (his first Olympics), he narrowly finished second to Robert Scheidt, largely due to a lack of experience at the start of the final race. It prompted 'the start of probably the most intense period of [his] life, from then until Sydney.'

He vowed to match or pass his rival in fitness and also not to be intimidated by him in competition, but instead to confront him tactically on the race track when appropriate. He also immersed himself in getting to know the waters of Sydney Harbour where the 2000 Games were to be held. He started beating his nemesis at the World Championships and in races in Sydney.

The final showdown between them at the Olympic Games came down to, unusually for sailing, a televised battle in the final race in which Ainslie in silver position, entirely within the rules, positioned his boat to slow down Scheidt in a series of eye-to-eye manoeuvres. It was like jousting on the water. Ainslie's poise meant he leapt from silver to gold medal by the end of the race. Reflecting back on what might have happened if he'd made gold at their first meeting four years earlier in Atlanta:

> I suspect it would have been very different. I would have been rushed into the limelight far more quickly than I have been … such close proximity to

success [by finishing second] made me even more determined to train much harder to try and win gold next time.[12]

Once again the intense sustained duel worked its motivational magic.

Motivational spur

Coming second then often highlights what an athlete or team needs to improve on, whether technically or in the whole training regime, and thus they can exact change as opposed to a complacent champion who is less likely to feel the need to adjust anything.

As Ainslie describes, coming second embeds an incredibly powerful motivational spur to do better. A top athlete or team that has ability and something to prove after Olympic disappointment may become almost unstoppable. Michael Johnson, who performed poorly at the 1992 Games due to food poisoning, and Jessica Ennis, who was returning from injury, both went on to dominate World Championships in post-Olympic years and then progress on to their first Olympic success. US gymnast Shawn Johnson, who won a gold and three silver medals in 2008, recalls a similar hunger:

> I remember the 2007 World Championships and making many mistakes and missing out on a medal. I was considered a serious contender on the balance beam. I just remember that feeling and the fire lit inside me to never want to feel it again.[13]

The trouble with finishing second too frequently, however, is that it can undermine an athlete's personal identity. There is a need for athletes to have a robust self-esteem with an identity that is not solely defined by performance results. This balance means they can maintain their emotional stability and work out how to improve. Jonathan Edwards, a former Olympic, World, Commonwealth and European triple jump champion, puts it clearly when he says, 'athletes, like everyone else, need to strike the right balance between who they are and what they do'.[14]

Final thoughts

There are, then, ample personal examples that finishing second can help you develop a clear vision of how to become a champion, but it seems champions only appreciate this with the benefit of hindsight.

But it's all about having time to make significant changes: in four years, or even one, quite a lot can be achieved. Interview answers of learning from defeat, made in the context of weekly professional team matches, don't truly reflect or reveal the lessons needed to be learnt following defeat; they are a form of irrational optimism. Making tweaks for the next week's game is possible but wholesale change is unlikely. Learning from defeat can have most impact in the medium to long term since, as we have seen, it can be a real catalyst for changing thinking.

16 Confidence

The golden but slippery nugget: confidence. A *Times* newspaper writer likened confidence to a bar of soap in the power shower of sporting life: 'Grasp it too tight and it squirts from your hands, reach to pick it up again and you are flat on your back.'[1]

The idea that confidence and self-belief are slippery, aren't easy to keep hold of and can come and go will be familiar to most people. It's the same for champions and coaches. Learning how to find and keep hold of self-belief is crucial and while it does not guarantee success it is something of a paradox, because it is difficult to have belief in something you have not yet achieved. A look at child-athletes making breakthroughs will help us: we consider school-age children who have achieved their first big international success, including Cathy Freeman, Michael Phelps, Ian Thorpe and 18-year-old footballer, Michael Owen.

Of course, previous accomplishments are a key source of confidence, but what other sources do athletes and coaches rely on to build their self-belief? To answer this question we draw on two stories of experienced sports professionals who, competing consistently at a top level, finally achieved their ultimate goal: Bradley Wiggins's 2012 Tour de France and Olympic double and Andy Murray's 2013 inaugural Wimbledon triumph.

Child champions

Child champions' breakthroughs are fascinating as they have no medal success at the top level to help build supreme optimism. They often defy the form books to break through to senior success while still at school. Take Cathy Freeman who, aged 16, won a gold medal in the 4 × 100m relay at the Commonwealth Games. Her coach had entered her for the trials after noticing that her training times would put her into the mix, and her tied third-place meant she made the Australian relay team going to Auckland. '[She] spent the first few days [in the athlete's village] with [her] mouth open, staring at everyone and everything.'[2] Problems with dropped batons in practice raised question marks about her selection, however, and self-doubt began to gnaw away.

But confidence has a social element. What others say and their behaviour around us matters. If others believe in you, particularly significant others, and make this abundantly clear, it is a real fillip. In this case it came in the form of the team's top sprinter, Kerry Johnson, who had been Freeman's number one supporter and looked out for 'the baby of the team'. Johnson even threatened the management that she would boycott the team unless Freeman ran in the final. Her pre-race advice to Freeman proved invaluable and with her final words, 'I think we'll win this today,' arguably helped convince the schoolgirl that she deserved to be there and was a valued member of the team. The baton exchange from Freeman to Johnson was perfect as they surged to gold.[3] Freeman's life changed in that moment; 10 years later she lit the Sydney Olympic flame and then a week or so after that stormed to 400m gold.

Likewise, the other person that helped instil self-belief in 15-year-old Michael Phelps was his coach, who ignited his desire to become the youngest ever swimming world record holder. But hormones were also at play. In the preceding year Phelps experienced his most accelerated growth spurt – performance improvements can be rapid with natural hormonal support. His mum was rather surprised when she recorded a two-inch height gain on the marks she made in a doorway at home. Then his coach lit the fuse by writing 'WR Austin' (World Record, Austin, Texas) on all the notes he left for Phelps over six months of intense training, all aimed at preparing to break the 200m butterfly world record. At the Austin meet and World Championship trials he was the first ever to swim under 1 minute 55 seconds.[4]

Ian Thorpe has also described the benefits of growth spurts, which caused a huge 5-second improvement in his 400m freestyle time between the ages of 15 and 16. Imagine the exuberance and confidence of seeing almost monthly gains in performance and beginning to realise through your training times that you are becoming rather good. Mix this with youthful naivety at not really taking in the significance of this achievement and his quiet confidence and there is a recipe for great things. Describing the experience of winning his five medals at the Sydney Games at the age of 17, Thorpe said, 'I had been devoid of nerves – dazzled by the lights and attention, unaware of the true pressure of an Olympic meet and oh-so calm.'[5]

At each major championships a new and exciting child champion emerges, sometimes reserved and humble whose self-belief is based on treating the event as similar to their intense training sessions. Young people often use their training and competition as a way of expressing their emerging identity and can perform on automatic pilot. At the 2012 Olympics it was a shocked 15-year-old Lithuanian swimmer, Ruta Meilutyte, whose astonishment and tears at winning gold made emotional viewing. Appropriately, it was Ian Thorpe who defended and rationalised her teenage success to a suspicious media.

When former England footballer Michael Owen spoke about his experience as an 18-year-old in scoring a wonder goal against Argentina in the 1998 World Cup he captured the clutter-free thoughts of youth:

> When I did it I wasn't surprised at all, now as you get older and look back you think what an attitude I had, I wasn't scared of anyone, I didn't even know who I was playing against. We'd have team meetings and they'd say you're playing against this man and this man: I didn't even listen, I didn't care. I just knew that I was playing, that I was going to score and I didn't

need to know about the opposition. You get older and you start worrying about things, you know, you just worry too much … You only have that not being scared as a kid.[6]

Not being scared sums it up nicely – the benefit of being a child. As he reminds us, life gets more complicated as an adult – relationships, mortgages, media commitments, expectations, elevated pressure, the weight of history and other athletes gunning to beat you.

Child champions' unique experience suggests that self-belief has a social element (coaches and significant others) and that their limited experience or naivety can actually be in their favour as they have no fear. Some young champions might also realise in hindsight that their confidence draws on two further aspects: firstly, how they feel about their preparation and secondly, the fuel of sustained improvements (aided by maturation of mind and body).

Where did Bradley Wiggins's 2012 confidence come from?

The first Briton to stand victorious on the Champs-Élysées podium of the Tour de France in 2012 backed up his win just over a week later by winning the Olympic time trial gold medal. How did he build his confidence to tackle such a supreme peak?

Early on in his career as a 15-year-old Wiggins had won his first national junior title and by the end of the same year he had won his first senior track race. Writing about it in his autobiography, Wiggins says:

> From [that] moment I never doubted I was going to make it. Some would call it arrogance, I would term it self-belief and if you don't have that as part of your make up you probably won't make it. You don't have to ram it down everyone's throat but you have to believe, deep down inside, that you are the best and you are going right to the top whatever gets thrown at you.[7]
>
> Natural talent can take you so far, and I would suggest I am the perfect example of that. My natural aptitude and competitive nature took me a long way down the road in the early years.[8]

His belief in his innate ability was a good starting point, indicating that he thought it was hardwired into him. If you believe that you have the characteristics to succeed, you realise your ability and confidence won't disappear overnight. The power of belief, even if it might not actually be true, has been shown to demonstrate the placebo effect. His innate belief in his abilities took a little bit of work and tough coaching to draw out. As we saw earlier in this book he was put together with his childhood role model Chris Boardman from the age of 23 and, due to his prolonged duel with the Australian McGee for supremacy in the sport, he raised his game to become a world-beater.

Fast forward 10 years to the 2012 Olympic Games. It is not often an athlete is described as being super-confident but Wiggins was, due to a combination of rigorous injury-free preparation and a string of successes. Wiggins, like many

Bradley Wiggins: detailed preparation, previous success, a familiar routine and voice in his ear

champions, is a student of his sport and he knew that apart from him only two other people in cycling history, Eddie Merckx and Jacques Anquetil, had won the Paris–Nice, Dauphine and the Tour de France races in the same year.[9] And so it was his innate belief in himself, his preparation and the season's successes that gave him the feeling that he was about to win the 2012 Olympic time trial race before he even got on the bike:

> The overriding thing with the time trial was that from the day before, going through the whole [pre-race] routine in the morning beforehand, it was the same process that I had been though on the Tour and every other time trial in recent years. So that put me in Hampton Court [at the start] on the Wednesday morning knowing what I'd achieved ... nine days before, feeling super-confident that I could win ... I knew I had it in the bag if I could avoid getting anything wrong.[10]

Yet, his coaches had to fix one thing to ensure the feeling of continuity and confidence was maintained. It was the voice in his ear. Sean Yates had been the person who accompanied and spoke to him by radio in his support car for all his time-trial victories that season. His coaches fixed it for him to be a Team GB member for a day, just to tick the last confidence box. Routine and consistency help maintain a feeling of control.

We've all heard the mantra of elite sport to concentrate on 'control the controllables' rather than worry about peripheral concerns. Well his support team realised that they could control the voice in his ear even if it took some logistical gymnastics.

Let's not forget the confidence gained from being a long-term member of a top performing team. His support team of sports scientists, coaches and team psychiatrist supplied the hard evidence of training statistics and the words, actions and team culture that had made this self-belief so assured. Their voices and the drip-feeding of persuasive words are a proven ingredient in the science of confidence.

What does the research say about confidence?

The Stanford University psychology professor Albert Bandura is *the name* in this field. Tags of 'the greatest living psychologist' must be hard to reconcile for Bandura, who is approaching 90 years of age as I write. His self-efficacy theory is the reference point for all subsequent work in this area. He investigated trauma, phobias and educational success and always came back to the importance of confidence and self-belief. His widely accepted theory says confidence is developed primarily from four sources:

- *Mastery experiences* (i.e. past accomplishments): crucial in the Wiggins example in both competition results and training preparation but less obvious in child champions making a senior breakthrough.
- *Vicarious experiences* (i.e. observing others, 'if Cathy can do it, then I can too'): we will cover this further in a moment, but consider the effect of Wiggins, earlier in his career, being in a team where everyone else is winning medals and the social modelling impact of this. In addition to live modelling of behaviour by others, Bandura also refers to 'cognitive self-modelling' – otherwise known as visualisation or imagery, i.e. imagining yourself in and mentally rehearsing successful situations.
- *Verbal persuasion* (i.e. positive beliefs expressed by a coach): we've already alluded to the social role of others in helping convince an athlete through words that they can succeed. Consider the actions of Cathy Freeman's mentor Kerry at her first international relay. Also the drip-feeding of positive words to Wiggins in training and the hours before racing.
- *Physiological and affective states* (i.e. the way athletes interpret nerves and other emotions): it is how champions attribute and use emotions such as nervousness that supports their confidence; most champions view nerves as facilitative, and accepting and understanding one's emotions helps support confidence (see chapter 17).

Some inquisitive English researchers who knew all about Bandura's ideas interviewed 14 medallists from Olympic and World Championships to see what they said about where their confidence comes from.[11] It is useful to see what medallists say compared to Bandura's theory.

The medallists, much like Bradley Wiggins, mentioned *performance accomplishment:* competition results, personal goals and personal bests unsurprisingly provided a major source of confidence. They also confirmed that *physical preparation* was identified as a further important confidence source.

But in the interviews the majority of athletes also talked about something rather different to Bandura: *mental preparation,* such as identifying and rectifying weaknesses, and structured goal-setting. 'Doing things in a structured, ordered way' along with leaving 'no stone unturned' helped to build confidence. Some medallists were more specific about their mental training practice, with for example anxiety-control, visual-imagery work and pre-competition routines all mentioned.

The medallists found that reaching agreed milestones with a coach was a major source of satisfaction and confidence. Some described how using training logs or diaries to record their progress helped convince themselves of their complete preparation and that they could not have done more. If a structured approach is also supported by expert analysts and scientists supplying compelling evidence of your performance level your belief in the process or system you have adopted will be stronger.

Just over half the group of interviewed athletes also revealed *social support* from stable relationships with family, friends and partners as sources of confidence. Presumably in Bandura-speak their social support might come in the form of 'verbal persuasion' of the wider perspective of life outside the emotional rollercoaster of being a top sportsperson. The opposite of this is when social support is lacking because there are unstable relationships that affect confidence and performance. For example in the years surrounding his divorce from Brooke Shields, Andre Agassi's ranking plummeted from 1 to 141.

But there was one rather interesting finding from a small number of athletes about *self-awareness* and confidence. It sounds odd doesn't it that they would attribute self-awareness and understanding the meaning of their sporting life to supporting their confidence?

The meaning of life

Some athletes said: 'I think I'm much more secure in myself, I know where I'm going, what I'm doing, and I know what I want, and I think you develop a level of confidence from that.'[12] For those pursuing dreams of getting to and staying on the podium, having a clear perspective of their overall purpose lays a sound foundation for confidence. If you are gripped by uncertainty as to the meaning of your sporting life, confidence will not come easily.

Dr Steve Peters, a psychiatrist working with British squads, emphasises this as a starting point for all his work:

> What I'm going to do [first] is to get someone to be happy within themselves, actually saying 'I feel good about myself, I feel good about where I am' and then we'll move forward because the chances are they will then medal.[13]

The story of a British 400m athlete, Roger Black, who had the misfortune to be competing at the same time as Michael Johnson is partly one of trying to work this out. At the 1996 Atlanta Olympics, in which Johnson was supreme in his gold footwear, Black reconciled the meaning of and happiness in his devotion to athletics.

The next time you hear an athlete say the seemingly bland statement 'I want to be the best I can be', it might reveal a little bit more about their thinking beyond a seemingly mundane interview response.

> ### Roger Black works out why he's continuing as an elite athlete
>
> I always say that for the first 10 years of my career, I was very good at running, but never really had that deep understanding of what it really meant to me and why I was really doing it. I think, when you line up for the big one, that's what comes through – if you are not totally at one with what this means to you and what this is about and why you have to run faster or jump a long way, then I think that can be expressed. You are at peace to do that, which is how I felt before my 400 metres final at the Atlanta Olympics.
>
> The problem with athletics is that you can do so well on natural talent. You come into it young and just do it – you don't understand what it really means to you because you're just good at it. When you get up against the best in the world, they're all very good. Often what separates us at that level is the ability to truly understand *why we're doing this*. It's not just jumping into a sandpit; it's not just running around a track. It's far more than that. It's about knowing you have to fulfil your potential.[14]

Roger Black achieved a fine silver medal in his 400m final against Michael Johnson. You can imagine how important it was for him to have absolute clarity about why he was doing it when he was up against the odds-on home-crowd favourite. I yearned for him to achieve his own success in Atlanta because, although he was few years younger, I identified with him because we'd attended the same school when we were teenagers.

Does a little self-doubt help?[15]

Every top sportsman wants to be as super-confident as Bradley Wiggins was in his 2012 Olympic time trial. In reality, those situations do not come around very often and in fact many champions would worry that too much confidence leads to complacency. They know from experience that nothing is guaranteed – but is self-doubt helpful?

A team of researchers set out to investigate this. The beauty of their experiment lay in its simplicity; they used a skipping rope test. Those who were 'moderately confident' at skipping were recruited and asked to do a one-minute practice run. Then half the group was given a different rope and told that this rope 'would be more difficult to use, and would possibly interfere slightly with performance due to differences in weight, length and stiffness ... In reality, the two skipping ropes were identical except for their colour.' This bogus information was a way to manufacture a state of self-doubt.

The performance of those using the different rope increased from the practice to the actual test. They concluded that slight reductions in confidence may promote greater effort and subsequent performance. Scaling up a skipping rope test to a world sports final is a quite a jump, but the principle that some uncertainty is a good thing still holds. Multiple champions, through the numerous finals that they have competed in, often recognise that there is always a niggling doubt that things won't work out, however confident they are. In fact, one of the warning signs of complacency for a coach would be if they weren't suitably nervous before a major event – now that would be a source of anxiety.

But, of course, the balance between confidence and a little self-doubt depends on the event and the athlete. Dan Pfaff, coach of Olympic champions Donovan Bailey (sprint), Greg Rutherford (long jump) and Paralympian Jonnie Peacock (sprint) has talked about the ego and a sort of confident arrogance needed in the power/speed events he coaches:

> They have strong self-esteem and self appreciation; probably a standard deviation above the average athlete … You need a good strong ego to do what they do. To stand on the runway in front of 80,000 people going nuts and you've got a chance of winning gold you better have some ego … they have to do a massive warrior stint when they get in that stadium.[16]

This talk of resilient ego and the kind of 'no fear' approach of youngsters reminds me of watching sprint finals. You never quite know if the way athletes present themselves to the public in the minutes before the race with introductions and so on is what they really feel: from confident swagger to confident seriousness? We never know. One could interpret Usain Bolt's playfulness before major races as a way of coping – he certainly was almost crippled with anxiety before his first major world success in front of a Jamaican home crowd at the age of 15. Over time a persistently confident athlete will work out with their coach their optimal levels of self-belief and the behaviour that works for them in those final minutes.

How did Andy Murray convince himself he could win?

Pages and pages have been written about Andy Murray's journey to ending 77 years of British disappointment at Wimbledon on the seventh day of the seventh month of 2013. Here we'll focus on five sources of confidence from which he was able to gradually convince himself he could win.

First, *physical preparation*. An enhanced training regime made him one of the fittest athletes on the tour. If you are supremely fit you can be confident that you won't blow up by chasing down every single point as he did. He was blowing hard at times but never wavered from his commitment to chase everything.

Second, *his Olympic victory in 2012* laid the foundation of how the Wimbledon environment could be his domain. But pay attention to what he did the evening before his Olympic final, it happened to be the so-called 'Super-Saturday' when Britain won three golds in the athletics stadium:

> I watched the athletics last night, it was amazing the way Mo Farah won. I do 400m repetitions in my training and when I'm completely fresh I can run it in 57 seconds and his last lap after 9600 metres was 53 seconds – so it is just unbelievable fitness – and it gave me a boost coming in to today and the momentum the whole [British] team has had has been so good.[17]

This is what Bandura would call a vicarious experience. While it is impossible to measure the effect on Murray's confidence of watching a team-mate in the same team colours pushing himself to extreme limits of success, his use of the word 'momentum' suggests at the very least he expected to be part of a British surge, and embraced the home support. As an aside, the science suggests that modelling effects on confidence work best when the person being watched is perceived as more similar to the viewer and there is social interaction between that person and the aspiring athlete.[18] So, as a thought experiment, if a British tennis contemporary of Murray had demonstrated world success earlier in his career it theoretically would have helped his confidence.

Third, he had a cunning plan, which had worked before. In defeating Novak Djokovic at Olympic Wimbledon a year earlier he had developed and used a more aggressive strategy of sometimes coming to the net and attacking his opponent's second serve that worked on the unique grass surface. Having trusted his *strategy* before, it enhanced his conviction that he could win, although in the higher temperatures of 2013 he played longer points, moving Djokovic around the court, relying on his supreme fitness. No game plan, no win.

Fourth, his *previous accomplishments* meant that logic was pointing towards a justified confidence. He had won an Olympic final at the same venue, he had beaten Djokovic on grass before, he had won his first Grand Slam event (the US Open). He could tell himself these things but he also had people he respected to reinforce and articulate this.

Step forward the calm respected coach. Fifth and finally, coach Ivan Lendl's *verbal persuasion* – we can only speculate on what Lendl said to Murray but the evidence of a change from previous finals was clear to see. For example, more first serves in, a stronger second serve and knowing how to work the home crowd – to gee them up when he needed them. And in the BBC post-match interview, when asked to relive the last point, Murray replied:

> I have no idea what happened. I really don't know. I don't even know how long that last game was. That shows how well I was concentrating.[19]

He lost three match points in the decisive final game, but he did not start muttering and shouting as in the past but oozed clarity of purpose and the intense focus that he described in his interview. For more on emotional control see chapter 17.

Final thoughts

If confidence is drawn from only one or two sources, say an athlete's recent win–loss record and beliefs about the advantages of their physical size, then it is likely to be fragile. A broader range of sources arguably produces a more resilient wholehearted confidence. Athletes early in their careers have fewer sources to draw on, and this is partly why it took Andy Murray a few years before he believed he could overcome the Djokovic-Nadal-Federer triad. Clearly champions' coaches are key since they often set and control the environment in which athletes operate.

Visualisation, which Bandura and many others recognise as being an important source of confidence, has not featured strongly in this chapter (see chapter 14 for more detail). But visualisation increasingly can be harnessed because with digital technology strong visual and audio stimuli make a very powerful tool for building confidence. Most elite sports teams and squads have performance analysts who trawl through performance data to spot patterns.

On my quest to see what makes athletes in different sports tick I visited the National Badminton Centre. I went into the performance analyst's room in which, with a few clicks of a mouse, he could play a video analysis of every top 50 player in the world. These videos allow detailed analysis of the strengths and weakness of every player their athletes may encounter, so that a personalised game plan for a player can be developed whoever they face. This strategic input is confidence building in itself.

These days every professional sports team, whether it be taekwondo or table tennis, has professional analysts on hand. But this digital archive can also be used for personalised confidence building. A former English rugby team captain explains how:

> We used to watch videotapes on a Friday night of us beating the opposition who were coming up next day, and we used to put it to good music, whatever it was. I remember how we chatted through with Tony, who we thought was a little bit low on confidence, and we put a special tape together for him: all the tries [touchdowns] he'd scored, to some great tracks, and played it to him and he loved it.
>
> And he ... said, 'Actually, these are the tries that play on my mind when I'm trying to build myself up. This is my favourite track of music.' And they put a special tape together for him, and he used to watch that just before we got on the coach to go to Twickenham [the stadium]. And it ended up [that] about four or five of the guys had their own tapes ... you've got to put them ... in a positive frame of mind because they're going into a very, very stressful pressure situation, and I think ... it helps massively.[20]

Although confidence is such a personalised phenomena, this is an example of a way in which even with a large squad of athletes individualised images and music can help with self-belief, visualisation, pre-performance routines (e.g. music) and reminders of past accomplishments.

The best athletes and coaches know how to instil and maintain confidence ... with a little help from technology and colleagues.

17 Keeping it all together
Nerves

While reading an autobiography of any sporting champion, you know you will read about anxiety: the type of nerves an athlete experiences just before competitions or a major test. The big question is how do champions cope with anxiety, and do they have any useful tricks that set them apart? It is an obvious topic to tackle because all champions have experienced anxiety or butterflies one way or another. During my research I interviewed four-time rowing Olympic champion Matthew Pinsent, because his autobiography includes a fascinating and authentic description of pre-competition anxiety. I spoke to him to get an insider's account of his most nerve-wracking moment.

Put yourself in Pinsent's shoes when, at 22 years of age, he went to his first Olympic Games. One day in 1992 he rose early in the morning for his Olympic final. His rowing partner, Steve Redgrave, had already won two gold medals at the previous two Games, and this fact only added to expectations.

The start is set for 10 a.m. to avoid the worst heat of the day. A nation waits and watches. Here is Matthew:

> My nerves were such that even the thought of food made my stomach churn. I found the couple of hours in the Olympic village flat a torture. I couldn't sit still yet I didn't want to waste any energy moving around. All the time I had these two voices in my head, one telling me that we are going to crush the opposition, the other telling me that it was all going to be a disaster. The success of the early heat and semi-final counted for nothing as I tried to keep calm. I tried not to think of the labels of 'world champion', 'world record holder' and 'favourite' too much, but there I was about to try and scale the pinnacle of my sport. At the time it felt far from fun. Right then it was purgatory.
>
> At last it was time to go to the boat, an hour before the race our coach, Jurgen gave us our talk. It was intense and made me feel worse still. I suddenly saw Steve pacing and jigging about almost endlessly and I never saw him that bad before – I couldn't look him in the eye any more, never mind speak. About 45 minutes before the race and we went on to the lake and the warm-up felt pretty rubbish with Steve telling me to take it easy and relax. What was supposed to be 28 strokes a minute was out at 36 – not a good sign. When we finally got to the start, I was struggling to keep it all together. I keep telling myself that this can't be healthy, 'I'll do this race and then get out of the sport for good.'

Like a handful of other champions he admits to wanting to have a Star Trek moment: to be beamed up to avoid this period of purgatory. But athletes need anxiety, it is the body's way of saying this is really, really important, let's get ready to go – here's some adrenaline and cortisol to energise you. It is a sign of readiness. Although deeply uncomfortable at the time, this was the case with Pinsent. The rowing pair won the gold by a staggering five seconds, a huge margin. Pinsent's rowing partner, Redgrave, has said that this 1992 final was the perfect final in his record breaking career, which spans over 20 years and includes five gold medals. Pinsent stored away the experience of facing this intense anxiety for the next three rowing finals in Atlanta, Sydney and Athens, in which his crew won gold each time. It's likely that as Pinsent sat on the start line in 1996, 2000 and 2004 he could then say to himself 'don't worry I've done this before, this is similar to Barcelona, I can do this'. This is why experienced athletes normally have the edge in tight situations; they've faced down anxiety and expectation before.

It's one thing dealing with voices in the head and hours of intense anxiety. Consider what it is like if you are also violently sick at the thought of an impending showdown. Tanni-Grey Thompson won 16 Paralympic medals (11 gold) as a wheelchair athlete over five Games. At her final Paralympics in 2004 she prepared for the 100m final after performing poorly a few days earlier in the 800m in front of an expectant live national TV audience – she had been devastated. Here is Tanni:

> On the day of my 100 metres final, I was perhaps the most nervous I had ever been in my life. Normally it is quite usual for me to be sick during the warm-up. Nerves affect everyone in different ways. Before this particular race I was sick 12 times … Going out on to the track for the final, I was sick one more time as we waited. The wait seemed to go on forever. As we lined up on the start line, I remember my hands shaking and I could barely keep them still as the starter called us to the line.[1]

Tanni's account of 13 bouts of vomiting before racing reminds me of what you sometimes hear in team changing rooms before they walk out. Some players deliberately have a bucket to hand as they too face being sick before they do battle. An extreme physical (somatic) component to anxiety and Matthew's description of the internal mental (cognitive) thoughts and fears are sobering.

Researchers have found that similar responses might also be felt by a novice runner doing their first fun run; it is not about the status of the event, but how people perceive it at whatever level. It is people's interpretation of the events and uncertainties they are about to face that causes the reaction. Andy Murray reveals that before every Wimbledon he gets a painful reminder what time of year it is with his …

> … usual bout of mouth ulcers. They come on before the Championships every year, the sign that although [he tries] to block out all that the tournament

means to [him] and everyone else in the country, [his] body will respond to the pressure in a way [he] can't control.[2]

The difference between fun runners and serial champions is that they have learnt over many years to expect these reactions and learn how to handle these intense physical and mental feelings. In fact, many champions would be deeply perturbed if they had no reaction before an important event. It would indicate that they are not ready.

Can you recall two or three moments when you had intense pre-event anxiety? It is very likely that you can. For me three stick out: a big 2010 speech in front of over 1000 people at the Barbican Theatre, London, a crucial moment in a 1986 World championships in Spain, which I went on to win and, in 1979, my driving test. Some people take the view, with which I agree, that emotions such as anxiety serve a function in our evolutionary past. Anxiety not only prepares us as animals to 'fight or flight' but also to vividly remember and store the experience, allowing us to refer back to it and learn from it. My recall of my most anxious moments bears this out.

We'll explore how champions cope and prepare themselves for anxiety and not just how it affects physical performance, but also what happens to your fine motor skills. For example violent shaking, vomiting and apprehension before putting in golf or taking a penalty throw or kick in basketball or soccer can have disastrous effects. Performing skilled movements with intense anxiety is a different proposition altogether from performing skills in a calm, relaxed state.

Beginning to get butterflies to fly in formation[3]

Psychologists have interviewed elite athletes to find out how they interpret anxiety. Elite athletes tend to interpret anxiety as helpful through their careers due to gradual soaking up and learning how to embrace and use their butterflies;[4] approaches such as pre-competition routines and use of self-talk and visualisation. As we'll discover later in this chapter, successful use of these techniques helps athletes control and rationalise intense nervousness as a natural part of competition. Coping techniques like these also help distract them from thinking too much. One of the key playmakers in his time in the New Zealand rugby team, Dan Carter, put it this way:

> I had 10 or 14 [international] caps under my belt by this stage and was able to rationalise my emotional state a lot better and realised what they [physical symptoms] were there for. I had learnt that they just emphasised a 'buzz' indicating that I was excited and ready for the game. This enabled me to control the symptoms mentally and overcome the negative effects [I] experienced previously.[5]

Serial champions, such as Carter, Pinsent and Grey-Thompson are able to draw heavily on past events and 'experience' to make sense of new and more demanding situations. Some authors have tried to pin down the nature of

Dan Carter: can players perform to the same high standards without the 'buzz'?

sporting 'experience' since champions are often said to draw on this. How well do you think their claimed explanation of experience works?

> ... the product of a process whereby knowledge is acquired and adapted so that action, reflection and learning takes place. This occurs as a result of exposure to a variety of personally significant incidents, both positive and negative in nature ... This can take place in different environments, be it training, competition, or lifestyle.[6]

Though slightly wordy, this explanation shows that it is the *range* of situations that make you experienced, rather than simply learning from mistakes. So, it is champions' interpretation of key events in different scenarios and the essential skill of being able to evaluate their own performance and incrementally develop their mental tools that allows them to see anxiety as helpful. But for some, debilitative anxiety can lead to a breakdown in performance, often known as choking. The phrase 'paralysis through analysis' is often used with choking. It is at the opposite end of the scale from being calm and confident.

What can be done to help prevent choking?

The elephant in the room and perhaps the most worrying thought for athletes, as they reach out and hope to perform smoothly approaching their golden moment, is 'will I choke?'. Writing about choking and the yips has gone mainstream. First there was Sian Beilock's 2010 book titled, *Choke*, and in the same year, former international table tennis player Matthew Syed described his own snatching defeat from the jaws of victory moment in a chapter called 'The Curse of Choking':

> I was trying as hard as I could; I yearned for victory more intensely than in any match I have ever played; and yet it was as if I had regressed to the time what I was a beginner ... My movements were sometimes lethargic, sometimes jerky, my technique lacked any semblance of fluency and coherence[7]

Then in 2012, Nicola Barker's acclaimed novel, *The Yips,* had as a central character a golfer who experienced humiliating anxiety, making even the shortest putt an agonising ordeal.

One of the most public examples of choking was in 2011. The golfer Rory McIlroy led by four shots into the final round of the US Masters. Towards the end of the final round his performance collapsed, and he finished 10 shots adrift. He said, 'I unravelled ... I just lost my speed on the greens, lost my line, lost everything for two or three holes'. But why does this happen?

As you may know yourself it is partly that thinking too much disrupts the fluent, automatic qualities of skills that Syed describes and partly that negative thoughts and acute uncertainty are distracting. Seventy national and international athletes across 19 different sports were asked to think about crucial competitive moments like this, when pressure is at a peak.[8] They were asked: 'where is your attention focused and what do you think about during these decisive moments?'

Athletes' replies – often they gave more than one example – were then categorised. The results are shown in Table 17.1 (opposite).

There were six categories of responses grouped into three themes in the left-hand column of the table. Firstly, a *facilitative* focus, in which athletes monitor themselves in a helpful way: presumably champions have refined and used this successfully in previous situations. The next two groups of themes are less helpful: a *distraction* focus, which probably means athletes are missing other important cues and information that might have helped them perform – for example, awareness of their opponents movement, and a *self*-focus, in which there is a danger of athletes losing their automatic flow, especially if they think too much about their movements, rather like Syed.

From this categorisation of athletes' thoughts, it seems they are most commonly distracted by worries and other irrelevant items when they are under intense pressure. About one in three athletes (31 per cent) described these distracting thoughts. So what? Knowing athletes' responses helps suggest ways in which coaches can assist athletes to prevent choking. The three most credible findings are:[9] The use of *pressure practices, routines* and *strategy.*

Pressure practices

The first and perhaps most obvious thing that champions do is to *practise under pressure*. Familiarity with pressure and anxiety should make it easier to deal with the negative effects. Think of airline pilots using flight simulator assessments or

Table 17.1 Athletes thoughts in high pressure situations: percentage of replies in different categories (with examples).

Themes	Statement category	%	Examples
Facilitative focus	Positive monitoring	58	I focus on my strengths
			I focus on 'keeping it simple'
			I concentrate on my breathing
Distraction focus	Worries	26	This is not going well
			I think about he consequences of failing
			I notice that I doubt my decisions
	Task irrelevant	5	I notice something or someone in the audience
			I notice what the TV/press cameras are doing
			I focus on the score
Self-focus	External task-relevant	7	I look closely at my flight of the ball
			I think about my position on the playing area
			I focus on my position against my opponent
	Movement execution	4	I think about the skill I have to perform
			I think about my follow through
			I focus on my feet placement

Percentages as stated in pp. 59–73 of Raul R.D. Oudejans, Wilma Kuijpers, Chris C. Kooijman and Frank C. Bakker (2011), Thoughts and Attention of Athletes under Pressure: Skill-Focus or Performance Worries?, *Anxiety, Stress & Coping: An International Journal*, 24:1, but examples and themes added by the author.

the military recreating battle conditions for their troops in training. The military also often use sanctions and punishments in their training to soldiers under pressure (see chapter 18 for more on this approach). Coaches and athletes need to sit down and think about how to create authentic pressure practices.

By becoming more familiar and comfortable with performing under pressure you start to see potentially stressful events as a challenge, and may even come to relish the opportunities they offer. Practising under pressure helps you learn coping techniques and enhance the sense of control and focus on what can be achieved, rather than what can go wrong. The anxiety might be similar but you feel more in control.

On a research visit to Barcelona I watched Espanyol, a top-flight professional football team, practise under pressure: timed breakaway phases of play with the ball passed out of deep defence to rapid counter attack. The added pressure of the head coach looking on may have been deliberate. The ball had to be quickly and clinically moved upfield against a threadbare but committed defence, and the goalkeeper then beaten. Not as easy as it sounds. You also hear of situations in which coaches have organised crowd noise to be played alongside practices to help recreate game conditions or practising when possible at the actual venue of a forthcoming game.

In basketball, shooting practices have been used as part of a trial. The gaze of watching coaches and filmed sessions, along with individual and team sanctions, were used to ramp up the pressure on players. After five weeks of practice using this simulated pressure they were tested in comparison to a control group who practised 'normally'. To liven things up and simulate intensity in the final test cash prizes were offered. The normal training group performed 5 per cent worse under high-pressure tests, while the pressure-acclimatised group performed 7 per cent better.[10] Pressure practices work as long as athletes interpret the training manipulations as authentic pressure situations rather than a coaching ploy without purpose.

In athletics, the British double Olympic gold medalist decathlete Daley Thompson's approach to practise was to feed off his competiveness by creating situations in which he would 'feel that sense of fear and disappointment'. His coach recalls:

> I remember doing training sessions with Daley where we would go out and peg where Hingsen [his main rival] might throw the discus and the agreement would be he would have one throw and one throw only to beat it.'[11]

In examples of manipulated high pressure, athletes continue to experience anxiety but no longer suffer poor performance. They are improving their ability to self-regulate the demands of the situation and to feel in control. The novelty of high-stakes situations is thereby decreased and athletes gradually learn how to exert some control. If you have control over a situation, you're more likely to view stressful events as a challenge. That's the theory, but coaches who use pressure practices must keep the range of situations varied, otherwise they quickly lose their realism.

The effects of becoming familiar with pressure situations are not just restricted to practices. There is evidence that exposure to moderate levels of adversity throughout life helps people to view pressure and stress as a challenge, whereas those who have experienced very high or very low levels see pressure as more threatening.[12] It is how athletes cope with key events that ends up shaping them. But paradoxically, dealing with pressure is also about routine.

Routines

Polishing a *pre-performance routine* is something champions and their coaches know is important. There is one kicking skill which is practised by children in backyards around much of the world. At the top level it is finessed with a detailed pre-performance routine that can win big games: the kicking of penalties in the various forms of football, American football, Australian rules football and rugby. One of the world experts, English rugby World Cup hero Jonny Wilkinson, has his own trademark routine before kicking.

The constituent elements of Jonny Wilkinson's pre-performance routine

Centring, focusing from the inside, slowing down the breathing, relaxing and channelling his power and energy from his core, just behind his belly button and down his leg and into his foot. When he does this he adopts, the strong position he became famous for with the [clasped] hands ahead of him.

He has also spoken of imagining a jeering mouth behind the goal and his attempt to strike the ball down its throat. Another technique involves an imaginary woman sitting in seat behind the goal, holding a can of Coke. As Wilkinson prepares to kick, he visualises the flight of the ball ending up knocking the drink out of her hands. This changed the emphasis of where he was aiming and it made him kick through the ball more.

Another is 'hardening' his kicking foot, which Wilkinson does by tapping his left toe on the grass before he kicks, usually in two sets of three taps, thus helping the foot to adopt the shape and the tension he wants when he hits the ball.[13]

Routines and thought processes like this partly give back a sense of control during intense moments. As Wilkinson has said it 'assures [him], very slightly it relaxes [him]'.[14] If it helps even a little bit it has to be worth pursuing.

Testing the use of pre-performance routines can be done be comparing performance in a group who develop routines with a control group that does not use one. For example, in a tenpin bowling experiment this resulted in a 29 per cent increase in performance.[15] Beyond experiments some analysts carefully studied the footage of real world NBA free-throws in play-off games identifying when players did and did not use their distinctive routine: a 13 per cent decrease in performance was observed when players did not follow their routine.[16] But why do routines work?

There are two aspects:

1. It helps focus attention on a relevant part of the task, e.g. Wilkinson's intense focus on the exact part of the ball he wants to strike. This helps block out external distractions (e.g. thoughts and crowd noise).
2. It directs athletes' focus away from detailed movements, allowing the skill process to deliver with minimal conscious involvement, e.g. if you overthink your movements, in driving a car you are in danger of producing jerky movements and not benefiting from your automatic ingrained skill.

Coaches and athletes need to find a routine that works and is meaningful for them. Wilkinson's example shows visual analogies are often a key feature in helping to take control of his demanding, high-pressure situation.

Australian Scott Draper is in the unique situation of having played both professional tennis and golf. Studying other competitors, he views the final part of a routine as being the important moment:

> Golfer Jack Nicklaus … might stand over the ball anywhere from 5 to 45 seconds until he felt completely ready to hit. At this point he would then have triggered movement (e.g. two waggles of the club head) and then he would swing … the trigger may be different for each person but essentially it tells the body, 'I'm ready it's time to go' and initiates the swing.[17]

From penalty kicking, free throws and golf putts to tennis serves, a whole range of personal idiosyncrasies emerge: a shuffle here, a shoulder shrug there, bouncing the ball a set number of times and so on. Athletes become more secure in their own routine and using their own mental space to recreate what they have practised so many times before. Look at how Andy Murray described his life-changing fourth championship point at Wimbledon 2013:

> You just do the routine things in that moment: towel yourself down, look for the two best balls, and get ready. But your heart is pounding in your chest that much faster, the adrenaline takes over.[18]

Strategy focus

A third frequently occurring feature of champions is maintaining a strategy focus. When you try too hard to concentrate on controlling a skill it can actually trigger a breakdown of that skill as Syed describes in his table tennis. So a strategy focus can be useful.

Those who set themselves targets of concentrating on movement or technique underperform compared to those who concentrate on broader strategy. Scott Draper describes his own strategy approach for a very pressurised bunker shot:

> I drew on all my previous psychology skill training experiences. When I got to the bunker I focused on where I wanted to land the ball and blocked everything else out of my mind.[19]

It sounds rather trite that a focus on strategy will help prevent choking but one of the main mechanisms involved is helping athletes deal with distraction. Of course, the reality is not that simple, but combined with pressure practices and routines, maintaining a strategic picture can help exert control over the situation.

Final thoughts

Authors Marc Jones and Martin Turner have suggested that the importance we place on events can increase the likelihood of choking. Using Rory McIlroy's US Masters example they explain:

> After the US Masters, McIlroy visited Haiti to see the people affected by a recent earthquake and was widely reported in the media as saying this contributed to him having a more balanced perspective about golf. McIlroy went on to win the next major golf tournament, the US Open.[20]

A sense of perspective on elite sport is sometimes hard to achieve when you've spent years training towards a goal. However, another source of perspective is provided in many athletes' home lives without ever visiting a disaster zone: young children. There are many examples of young children exerting a strong dose of realism into their bizarre sporting lifestyle which can often help see their results as yes, important but certainly not a matter of do or die.

Having perspective on life outside sport highlights how anxiety cannot be studied as a discrete stand-alone component. It is unequivocally connected to all sorts of other influences: confidence, preparation, coaching, experiences growing up, personality, the support systems that surround an athlete and the place that elite sport plays in an athlete's life and its contribution to their self-worth.

Perhaps it is, more than anything, the mindset and expectation that we take into an important event that shapes how we interpret anxiety. Now with young children himself and after years of competing, cyclist Bradley Wiggins articulated his optimum pre-race mindset of having ...

> ... confidence that you have done the work to the maximum of your ability, and all you have to do is empty the tank, be the best athlete you can, and accept what you get from it in the end.[21]

Other athletes express similar approaches in which, yes, they'd be really disappointed to lose but are able to accept it if their preparation has been robust. Framed in this way the event is less threatening and athletes are able to accept anxiety or nerves as part of the buzz of competing. One thing is for sure, you cannot reach the top and stay there without learning to live with and deal with expectation, pressure and anxiety. Experience counts.

18 Under pressure
New approaches

The subject of pressure – and the related anxiety – is one of the most written about subjects in performance psychology. Helping people reach their potential under stress is something of a holy grail in the business, sport and research worlds. We are awash with various positive psychology books. So let's explore what champions might be writing about in their autobiographies in 10 years' time. Here are two promising advances in pressure and anxiety research – bizarrely both stemming from the same sport, cricket, but also applicable to baseball and most other stressful sports requiring skilled movements and decision-making.

I've always been interested in the intense pressure that is created in cricket and baseball. Batting players have solid balls pitched towards them at 90 miles (145km) per hour, scary enough in itself; then, if they get 'out', the opportunity to ponder on their errors is considerable while the game carries on without them. They then have to get up and do it again in the next innings of a game in front of their teammates and spectators. Bowlers, pitchers and fielders face similar multi-layered angst and potential for public embarrassment.

I was surprised then at first, when a new development in training the English youth cricket squad was heralded as a step forward. It uses an old friend from education and army training: punishment. It might sound like a *Back to the Future* storyline in which 1950s past practices come to life again, but more accurately in cricket *punishment* has been skilfully used to create an environment with challenges in which there are *consequences* for underperformance and this can help desensitise players to pressure.

The intelligent use of punishment

I was intrigued to know what was involved with this new use of punishment in cricket training – it felt counter-intuitive. Punishment is rather a taboo subject among many educationalists and psychologists who would rather create a supportive environment in which there are plenty of rewards. What is going on, and what does it have to offer other sports?

Those leading English youth cricket identified that their sport at world level, like many others, is a harsh environment in which players need resilience and toughness. They argued that, in effect, the punishments of humiliation – letting down teammates, playing in front of hostile crowds, sitting out an innings while ruminating on failure, let alone the threat of injury from a hard ball – are ever-present. So, with the help of an eminent psychologist English youth cricket leaders set about creating a special pressured practice environment with the intelligent use of punishment.

They based their new ideas on how personalities differ and respond to threatening situations differently – a personality framework (reinforcement sensitivity theory) that suggests that individuals respond to rewards and/or punishments, shaping their behaviour. In very simple terms, are you more sensitive to chasing rewards or avoiding punishment, or both?

The professor who devised the new training, Lew Hardy, investigated national youth squad cricketers and found that those that choked were those most likely to chase both rewards *and* punishments, and this subtlety affected their behaviour and decision-making.[1] For example:

> one might imagine a batsman who at one level is motivated by the prospect of winning the match for his team (i.e., reward) and at another level is worried about avoiding being dismissed [getting out] easily and letting his team down (i.e., punishment). The conflict engendered is likely to lead to high levels of behavioral inhibition, which might manifest itself as a lack of composure and decisiveness in shot selection.[2]

The people who coped with pressure best were those that responded most to punishment cues, such as the threat of being dropped from the team, and were far less bothered about reward cues (e.g. press coverage). They are vigilant towards the future, particularly looking out for the threat of potential punishments in advance. If they pick up on a threat, it acts like an early warning system, and they mentally prepare for it. This constant looking ahead gives them more time and opportunity to implement effective coping techniques compared to a person who is inhibited by what Hardy calls the reward and punishment dilemma and thus often makes poor or panicky decisions.

What did they actually do to put theory into practice? Over 46 days, spanning two winter seasons, Hardy worked with the national youth squad coaches, including a challenging tour to India, to implement a new training regime with high expectations based on 'actions having consequences' in the form of punishments. The new approach was highly demanding – players were immersed in all things cricket from around 6 a.m. to 9 p.m. on most training days.

I noticed that Hardy's CV showed where some of these ideas may have come from: he'd worked before with the army, considering approaches to army training – his ideas in sport are not so brutal as they first appear. At the initial meeting of the national squad, standards of behaviour, dress, performance levels and attitudes were explained and the new training philosophy was carefully described to parents and young athletes (16–18 years old), with the option to opt out if they wished.[3] None did.

A list of consequences was published and regularly reviewed. The consequences were designed to be unpleasant and meaningful, for example, cleaning the changing rooms and toilets, missing the next session or repeating a test in front of the group.

The real difference between this training and an army boot camp was the way in which the purpose and vision of this approach was explained. It was presented in an inspirational way as preparing pressure coping techniques for use as a senior international player – that is to say it was couched in terms of being a transformational form of training. Famous senior ex-national captains (Michael Vaughan, Graham Gooch, Alec Stewart) personally attended the session to reinforce this message, which is obviously a useful fillip for any new programme.

The coping techniques included those we've already mentioned in early chapters: goal setting, imagery techniques, self-talk, anxiety regulation, cognitive reappraisal of threatening situations and pre-performance routines. A learning orientation was also encouraged, and when the youth athletes were refining their playing skills they were encouraged to experiment and make mistakes – the punishments did not operate in these sessions. As we know, learning skills is largely about making mistakes, adapting movements and decisions and incremental progress, and this is best done without the threat of cleaning the toilets!

So did it work? As observers, we'd tend to look for quantitative numbers rather than qualitative judgements as proof of improvement: statistics feel more valid. The fact that some lessons from the programme are continuing to be used in cricket suggests that it has been received favourably. Here, though, are some of the main results from 'before' and 'after' measurements of the squad members.[4]

First one test, for *indoor batting*, which would scare most people. Facing a machine pitching 24 fast balls (at 85 mph/137 kph) and trying to score points by hitting the ball to certain zones: a 20 per cent improvement was recorded after the new training regime.

Next, competitive performance statistics, drawn from assessment of data such as batting/bowling average and strike rates: a 12.5 per cent improvement.

And a third example: the multistage fitness test exposes participants to sustained physical adversity which requires high levels of persistence and determination: a 9.5 per cent gain.

The results were also compared favourably (and declared statistically significant) against a supposed control group of young players of a similar standard who had missed out on the initial squad selection and received the same number of days training but in a traditional format (e.g. net practices, fitness sessions).

This bold new 'consequences/punishments' approach to training is different to the use of pressure practices alone. It is creating a holistic high-pressure developmental environment with carefully designed challenges in which the narrative of mental tools, toughness and responding to pressure is consistent. It must take a lot of careful planning, and the inclusion of a tour to India as part of the process was in itself a huge learning experience for any player. Other sports could learn from this approach as long as they carefully briefed coaches, parents and others since there could be misunderstandings around use of the taboo word 'punishment'.

Perhaps this intense, carefully choreographed approach can only be effective if the young athletes already have a fairly well developed mental toolbox. At national youth squad level or its equivalent this is likely.

> We do our young people [generally] an enormous disservice since we teach them that the world is full of opportunity and good things will happen to you and the worst thing that should ever happen to you is that you don't get rewarded ... and so they grow up, slowly, to expect this is how the world is and they get into their teens they find out this is not how the world is, there are all sorts of consequences for all sorts of things and they get let down and they get angry ...
>
> It helps you [as an athlete] to judge the seriousness of consequences and have a perspective and I think perspective is a pretty key thing in choking.[5]

The word 'perspective' is again used in connection with choking. The value of champions being reminded of life outside sport or getting some perspective is important when dealing with anxiety, choking and pressure (see the example of McIlroy's visit to Haiti, pp. 177).

The power of a champion's vision

Now let's focus on another 21st-century initiative. Some sporting headlines in the mid-2000s revealed that scientists had proved that sports experts had a different way of looking at things compared to non-experts – so-called gaze strategies. I wanted to find out the implications of this for champions' paths and the very latest work on something called the *quiet eye* phenomenon.

Athletes at the top of their game often look like they have all the time in the world to play their shots or make their moves. They don't necessarily have faster reaction times, but they can anticipate what is about to happen because they've watched it unfold in front of them so many times before; they have implicitly learned movement cues and patterns. They can look ahead, interpreting the way their opponent is moving before the opponent has fired the ball towards them in sports such as tennis, hockey, football, rugby, baseball and cricket.

Wayne Gretzky famously said, 'A good hockey player plays where the puck is; a great hockey player plays where the puck is going to be', while in rugby union Irish player Brian O'Driscoll is used as example of someone who is different to others in his reading and anticipation of the game.[6]

'Looking ahead' in cricket was first studied in Australia. Top batsmen have the ability to pick up advance information to anticipate the flight of balls bowled to them at speed. Video films of approaching bowlers were shown to a range of batsmen. Experts whose focused gaze was on the bowling arm and hand were far more attuned to anticipatory cues, which gave them an advantage compared to moderate players. They were able to work out, to varying degrees, where the bowlers were going to place the ball.[7]

The implications of this are that, in amassing hours and hours of practice, not only are champions learning how to hit and move well but they are also learning how to anticipate what is about to happen. Reading tactical plays and other people's body language helps signal this – so experts pick up a lot subconsciously from an opponent's dip of their shoulder or the way they change their weight distribution ahead of a shot.

David Epstein illustrated this well in his look back at the 2004 Pepsi All Star Softball Game, in which the National League baseball sluggers were up against soon to be Olympic gold-medallist pitcher, Jennie Finch.[8] Under a title of 'Beaten by an Underhand Girl' he shows how Finch's 65mph (105kph) underarm pitches in softball continually blew the ball past the very best bemused baseball players including renowned hitters Barry Bonds and Albert Pujol. These experienced professionals were more used to dispatching pitches thrown overarm at 95mph (153kph). Much mirth and bravado from teammates resulted.

Epstein's explanation draws on the same research we have glimpsed here to conclude that 'the only way to hit a ball travelling at high speed is to be able to see into the future, and when a baseball player faces a softball pitcher, he is stripped of his crystal ball'.[9]

If this crystal ball is all about refining anticipatory cues, you can see how in the future digital virtual environments might play a hand. In the future, skilful use of video and game animation will help champions' hone their decision-making and game-reading skills – though it is too early to identify the impact this might have.

The quiet eye

A detailed focus on champions' vision might also be a fruitful avenue in future anxiety research. In many fine motor control tasks the eye fixes on the site of action beforehand for a short interval of approximately a second. When taking a penalty kick, Jonny Wilkinson looks first at the target, then fixes his gaze on precisely which part of the ball he intends to strike. From receiving a baseball to golf putting, the visual information collected in these final seconds is crucial. It is now possible to measure this precisely, since scientists have the equipment (eye trackers) to interrogate these important final gaze sequences and timings. Additionally, some important results are emerging in relation to anxiety. This measured gaze is called the *quiet eye* – a measure of optimal visual attentional control.

Recent research has demonstrated that this *quiet eye* phenomenon is:

- impaired with anxiety – the gaze that fixes on one spot becomes shorter and more sporadic.[10]
- earlier and longer during successful performances than unsuccessful performances.[11]
- helped by quiet eye training since athletes who have undertaken this training have lower heart rates and less muscle twitchiness, indicating less performance anxiety.[12]

Impressive performance improvements have been reported for national/ international athletes in volleyball, basketball and shooting who have been quiet eye trained.[13]

Hayley Wickenheiser, a Canadian ice hockey (four golds, one silver) and softball Olympian takes up the story of being tested and what it meant to her.

Hayley Wickenheiser's look forward[14]

Hayley wore a mobile eye tracker on her head 'that filmed exactly what I was looking at while shooting … An external camera was also set up to record my skating and shooting movements in the same time frame'.

Hayley Wickenheiser: she first played for Canada aged 15 and has played in the men's professional game

She had to perform with other ice hockey skaters pressuring her and shoot at a skilled goaltender. For each type of shot, Hayley had to try out two strategies:

An *eyes up strategy*: 'I was to keep my eyes on the goaltender all the time and shoot … the idea is to play cat and mouse with the goalie and exploit any errors. And second, an *eyes down strategy* 'I was to look at the net early as the play developed and determine in advance where I wanted to shoot and then keep my gaze down'.

The main results were:

'I used two … fixations during each play, with one on the net/goaltender and the other on puck/stick that together added up to about 500–600ms (just over half a second) …

Overall I learned that it pays to use the *eyes down strategy* involving an early fixation of about 400ms on the net (prior to backswing) … followed by a brief glance down to the puck prior to the shot (150ms).'

She summarises the potential: 'many athletes intuitively "know" but do not "understand" how they learn or what they are actually seeing during competition. Quiet eye testing and training can help a coach and athlete look into this … on "seeing" what is really important in crucial situations'.

Again it is fairly early to see where this type of testing and subsequent training may end up. But it offers athletes an approach that directs their attention to appropriate visual cues under their control rather than a focus on trying to deal with their thoughts. Being able to measure these gazes may help coaches and athletes understand more about how they perform well and why things may go wrong under pressure.

Imagine if you were a developing teenage athlete learning how to deal with pressure; would you rather focus on technical aspects of concentration or discussion of emotions and feelings? Is the former more tangible and less threatening than the latter?

When I learnt how to play golf all this talk of how to control anxiety came flooding back. I knew I had to fix my gaze on the ball, but if quiet eye technology becomes more mainstream it might lead to knowing which part of the ball to look at or when and for how long is most effective. Maybe these new discoveries will reveal some of the answers and speed up the learning process

Final thoughts

There is a contrast here between the re-emergence of old-school thinking using challenges with consequences/punishment in a structured way and using the latest technology to investigate what athletes look at.

In terms of impact, at the time of writing, intelligent adjustments to the training environment of developing athletes is likely to have greater reach and results than eye technology. Careful use of structured challenges and more informed coaches who understand how to prepare their athletes for intense expectations and pressure can make a difference. However, who knows where we will be in a decade's time, with vision and digitally related technologies able to create their own pressure-training practices?

Part IV

The coach

19 What I wish I'd known about Olympic coaching when I started

While I was training to work in education, I became very good at, what was then, the new sport of windsurfing. I then became the sport's first national coach. And a year later I was literally thrown in at the deep end in the Pacific Ocean to coach at the venue of the Seoul Olympics. During nine years of coaching I made plenty of mistakes, but gradually worked out an effective approach to coaching, particularly at junior level. Though the national squads began to win World and European Championship medals, the Olympic podium eluded British athletes until 2004; after which point Olympic medals were achieved regularly.

The benefit of hindsight is a great thing and I, along with many coaches, will, no doubt, acknowledge that there are things we'd have wished to have known about coaching and leadership when we'd started out. These next two chapters, therefore, explore the experiences of seven champions that, in hindsight, have helped me make sense of coaching. These experiences highlight the key contribution of coaches to shaping champions.

First, let us consider why coaching is as much an art as it is a science. Successful top level coaching behaviour isn't entirely tangible because, irrespective of theory or research, what an effective coach does is partly beyond our understanding – it is complex and multilayered,[1] not easily dissected or analysed by theories. Coaching is largely down to relationships and understanding how athletes think; but it is not like a surgeon–patient relationship that draws on a recognised body of medical knowledge which is then applied, often via observation of symptoms and testing, to rationally solve problems i.e. using *just* a scientific approach. Elite coaching is often a long-term relationship which entails coaches to prepare athletes to strive, often beyond what they thought their bodies were capable of, under the most intense pressure. Sometimes this has to be achieved by leading a team in which multiple experts interact and a champion's coach has to blend all this together.

A coach must also manage change: change in technology, rules, training methods, funding and individuals' emotional maturation. Relationships and groups alter and change over time, so the art of coaching needs to be combined with the technological and human sciences.

Only a handful of champions have had the same coach from their teenage years to their zenith, athletes such as Michael Phelps and Jessica Ennis. Many athletes have a transient relationship with coaches and champions in a position of power (knowledge, money, or other) can decide to move on – they have choice.

Champions have choice

High-earning professional tennis players, golfers and track/field athletes, along with other sports players of individual sports, are often in the position to seek out a coach who they think will most benefit their progress. Their choice of coach to help move their performance on is interesting. It partly illuminates what athletes are looking for in their relationship with their coach at different stages of their career. Unusually compared to other sports they are sometimes in the position of the employer, hiring and firing their support team and coach. How did Andre Agassi and Andy Murray, for example, identify the right coach at the right time for them?

Imagine that, like Agassi, Murray or Michael Johnson, you are near the top of your field. With the help of colleagues and other members of your team you start evaluating who might be able to help you reach that next level. Consider the brief bio-pics of coaches in the box that follows, drawn from my own experiences, and think about which characteristics would appeal to you if you were seeking a coach to help you progress.

Coach X

Your coach is respected by those they work with and is good at the big strategic picture of where your sport is headed. They have studied in depth and consider they are knowledgeable in most areas of training; they draw on other sciences to support performance as long as it is communicated well. They believe that tactical acumen in competition is one of the keys to success and have published a book about this. This coach also considers that success follows from careful goal-setting, with individuals being monitored throughout the year and their progress recorded. They make difficult decisions that a group would struggle to reach.

Coach Y

The good reputation of your coach is largely based on their considerable charisma and ability to lead others. Over time they have established their own formula for success which they often use when deciding the types of training to focus on. In particular, their experience suggests that the quantity of training and being the fittest is important and often provide memorable phrases to motivate performers when training gets tough. They are particularly good at managing the media to shape expectations and create/relieve pressure on others. As a result they lead and motivate from the front.

Coach Z

Your coach concentrates on the quality of training and gradually challenges you as you improve by introducing new variables and 'raising the bar'. They are very good at developing sessions that have feedback built into them so that athletes can assess their development and contribute to decisions as to how to shape training further. They successfully collaborate with other experts to build in other perspectives. This coach is not a 'big' character, but they do have a clear vision of what they are trying to achieve. They are good at communicating this as well as interacting with others at all levels.

These are purely an illustrative tool to start thinking about the choices champions face. The coach portraits were originally written for an online Open University Interactive called 'Olympizise Me'[2] to engage people in considering how different variables, including coaching, contribute to sporting success. All three coaches might be attractive choices for different people depending on their past experiences and personality.

Andre Agassi's decision to employ Brad Gilbert as his coach was a very successful move. Gilbert, who was at the end of his playing career, caught the attention of Agassi's manager after he had read Gilbert's book *Winning Ugly*. The three of them met for dinner. There was a slightly prickly atmosphere to start with as Gilbert insisted they sit inside to avoid the mosquitoes and then rushed out to the store next door to buy Bud Ice, the only type of beer he tolerates. It turned out, however, that Gilbert was a talkative and passionate student of tennis and, once invited to comment, gave an uninterrupted 15 minute analysis of Agassi's game. When he visited the bathroom during the meeting, Agassi turned to his manager and said, 'That's our guy'. They start working together the next morning.

Amazingly for such an instinctive, quick decision, their professional relationship lasted for almost eight years and included six grand slam victories, three-quarters of Agassi's total haul. The gut instinct that they could work together suggests that this decision was partly based on personal chemistry and mutual respect: Agassi for Gilbert's reputation as a smart player, and Gilbert's admiration of Agassi's game.

Coach-athlete relationships like this are interesting because the athlete is an employer, in a sense, and has some power and control. Yet the athlete needs to reconcile that with the need to accept the lead and advice of the coach they appoint. After all they will be travelling the world in each others' pockets. But like any interpersonal relationship there are a few fundamental aspects that characterise how well people relate to each other. Think of your own relationships with others. Things like respect, understanding, honesty, trust and communication. As a young coach I did not quite appreciate that building relationships is central to your role as a coach.

Agassi's quick assessment that this was someone he could work with must have been influenced, in part, by Gilbert's knowledge of the game and specifically his analysis of tennis match play strategy, but would also have been due to intangible personal chemistry. With his new coach Agassi gradually heeded his strategic and tactical advice and the beauty of Gilbert's message was its simplicity:

▨ Aim for steady, consistency – this is enough to win 90 per cent of the time;
▨ Attack your opponents weaknesses – instead of you succeeding, make him fail;
▨ At the start of a grand slam tournament, count backwards from the 21 sets it takes to win a slam – make this your goal and when you win a set, say, 'that's one down'.[3]

Strategy can often be over complicated, but this three-point plan is appealing in its clarity. Some people, such as speech-writers, call it the rule of three: a triad of three concepts to express an idea, emphasise it and make it memorable. I wish I had known about this simple device as a developing coach, particularly when explaining strategy and tactics. The device has been useful in the Olympic movement i.e. Faster, Higher, Stronger.

After a period of adjustment to his game, which included a number of losses, Agassi eventually started to improve and became the first unseeded player to win the US Open in almost 30 years. After the win, Agassi described his contentment with having a new five-person team in place: his new girlfriend, new coach, new manager, conditioning expert/friend and a surrogate father (a former preacher).

However, one champion's dream coach is another's poison. Andy Murray's relationship with Brad Gilbert in the noughties lasted only 16 months, perhaps caused by tension between the American extrovert and the more reserved Scot. It illustrates the individual nature of coaching relationships, demonstrating that a coach may connect well with one athlete, but then struggle with another.

After Murray's episode with Gilbert, he assembled an effective team around him and, in late 2011, he picked up the phone to Ivan Lendl to discuss the prospect of him becoming his coach. Describing the decision behind it, Murray said: 'At that stage of my career, I was feeling like I was a loser: nothing more, nothing less. You wouldn't believe the abuse I would get walking down the street …'.[4] But he was intrigued by Lendl's playing career: 'I liked the fact that people had found him difficult to appreciate and he wasn't all about the fame: it was about the winning for him'.[5] His mother Judy describes the decision process in Murray selecting Lendl as his coach in the box below.

Judy Murray explains Andy's coaching change

He had been No.4 in the world for a few years, so perhaps 'he had got stuck a little bit'. He had beaten the top guys but they were more consistent and won the big matches. What might make the difference? A coach who could help 'reset [his] focus when [he] started to get a bit distracted' and someone that had direct empathy and understanding of what it is like to play a grand slam final.[6]

Andy Murray: he climbed the mountain to US Open, Olympic and Wimbledon success, but his big challenge has been to bounce back from back surgery

When Andy met Lendl over lunch the two apparently got on, having the same work and training values and also a similar sense of humour which was a good starting point for a very successful two-year partnership.[7]

Lendl had immediate respect since he had experienced similar success and failure and he gave the support team leadership – he was able to contribute not just to the on-court side of things (technically and tactically) but also the conditioning side, helping the team make sound decisions about how to manage his schedule in preparation for peaking for the bigger events. Judy Murray admired Lendl's total focus on the goal and all the other aspects being stepping stones towards that goal.[8]

His new coach succeeded in reining back outbursts of self-directed rage and fury from Andy on court that undermined his performance. Judy reports that Lendl helped Andy to manage the frustration of losing points at critical moments.[9]

Both Andy and his mother's comments reinforce the idea of mutual respect, the crux of which was the shared rollercoaster experience of playing in grand slam finals and feeling like an outsider. You can imagine that this common ground would help develop a closeness, shared commitment and empathy. But their example introduces a new idea: the coach as leader. In my time as a national coach I'd wish I'd appreciated more about the distinction between leadership and management. It is all too easy to get stuck in the details of day-to-day management.

Coaching: a form of leadership?

Coaches working at the top end of sport can often, like I did, get bogged down with management and forget about arguably their more important role as leaders.

Increasingly an explicit distinction is made between the two functions of leadership and management in both business and sport. Leadership is concerned with developing a sense of strategic purpose and direction for the squad/organisation and influencing others to share this purpose and work together towards achieving it. Management, on the other hand, is about day-to-day maintenance of the squad/organisation and planning and implementing how it operates. So the leadership Judy Murray was talking about was the vision and strategic direction of the team surrounding Andy: from those concerned with his commercial management to fitness, nutritional, sports medicine, massage and video analysis personnel. Lendl articulated where they were headed and gave them a sense of purpose, particularly focused on Andy's readiness for the grand slam events.

Table 19.1 shows the differences between a leader and manager in more detail.[10] There are two particularly interesting messages in this table. The first is the leader's focus on change and innovation, investigating new ways of approaching a problem. Their questioning can sometimes challenge the status quo. Second is a further metaphor I use for leadership vision and future direction, which liken to knowing where you want to get to, but having a map and compass to guide you and the team to get you there. This translates to developing goals and a strategy to achieve the goal.

Table 19.1 Leaders and managers

Leader	Manager
Develops vision and future direction to put the athlete on the podium	Establishes plans, budgets and allocates resources to achieve vision
Communicates shared sense of vision and values	Organises implementation plans
Inspires, energises and empowers	Controls implementation, solves problems and monitors results against plans
Focuses on change and innovation	Focuses on administration, maintenance of progress and achieving agreed results
Focuses on people	Focuses on systems and structures

A few years into my new Olympic role, my experience with the athletes I worked with was that they had a chip on their shoulder because they felt they weren't quite as good as others in Europe, particularly the strong French squad. I thought an easy way to start changing this was to start taking our best juniors to the French championships, where all competitors use identical equipment, to show them that they were on equal terms. The squad was so fired up that they won the Under 15 and Under 19 titles – much to the frustration of the hosts. It marked a turning point in my coaching as I gained confidence from my decision and the squad culture started to change.

An example of the successful fusion of leadership and management comes from Team Sky's Dave Brailsford. His *leadership* of the coaches, sports scientists and athletes established a 'vision for excellence' and an 'attention to detail' which have resulted in a dominance of the sport and back-to-back Tour de France victories for Team Sky. However, in order to achieve excellence in this area, it is necessary for Brailsford and other *managers* to implement the strategic plans, including in the more day-to-day tasks: the recruitment, selection and induction of suitable staff, managing resources to ensure that the appropriate facilities, time and equipment/technology are available and effective media handling to attract and sustain sponsors. Much of this might be delegated but then Brailsford, as manager, has to find and monitor the right people to implement these crucial background elements.

For those head coaches leading large sports operations, leadership and management are essential and closely related:

> Organisations which are over-managed but under-led eventually lose any sense of spirit or purpose. Poorly managed organisations with strong charismatic leaders may soar temporarily only to crash shortly thereafter.[11]

How many times have you seen professional sports teams instigate change by bringing in a new charismatic coach to stimulate short-term improvement?

Charisma, quirkiness and a sense of humour do have a role in coaching as long as it is free of personal promotion and ego – the case of Jose Mourinho in soccer springs to mind but I'm wary of the ego he brings to the role. One former Australian rugby coach, Eddie Jones, expressed it nicely:

> The players, I think, get enjoyment out of being able to mimic the [silly] things I do and say, so I leave them in my repertoire. I know they think some of the expressions are right funny, but I'm happy about that because I think they'll remember it and it gives them a laugh. It's all part of the psychology of coaching.[12]

Coaches as managers can change the culture of a squad. This is often through adjustments such as accommodation, time keeping, clothing, the tone of communications. Athletes and support staff absorb a culture in the same way that you pick up an accent. Leaders such as Dave Brailsford would argue that one of the ways to change things is to focus on the detail. Sometimes small symbolic changes, such as the look and feel of a home changing room, are used to help buttress change and excellence.

I am reminded of the idea of nudging people towards change. Nudge is a behavioral science concept which argues that positive reinforcement and sometimes small suggestions can influence change at least as effectively as compelling people to do things. The authors of *Nudge* explain:

> A wonderful example of this principle comes from, of all places, the men's rooms at Schiphol airport in Amsterdam. There the authorities have etched the image of a black housefly into each urinal … 'it improves the aim' … staff conducted fly-in-urinal trials and found that etchings reduced spillage by 80 per cent.[13]

Small symbolic changes can give direction and purpose to individuals and groups.

How do athletes learn in elite sport?

Coaches as leaders teach new ways of thinking and approaching performance yet we very rarely stop to think how athletes learn. I now realise that coaching practice is shaped by how coaches imagine athletes learn.

Educationalist's often learn about 'behavioural', 'cognitive' or 'constructivist' theories that are based on assumptions about how an expert's knowledge is developed. For instance, one of the first bits of behavioural theory I learnt was about the salivating learner (cf. Pavlov, his dogs and behaviorist conditioning). This approach is about how people respond to stimuli and reinforcement suggesting that drills and practice lie at the centre of elite athlete learning.

My early indoctrination into this was combined with another view. I thought coaching was driven mainly by what the coach knows and how this understanding is acquired by athletes, i.e. how knowledge is passed on. How wrong I was; learning theory has moved on to recognise the social side of learning. With this view athletes 'construct' their own mental frameworks through interaction with the elite sport environment. With such a 'constructivist' view, understanding and experience are in constant interaction, through participation, mingling with others and practice. My revised view of learning now is that athletes gradually learn how to become elite athletes through their interaction with the elite training environment and constructing new meanings from experiences – knowledge and skills being passed on informally just as much as formal teaching.

Learning does not occur in a vacuum; squad and coaching culture and symbolic systems shape it. For example, does a team player learn how to make the right passing decisions just through coaching? No, other elements are just as important – informally chatting to colleagues, watching videos of other games, gradually learning how to assess risk/reward and symbolic gestures within a squad such as any 'player of the month' or similar awards.

This hindsight view represents a more holistic approach to an athlete's learning with the coach's knowledge as only part of the picture. A similar holistic perspective of developing the whole athlete had an impact on how Michael Johnson chose his coach.

Michael Johnson's beauty contest

Michael Johnson, as one of the top young athletes in the USA, had a type of contest with coaches coming to meet him and his parents at his house and promising the world to attract him:

> They all wanted me to go to their university … I'm not sure what I was looking for then but when [his future coach] came in to my house I just got a feeling that he genuinely cared about the athletes [in his programme] as people and he wanted us to become successful people in athletics or otherwise.
>
> [He] set himself apart from all the other coaches … by talking about the degree I would earn at Baylor [University] and not just the events I would run in. It was clear to me and my family that here was a man who truly cared about the athletes he coached, about our future as well as our athletic present.[14]

Hearing this, you realise that it is not just about the surface appearance of caring for athletes but genuine concern and having the interpersonal skills to convey this. It also reinforces that an athlete's whole environment contributes to their progress, not just what takes place in training. One lesson soon learnt in coaching is that driving many hours to visit athletes at home is hugely valuable in starting to understand them and their families.

Self-aware coaches

Canadian researcher Jean Côté spent a few years trying to work out what else you needed beyond a *professional knowledge* (e.g. tactics, training), a holistic view and interpersonal skills to be an effective coach. To be really authentic as a coach who cares about athletes, you also need *intrapersonal knowledge* or self-awareness as it is better known.

Côté characterises it as:

> … effective coaches … are aware of their strengths and limitations, and are prepared to act on insights gained. The development of this awareness occurs through constant reflection about current and past actions.[15]

In chapter 15, you will have read about Danny Kerry, Great Britain's successful hockey coach. A reflective person, Kerry explained how his self-awareness gradually led to improvements in his coaching. Danny's first Olympic Games turned out to be quite a bruising experience. In Beijing he had a tough time: 'You name it, everything happened. There are things [unspecified] that I had to handle as a young first-time head coach that you wouldn't wish on your worst enemy'.

He coped with the challenges, but since he was so involved with the pressure situations the use of detailed interpersonal skills suffered. In his post-Games review there was a focus on how he had handled the relationship side of things which hurt him at first. He had neglected talking to his staff, the athletes, 'putting an arm around a shoulder here or there when needed, I was too busy in my room working on the analysis and process, on how to play against Argentina in the next game'.

The review also concluded that tactically, technically, and the strategic planning and programming had all been done excellently.

The feedback hurt, because [he] really [does] care about people, although [he] obviously wasn't showing it and they just weren't seeing it. So [he] then worked incredibly hard to take and show a real interest in other people.

Danny's explanation of withdrawing into his own personal comfort zone of match statistics and analysis while under intense pressure is something that we all perhaps do. We have a preference for acting in certain ways so then when we feel pressured we often return to what we know best. In a study of Olympic coaches under pressure, most coaches talked about controlling your own emotions as being important attribute for a coach at the Olympic level.;[16] One coach described themselves as being, 'pretty unflappable, you know, completely calm in a crisis, probably more measured than I should have been, very measured, very considered … ' In the same study, displaying confidence was also seen as essential for successful coaches along with athlete communication and empathy.

Hats off to Danny for demonstrating the importance of self-awareness and honesty in your own coaching. If only I'd appreciated this as a young coach and had the maturity to try to do something about it; though perhaps you get better at this type of thing with age as it is partly about being personally open to change. Something that often comes with maturity, confidence and understanding after years of experience.

Can shared leadership work?

The world of professional team sport certainly takes the meaning of coaching as leadership under pressure to a new level. Constant weekly selections, games and the need to handle a range of players from nervous newcomers to experienced pros. An unusual probe into elite soccer in Norway looked at the type of leadership newcomers and experienced players preferred while on a losing streak compared to a winning streak.

When the players were trying to dig themselves out of a hole in the losing scenario, they preferred more instruction, positive feedback, social support and democratic leadership. This is not surprising for a team in a slump but – democratic leadership – it is not something I'd heard of as a novice coach. What does it mean? Here is how the authors described democratic leadership:

> … to take more responsibility, have more influence and potentially participate more in the decision-making and leadership process … [with] greater player involvement in the coaching process …[17]

This is exactly what happened with the England Rugby team as they progressed to the final of the 2007 World Cup. They suffered a 36-0 defeat in their first game and were written off. This defeat stimulated senior players to take more responsibility as a team which saw them dramatically improve their performance and reach the final. Democracy doesn't mean taking a vote on everything, in this instance, but rather creating a change in power relations between coach and athletes so that there is collective responsibility and shared leadership. In most teams there are three or four experienced players who, if they can be harnessed to work together, can contribute to leadership, provided the coach does not feel threatened. It takes an open-minded coach to relinquish some of their control.

What about youth versus experience? In Norway, less experienced players wanted social supportive as well as a more democratic coaching approach; it seemed younger players did not respond to traditional 'coaching as control'. Some claim that a new breed of coach of this ilk is emerging. Respected sports scientist Ross Tucker has written about South African cricket coach Keith Upton, who is turning coaching as control on its head (see box below).

It demonstrates that there are many different interpretations of what 'good' coaching means. As a young 25-year-old novice coach I doubt I would have had the confidence or interpersonal skills to adopt this approach unless I had experienced it myself as a youngster – it is therefore a catch-22 because it takes a unique person with well developed emotional intelligence to achieve this more democratic approach.

A new genre of coaching?[18]

As a coach of India and South Africa (with Gary Kirsten), and then of the Indian Premier League's Rajasthan Royals, Keith Upton has lead his squads to World Cup and No. 1 World Rankings and club success.

The professional team sport norm is that the coach is the all-knowing, all-seeing, head of a team of specialist assistants and analysts who collectively provide data and information vertically downwards to the players. Upton's approach is to recognise how expertise is constructed socially, giving more power to the players, allowing them to drive their own technical, and personal development through exploration, failure and support from more experienced colleagues. A sort of squad collective wisdom that the coach draws out. 'Information flows sideways, peer-to-peer, with the coach facilitating' this approach.

What does coaching effectiveness look like?

Jean Côté came up with a framework for answering the question of 'what constitutes a truly effective coach?' His framework would have been useful to me. If someone had sat down and discussed it with me at regular intervals early on in my career, this would have helped me understand what I was aiming at. I had thought coaching was all about results:

The elements of effective coaching[19] (adapted)

Effective coaching is underpinned by three type of integrated knowledge:

Professional coaching knowledge
For example, expertise in the tactics / techniques of the sport and understanding of *some* of the following: physiology, nutrition, conditioning, biomechanics, materials science, teaching, psychology, medicine and other related sciences.

Interpersonal knowledge and skills
For example, the ability to communicate in writing and orally to a range of personnel including excellent one-to-one skills.

Self-awareness (intrapersonal) knowledge
For example, awareness of personal strengths and limitations, and a willingness to act on insights gained from reflection about current and past actions.

Effective coaching is demonstrated by the coach being able to improve athletes holistically. These outcomes are sometimes known as the 4Cs.[20] Developing athlete:

competence – technical, tactical, mental and physical skills to be the world's best;

confidence – belief and confidence in the capability to perform at the highest level under intense pressure;

connection – to foster a climate in which successful bonds develop with coaches, colleagues and the support network; and,

character – to support ethical and moral decision making including empathetic understanding of others and a sense of right and wrong (e.g. sportsmanship).

Based on this framework, an elite coach job description almost suggests the need for a superhero who is good at everything. Certainly in terms of professional knowledge coaches can use many different disciplines but are rarely experts in all. Michael Phelps's coach Bob Beaman, for instance, holds a degree in developmental psychology so knows a thing or two about child development – particularly relevant in Phelps's case due to his ADHD-related 'inconsistent focus' and his 'duelling moments of indifference and determination' as a youngster. Cycling conditioning coaches often have a physiology background; long-jump coaches are often expert in biomechanics and any sport that requires competition over a number of days (e.g. tennis) will have nutritional expertise in their team. Increasingly, the overarching discipline of sports science is the underlying knowledge base for many elite coaches with these coaches relying heavily on their playing careers to provide their sporting knowledge.

If Michael Johnson had actually written a job description when searching for his coach, he'd probably have included another 'C'; in both his autobiographies he constantly highlights the value he placed on consistency, i.e. for his coach to be the same person 'when [he won] as when [he lost], the same today, as when [he was] a world champion'.[21]

So it's clear that effective top level coaching draws on integrated types of knowledge (professional, interpersonal and intrapersonal), which might mean one coach tackles a problem completely differently from another (e.g. taking a psychological compared to a mechanics approach). This is often why coaching teams are assembled, drawing on different expertise, but the person with the best interpersonal and intrapersonal skills would ideally have the closest day-to-day relationship with a champion.

In choosing his coaches Andre Agassi would probably place more emphasis on 'inspiration' and 'strategy', while Andy Murray would focus on 'mindset in grand slam finals'. Michael Johnson chose his coach for his authenticity as someone who had a holistic approach to those he coached: athletic, educational and overall development. The choice of coach all depends on the athlete, their situation and needs. There is no stereotypical personality or knowledge base for success in coaching however formulaic effective coaching frameworks or even job descriptions may make it look.

Final thoughts

What about my own preference for coach X, Y or Z? Personally speaking now as an athlete, I would opt for coach Z as this type of coach reflects my belief in how to improve performance with a focus on quality training that progressively challenges you while also having feedback built into sessions, which would certainly inspire me. As an athlete I'd also gain confidence in good collaboration with leading experts in other fields and a coach who can clearly explain their vision of what they are trying to achieve and are able to justify it. My inquisitiveness as an athlete would always want to know 'why?'

The main coaching attributes from this chapter that are important for a coach developing their skills are:

- the importance of self-awareness and interpersonal skills;
- the emphasis on relationship building in which honest communication is possible;
- the ways in which concepts can be explained with clear memorable messages, devices such as 'the rule of three' may help;
- recognising how athletes learn by constructing meanings from informal interaction and other sources;
- acknowledging that much of coaching is leadership and
- knowing what is meant by 'holistic focus' on an athlete i.e. developing their confidence, competence, connection and character.

Much of this represents the intangible 'art' of coaching. The 'science' of coaching at the top level is increasingly dealt with by sports science or management systems specialists, but a coach needs to learn how they can use and manage their input. Blending the art and science together into a clear vision is the real skill of champions' coaches as this can impact on development towards podium performances.

20 Learning from behind the lines
Coaching stories

Myths about coaching abound. This chapter tells some little-known stories about the coaching of four champions, with a view to changing the way you think about coaching and the impact it can have on athletes and champions as we briefly helicopter into the worlds of Mo Farah, Jack Nicklaus, the Arsenal football team and Roger Federer to see what we can learn.

Each story addresses a different theme, moving from coaching innovation, to coach independence, to managing multinational player squads and ending with controlling emotions in tennis. We start in the United States.

Alberto Salazar: from near death to Olympic redemption

Double Olympic and World 5/10,000 metres champion, Mo Farah, switched his coach, his location and his training regime under the guidance of Alberto Salazar. It is clear that Salazar's approach is a great example of coaching leadership and, in particular, a focus on *change and innovation*. Innovation is all well and good, but what is important is choosing what to innovate and using science and evidence to guide the changes you make.

Alberto Salazar was a leading marathon runner in the USA in the 1980s during a running boom period, but he suffered due to almost obsessively overtraining. He now focuses on ensuring that his athletes – a group of eight or so funded by and based alongside the Nike headquarters in Oregon – don't make the same mistakes as he did. His overriding philosophy is to train smartly in terms of effective use of the athletes' time but also effective use of emerging technologies to avoid injury.

Another focus of his coaching comes from the 14 minutes Salazar was declared clinically dead when he collapsed with a heart attack in 2007 – you can only imagine how this could give you a unique perspective on sport, training and life! Following this event, Salazar wanted to make a difference to his athlete's lives, not just their running. Salazar is a great example of a coach addressing the person as a whole; for him it is about enriching and releasing the talent of those he guides.

Before any athlete joins his group (which also includes US running star and Olympic silver medallist Galen Rupp), Salazar ensures that there is democratic acceptance of the athlete joining them. All the athletes vote and more than one dissenting voice closes the door – Mo was unanimously accepted.

Mo Farah's decision to change and move across the Atlantic was prompted by ambition and earlier defeats. In 2010, after winning the European Championships, he did not stand still, but wanted to take it to the next level: about 1–1½ seconds faster. Mo had the vision of what it takes to succeed. He had lived and trained with Kenyan runners in London and also went away to train in Africa for long stretches, but was often without coaching support and family on such trips. Once accepted by Salazar's group he jumped into the change with both feet, moving house and his young family to the US. A total commitment to becoming world class and closing the 1½ second gap.

Farah and Rupp thrived together as training partners in Oregon, each learning from the other. Unusually in coach–athlete relationships, Salazar had coached Galen Rupp since the age of 15, and Rupp's relationship with Salazar had developed from that of between adult and child to that of peers:

> When I first me him [aged 15] he was a father figure to me, I wouldn't question anything he said, I'd just nod my head and do it without thinking twice about it. As I've got older, gotten married and stuff our relationship has changed ... that is a real testament to Alberto that he has been able to change and really adapt ... I think it drives him nuts sometimes when I question stuff, but in the end he likes it, we can talk freely ... we both really care a lot about each other.[1]

Notice how their relationship has developed into one of mutual respect and one involving honest communication without hierarchical power differences.

One aspect of training that Salazar focuses on with Rupp and Farah is economy, efficiency and injury prevention: the mechanics of movement. Salazar has become an expert in running biomechanics, as he understands that even the smallest increases in running efficiency make a big difference over long distances. He has consulted with the sprinter Michael Johnson, among others, about the most effective movements for his athletes, going against the received wisdom of long-distance athletic events. He has said, 'when you don't have good biomechanics it will ultimately lead to injuries'.[2] Salazar's myth-busting approach advocates a great deal of strength training in the gym, which is unusual for endurance athletes. This helps overcome any muscular imbalances and maintains optimum running style as athletes fatigue: these were both problems that Salazar knew had to be addresses to close Mo Farah's 1–1½ second gap to truly become world-beating.

Staying injury-free is a key focus. Salazar's relationship with his athletes means that their open honest communication with him, for example reporting slight muscular or tendon soreness, means that their training is immediately adapted to a reduced weight-bearing regime: sometimes to water-based work and/or an Anti-Gravity Treadmill (AlterG) originally developed for use by NASA astronauts. Salazar was an early adopter of this AlterG technology, which uses differential air pressure to adjust weight-bearing loads, and it is now a commonplace training and rehabilitation tool. Due to these adaptive training methods, Farah only missed eight days of 'normal' training (due to slight soreness) in the year preceding his Olympic victory. Research suggests that 36 per cent of elite athletes across all sports will get at least one injury per season, with each causing on average 15 days lost to training.[3]

At the 2012 Olympic Games, astonishingly, Farah and Rupp occupied the top two places on the 10,000m medal podium. Farah then went on to win the 5000m and 10,000m gold medals at the 2013 World Athletics Championships, but Salazar's mission is now to help Farah sustain this success, and eventually convert to his own event, the marathon.

The close relationships and atmosphere of a small, tight-knit training group is a very specific example of an environment that is supportive of an athlete switching to a new regime, which is a huge risk for an athlete. It is also an example of a coach's vision leading to change, often against the received norms in his discipline.

Increasingly research is suggesting that there are probably feedback-related behaviours that top coaches should do but often don't. Let's take a look at the example of athlete independence.

Independence: Coaches speaking less

Coaches were not surprised when a number of recent talent-development books emphasised the importance of quality and quantity of practice in the development of champions. After all it is the coaches who create the practices and build in the rich feedback loops that Matthew Syed describes:

> … great coaches are able to design practice so that feedback is embedded in the drill, leading to automatic readjustment, which in turn improves the quality of the feedback, generating further improvements, and so on.[4]

Michael Johnson's coach Clyde Hart introduced feedback into Johnson's sessions by use of a beeper sounding every few seconds and wired into trackside speakers to give Johnson pace feedback in every session he did for 15 years. Like a metronome in music, it helped him to judge his rhythm and speed, enabling him to instantly judge his form at key checkpoints and refine his technique and tactics.

Feedback and instruction are often seen as the key role of coaches. In fact, champions' practice is most effective when the coach creates a thinking athlete. It is then not all about feedback, but about creating athletes that can determine what they have done wrong and how to correct it independently.[5] Golfer Jack Nicklaus illustrated this point when he said:

> Jack Grout taught me from the start. He said I need to be responsible for my own swing and understand when I have problems on the golf course how I can correct those problems on the golf course myself without having to run back to somebody. And during the years that I was playing most of my competitive golf, I saw Jack Grout maybe once or twice a year for maybe an hour … But he taught me young the fundamentals of the game. He taught me how to assess what I was doing. When I made a mistake, when I was

doing things, how do you on the golf course fix that without putting yourself out of a golf tournament and then teaching yourself.[6]

This strategy is at odds with what coaches, often do because giving less feedback is counterintuitive: it challenges the coach's control and the cultural norms of many sports. The idea of gradually reducing or fading out coach feedback is to reduce coach dependency and get athletes to think more and make their own decisions just as they need to do in the heat of competition.

A sport's 'cultural norms' will largely influence how coaches behave and run their sessions – coaches often base their coaching model on how they themselves were coached and these behaviours are perpetuated, sometimes meaning that practices can become deeply ingrained in the culture of a sport. As a result there are numerous cases where what coaches do is considered contrary to the scientific principles. For example, coaches in elite adult judo have been described as highly autocratic, showing low levels of social support and using their behaviour as part of a 'toughening up' process for their athletes.[7] Although the athletes did not like this coaching behaviour, they acknowledged it to be effective, illustrating that the culture of the sport strongly influences what coaches do. I can imagine judo coaches throwing their arms up in horror. I'm sure at the top Olympic level coaches have strong individual relationships with the likes of Gemma Gibbons or Kayla Harrison, but this research suggests the culture of judo squad coaching is largely based on approaches in which communication and influence is likely to be mainly from coach to athlete.

Looking at professional coaches' central role in soccer a 'traditional' approach to coaching has also been described by a number of studies in English Premier League (EPL) clubs. This 'is characterised by a highly directed, autocratic and prescriptive approach to instruction'[8] with limited player independence.

For example, when the proportion of time coaches spent on different tasks during practices in EPL soccer was measured, some interesting results showed up. Instruction (60 per cent) was by far the most common activity, proportionally followed by lots and lots of praise (15 per cent), with observation (13 per cent) occupying less time and far less time used for the coach asking questions (3 per cent). The remaining 9 per cent of the time was largely made up by the coach managing and hustling along the session.

This somewhat contradicts the lessons that Jack Nicklaus gleaned over the years about being encouraged to think and work things out for himself. With 60 per cent of the time being used for instruction, including feedback, it suggests rather too much information and talk in sessions. Also, although praise is designed to build confidence, some have concluded that the overuse of praise could be regarded as a sign of rather unspecific feedback that can dilute its motivational effects.

An interesting finding is that, in a similar study of top-level football coaches in Norway, the coaches employed silent observation two and a half times more than English coaches (37 per cent as opposed to 15 per cent). Guiding individuals to work things out for themselves is one thing but perhaps the real craft for team coaches is to set up situations in which groups respond to and fix problems.

In one-to-one coaching the coach might come to feel like rather a spare part as their athlete becomes independent. Consider world 800m record holder David Rudisha's coach and mentor, Father Colm O'Connell, who has never been abroad to support him at major events – for him, his work is done.

Arsène Wenger gets personal

Frenchman Arsène Wenger has been the longest serving football manager (or head coach in US terms) in the English Premier League, having joined Arsenal Football Club in 1996. His intellectual 'Le Professeur' media tag has stuck as has his love of a multicultural squad. Coincidentally his club is part of a wider transatlantic enterprise, which owns a number of American team franchises.[9] Two comments Wenger has made are particularly relevant here:

> … in football you do need special talent, but when a player passes the age of 20, what is in the *mind is more important* than the rest and that's what makes a career.[10] [my emphasis]
> For me being a football manager is being a guide. A guide is someone who leads people somewhere … he has to identify what he wants … convince everybody else and try to get the best out of each individual.[11]

Wenger's interest in the mind and a personal guiding approach is said to work, because he emphasises his core underpinning values, which are articulated and embodied throughout a squad helping to provide direction:[12] values such as multiculturalism, respect, honesty, fairness and trust. He also has to convince every player of the importance of team solidarity: the emotional bond of going through something together can give individuals far more than just concentrating on themselves. Wenger describes the crucial age for young professionals when they are 19–22 years old as:

> a period in your life when your ego is massive … the world turns around you – and that's a normal development thing for a person. But at that age [he believes] a leader has a big part to play to give this understanding that, OK, you are important but all together *we* are even more important.[13]

The leadership expert Mike Carson, who interviewed Wenger for his book *The Manager* says that a leader who can create belonging and fulfilment in the work of his squad will influence them at the deepest level. Leaders should strive to create a sense of belonging that is purposeful, intimate, lasting and fulfilling.[14]

This is easier said than done in football, since a number of practices work against it. The need to create belonging is therefore even more important. Wenger identifies:

> one of the difficulties in [a coach's] job is that [you] have 25 people who fight to play on Saturday and on Friday night [you] have 14 who are unemployed and [you] tell them on Monday, let's start again you have another chance.[15]

Those who don't play feel useless and vulnerable every week and often start asking themselves and maybe the management how they might fit into the team. As a result their sense of belonging is threatened with every team selection. This highlights the importance of how a squad's culture needs to give a sense of belonging, respect and credit to athletes and players who, in this situation, are not able to demonstrate how good they are.

Squad culture can also be the glue that helps bind people together, but the underpinning values and behaviour boundaries also need to be crystal clear. At Arsenal, Wenger had athletes in the squad from 18 different countries, which provides a different challenge:

> For example, being on time isn't the same for a Japanese man as it is for a Frenchman. When a Frenchman arrives five minutes late, he still thinks he is on time. In Japan when it's five minutes before the set time he thinks he is too late.
>
> That means you have to create a new culture and identify how we all want to behave and create a company culture. That way, when someone steps out of line, we can say: 'Look, my friend, that's not what we said.' So it's important to have clear rules and everyone knows and agrees with it.[16]

After almost two decades in the job you can see that Wenger has a particular clarity in how he operates. He also emphasises an appropriate mental mindset by encouraging his players to have autonomy and look at their own standards off the field as much as on it. Carson reports that Wenger constantly invites players to assess how they think they are doing and is keen to see how accurately they evaluate themselves.

Overall Wenger's holistic approach with his squad is based on a commitment to working with emotions, identifying beliefs and motivations and reinforcing players' self-regulation.

Moving on from the complexity of guiding football squads to the individualism of tennis (quite a jump!), emotion is the common theme. It is something that often surfaces in players from both sports, but the spotlight is often particularly focused on the emotion–behaviour link amid the cauldron of grand slam tennis tournaments.

Roger Federer learns to be ice cool

Consider the performance cost of temperamentally going over the edge and losing it in competition. From 'red-mist' antics causing lost points or even dismissal from the field (examples include Lee Bowyer in football, for Newcastle vs Aston Villa, 2005; Wayne Rooney in football, 2006 European Championships for England versus Portugal; Rodney Harrison in the NFL, who coaches voted the 'dirtiest player' in a 2008 anonymous poll conducted by ESPN; and Dwayne Wade in the NBA, 2012 for Miami in Charlotte Bobcats vs Miami Heat), biting opponents and resultant bans (Mike Tyson in boxing and Mario Balotelli in football) to simply getting wildly annoyed with themselves or the umpire (e.g. numerous tennis players).

It seems difficult to believe that Roger Federer had a problem with his temperament now that he is known as a supreme champion of such poise, unflappable calm and confidence. Yet in his developing years he would often curse and toss his racket around, causing his then coach to intervene. Federer explains the depth of the problem:

> It was bad. My parents were embarrassed and they told me to stop it or they wouldn't come along with me to my tournaments anymore. I had to calm down but that was an extremely long process. I believe I was looking for perfection too early.[17]

His biographer claims that a turning point came at the US Open, aged 17, when he demolished a racket on court and his coach at the time had to make him realise he should be more patient in his strategy rather than taking glamorous high risk shots. Federer also started working with a sports psychologist for a few years to help him improve his game:

> Back then I wanted to show everybody what I was capable of, the difficult strokes I had mastered … but at some point it became clear to me that I would get more attention if I were among the top players in the world.[18]

When he started to maintain control he mused: 'I don't know if this has something to do with the big stadiums. Perhaps I'm more ashamed when I lose control there'. These days a smashed Federer racket is the tennis equivalent of a unicorn sighting. The last known instance of Federer racket abuse can be found on YouTube from Miami 2009 – needless to say he lost 6–3 in the third set.

More recently Andy Murray's muttering and verbal self-abuse – at the more mature age of 26 – has been the focus of coaching interest. His mother, Judy, has stated the influence on Murray of coach Ivan Lendl, himself known for his poker-face on the tennis court as a player. Lendl's deadpan expression continued courtside in his two-year stint as coach. Lendl succeeded in reining back Andy's verbal outbursts of frustration and anger, which seemed to distract him at crucial pressure moments. Most of these outbursts were self-directed, and Lendl helped Murray to control these tendencies when crucial points are lost.[19]

Judy Murray's analysis is that Andy's improvement means he is better able to reset his concentration than he was before. It is no use letting too much emotion unnecessarily drain your energy, especially on something that has already happened, and Judy considers that the more emotionally calm you can be throughout a long match and grand slams the better.[20]

This key feature of Murray's new approach was to prove vital in his first Wimbledon Championship win in 2013. Controlling temperament is an absolutely key attribute in all sports, but it can take a while to master. Fortunately, in Murray's case, Lendl was a respected coach who was not afraid to confront the behaviour and make a few home truths known.

Final thoughts

These four separate stories have now helped me make sense of the coaching part of my career. Top coaches' experiences highlight their contribution to shaping champions, and if you were in the position of choosing your own coach after reading the last two chapters, you might consider the underpinning values and principles that guide their coaching. For example, the likes of Alberto Salazar, Arsène Wenger and Ivan Lendl appear to have clear philosophies, all slightly different, which help give clarity and consistency to their coaching.

You might see how a coach uses power relations in their interactions with athletes and if this feels appropriate and is a mutually balanced relationship. Power and control might be necessary in squads but it may get in the way of coaches and athletes talking freely and being honest with each other.

The extent to which a coach adapts to change and new ideas, including use of innovation is important. Sometimes change can be pursued for its own sake, as new fads and technologies emerge but I was struck how Salazar's mission was to pursue *quality rather than quantity* in his training. Training smartly and staying injury-free is a key part of becoming successful so a coach's ability to use new ideas appropriately is important.

Most champions are good at evaluating their own performances, and working things out for themselves. This therefore frames the coach's role as one of trying to embed feedback into most training sessions and creating an environment in which top athletes can thrive. Some individuals seek minimal and subtle coaching input others prefer far more. Personally I would favour the former.

Good top-level coaches are often recommended by others. Of course, this is not always reliable due to individual differences but it is worth exploring how much of a sense of belonging a coach creates. Champion coaches know that creating a sense of belonging and squad solidarity is vital. The team is paramount in Wenger's Arsenal squad, but in an individual sport like athletics Salazar's training group seem to be purposeful, and he has created something lasting and something fulfilling. Is a coach who can create an authentic sense of belonging likely to be more effective and perhaps more likely to be more recommended?

And finally, a coach who coaches the whole person is likely to focus on guiding the temperament and self-control of those he works with in positive ways. A coach who is steady and consistent but also passionate will model the behaviour of those he or she guides. In my opinion self-regulation is something champions and coaches need to master.

These personal conclusions, if they could all be realised in one coach who also had the right type of interpersonal and technical knowledge would shape the progress of most but not all champions. Successful coaches do best when they can respond to individual differences among athletes.

Two particular specialist and challenging individual characteristics – responses to pain and personal mental health – are considered in the following chapters.

Part V

Specialist characteristics

21 Do champions think differently about pain?

There are still some unanswered questions about individual differences that are connected to coaching. First off: is champion athletes' tolerance of pain in training and competition different to that of the rest of us? The mystery of how champions endure and think about pain has been nagging me. Increasingly my research has shown extreme accounts of how champions' view suffering and pain: particularly among endurance athletes. Not the pain of an injury but the lung-bursting, limb-burning, head-throbbing sensations you feel when you push yourself to the limit. Three descriptions of enduring pain from Chris Hoy, Chrissie Wellington and Alberto Salazar, each with a slightly different perspective, are used as we start this chapter to explore deep, long-lasting pain.

Chris Hoy, while sharing a room at a championships with his childhood hero and former world record holder, Graeme Obree (opposite), listened intently to what Obree said and it stuck with him:

> You always think you're at your limit ... and that you can't go any harder – but just when you think that, push a bit harder ... it's like holding your hand in the fire ... it's a case of who can deal with the pain the longest.[1]

Applying this to his own subsequent career performances, he went on to reflect:

> The important thing is this: that only *you* know. When it comes to that crunch point, usually on the final lap, or in the final few seconds of a race or training session, when your body is screaming at you to stop, all you've got to do is throttle back half of one per cent to make it bearable, or tolerable. It's a miniscule drop-off in effort; and nobody would know – not even the coaches studying you ... you can kid other people but you can never kid yourself.[2]

Let's call this the *committing 110 per cent* perspective; the inward satisfaction and confidence of knowing that pain did not prevent even the tiniest drop-off in all-out effort.

Next, Chrissie Wellington, an expert in the mind-games of ironman suffering, having won the event four times. She says that pain is never far away in an endurance athlete's life and compares pain to a conversation between your body and your brain:

The brain is the master computer of the body … It's a question of testing the limits. The brain is programmed to protect us, and that can mean imposing limits on what it thinks we can or should do. Constantly push at those limits, because the brain can be way too cautious … We should constantly question it, fight it. That means enduring pain … What the good triathlete should relish is the pain, that is our brain's way of telling us that it doesn't like how hard we are working.

… This is not gratuitous masochism. There is a very real process of refinement going on. You are not just working your muscles and lungs, you are working your brain to learn to accept each new level of exertion as something that can be endured safely. The brain – at least, the safety-first part of the brain – will try to dig its heels in.[3]

Wellington's description seems to be about *exploring beyond the brain's pain limits*. She views the brain as rather conservative in the limits it perceives as 'safe' for well-being.

And the third perspective comes from Alberto Salazar, coach and former four-time winner of the New York/Boston Marathons. His athletes Mo Farah and Galen Rupp dominated the World Championship and Olympic podiums in 2011, 2012 and 2013:

[he] think[s] pain and discomfort and fear and anxiety are really what you should be looking at [rather than athlete's mental toughness]. Anybody can take pain and discomfort when you're succeeding. It's really your ability to deal with that pain, discomfort and fear and not have it negatively affect your running. It's not like you ever give up and say, 'Well I can't take this pain, I've got to back off.' It's the negative thoughts that creep in – I'm not doing well, I'm not handling this well – that make you back off. And I think – and again this is something we know from other sports – often runners will think, 'I have these negative thoughts, I'm a wimp, I'm not tough' and stuff. And the more that you sort of, I don't want to say embrace it like you have to be some sort of masochistic person, but the more you expect it, that this is natural when you're going all out and you're on the edge that the doubts will come. And learning to deal with that in a scientific way, and through sports psychology and learn that you can deal with that and perform even better.[4]

Salazar's perspective is that *reaffirmation and self-belief of pain tolerance* is all part of mental preparation: so when it hurts like hell during adverse periods in competition the confidence is there to deal with the deep pain. A sort of pain-training confidence builder: despite the acute suffering inwardly saying 'everything is still all right – I can deal with this!'

What do you think … are champions actually different to the rest of us? Certainly, athletes who train at eye-popping race intensity week-in, week-out, provided they rest properly, stimulate great physiological adaptations and benefit. But it seems that all three examples really are exploring the edge of what they can withstand.

An explanation or framework that explains the difference between champions' approach to pain and the rest of us is needed. Initially, I thought an explanation might be found in the cultural norms of the sport: for example, you often see elite rowers falling off their ergometer after being tested. So in a sense, an athlete's view of pain is part of the socialisation process, as they start out and continue up the ladder in a particular sport, to the extent that in the end it becomes an accepted norm in sports like cycling, rowing, swimming, running and perhaps combat disciplines. Pain becomes part of the furniture such that athletes talk about it surprisingly infrequently: it becomes part of their daily lives.

But when Wellington talks of *exploring beyond the brain's pain limits*, I felt that I needed to dig deeper and find out what causes the limits of performance, particularly in self-paced endurance sports. How is pain and fatigue tied up in this? Without knowing it I'd stumbled into a major scientific debate about the limits of performance, which potentially involved a major realignment in neurophysiological thinking over the last decade. This rethink in the science of endurance and self-pacing has implications for clichés like 'it's all in the mind', 'no pain, no gain' and 'it's the leg's that go first'.

I'll explain with the help of South African researchers Tim Noakes, who pioneered the new thinking, and Ross Tucker who studied with him and makes science accessible on his excellent *Science of Sport* website.[5]

Traditional views on the limits of performance

Earlier explanations of fatigue use the 'peripheral fatigue model' or the 'catastrophe model', basically taking the view that fatigue is all about physiological limits. This suggests you have absolute physical limits as to what your body can sustain and we slow down when this is reached.

Fatigue, according to this view, is the result of physiological failure causing the athlete to stop or to ease off, which is partly where the saying 'the legs have gone' comes from. Failure might occur anywhere in the body systems – but failure in one or more of these is most likely: failure to supply enough oxygen to the muscles, failure to keep lactate and other debilitating byproducts of exercise levels down, depletion of the energy that supplies muscles (glycogen), or overheating. Once this catastrophic failure point is reached, this view suggests an athlete has to slow down or stop altogether, and not surprisingly the resulting fatigue is debilitating.

Something like this has happened to me: what is known as 'bonking' in cycling. This means running out of glycogen (a form of sugar), so you feel weak and lightheaded – rather like being drunk. In the 2013 Tour de France, the eventual winner, Chris Froome apparently 'bonked' while climbing Alp D'Huez, and finished three minutes off the day's leader as a result. When you run out of fuel, glycogen stored in the muscles and liver becomes depleted and the body proceeds to get most of its energy from fat. Fat doesn't provide energy as quickly, nor does it fuel the brain as efficiently, hence the sluggish 'drunkenness'.

This traditional catastrophe view sees fatigue and pain as our body coming up against its physical limits. When it hurts on a tough running or cycling hill climb, the inner frustration and public shame of quitting hangs over you, but in my instance I knew that I could probably have kept going if I really, really needed to. If you believe the traditional view of pain caused by catastrophic failure, you might take comfort in the biological explanation that your system or fitness met its limit. Anyway, that's what we used to think.

In the 1990s, Professor Tim Noakes asked the question: why don't more elite runners die from heart attacks if they have to slow down and stop because their bodies approach their physiological limits? Surely those elite athletes with the willpower who pushed on would often be close to death?

Only two public examples spring to mind. The wobbly, zigzag path of Dorando Pietri as he repeatedly fell on his way to the finish of the 1908 Olympics; he was not close to death. Rather it is said he indulged in some mid-race strychnine (a stimulant) and/or perhaps his demise was hastened by the brandy he used to refresh himself. More serious was the cyclist Tom Simpson, who collapsed on Mont Ventoux on a blistering day of the 1967 Tour de France. We'll return to him in a moment.

Noakes's ideas began to take shape and he started to realise that, rather than catastrophic failure causing fatigue, something forces the body to slow down to protect itself well *before* that point. As Chrissie Wellington suggests, the brain is programmed to protect us in anticipation of trouble ahead. He turned his attention to what happens with prolonged exercise in heat.

Fatigue and pain as illusionary symptoms

When the body temperature reaches 40°C, the point at which heatstroke sets in, the catastrophe theory says that the brain fails to activate muscle fibres and you can no longer continue to exercise. Noakes and Ross's alternative explanation states that there is anticipatory regulation to prevent bad, dangerous things happening to the body. A key component of this is the idea that fatigue is not a physical event but rather a brain-derived emotion that can be illusionary: it is used by the brain to regulate how hard we push on.

Noakes suggests that performance is regulated by the brain processing information from numerous different sources in addition to body systems (see Table 21.1 opposite) and it responds well before the 40°C temperature limit is reached. Looking at the table you can begin to see how the overall perception of fatigue comes from a complicated mix of mental and physical inputs. Fatigue and pain contribute to the athlete slowing down, with the effect that the athlete produces less heat. So 'you don't slow down because you are hot, you slow down in order to prevent yourself from getting hot'.[6]

In the case of Tom Simpson in the Tour de France, the athlete had ingested amphetamines and his death is generally attributed to doping, but the real reason he died, Noakes and Tucker claim, was because the drugs dampened his brain's perception, the anticipatory regulation of what was safe, allowing him to ride himself to death.

Further unresolved questions remain. Why is it that only between 35 per cent to 50 per cent of active muscle fibres are used during sustained exercise?[7] Without

Table 21.1 Some of the inputs to the brain that influence performance.

Mental	Physical	Features of the event	Other
Emotional state – how you feel	State of recovery from previous exercise	Prior experience of event	Deception information – false time, distance covered, comparisons to previous pace
The extent of mental fatigue or sleep deprivation	Pre-exercise whole-body cooling	Knowledge of distance to end-point	Placebo effects
The level of motivation	Chemical agents including the stimulants – amphetamines, caffeine and others	The presence of competitors	
Monetary reward	Tasting, not even swallowing, a sweet carbohydrate drink		
The degree of self-belief, including superstitious beliefs			
Listening to music			
Training in psychological skills			

Noakes, T. (2012a) Fatigue is a brain-derived emotion that regulates the exercise behavior to ensure the protection of whole body homeostasis. *Frontiers in Physiology*. B:82.

knowing it, your body still keeps something in reserve even when you try supremely hard. This makes it difficult to explain how any physical limit forces you to slow down (as is the case according to catastrophe theory). In fact, what happens in every self-paced endurance sport (such as distance running and cycling), is that athletes pace themselves at a sustainable speed in the middle part of a race to be able to produce an end spurt. The big question for scientists is to what extent there are unconscious elements to this pacing strategy. The argument, and increasingly the evidence, indeed suggests that there is an unconscious element with things like heat, music and previous experiences influencing how you set your pace.

Ross Tucker's view of the end spurt – from an anticipatory regulation perspective – is that the final effort is possible because earlier in the race the brain has conserved resources in response to numerous inputs. Since the finish line is approaching, and the physiological changes are no longer deemed harmful or potentially limiting to continuing exercise and the muscle reserve can be activated.

This connects to what Galen Rupp says about him and Mo Farah training together:

> We can be dead tired and then [Alberto Salazar] will have us run a really fast last interval and that kinda shows you that even though you are dying and you might not have anything left you are always able to pick it up and run fast … You can always try to dig down and find a bit more; it's not going to be easy and its going to hurt a lot, but that energy is always there … we replicate that feeling day in day out in training and *we want* to replicate that feeling so that we're prepared when that time comes in a race.[8]

The range of inputs that contribute to anticipatory regulation, identified by Noakes in table 21.1, all centrally interact in the brain and therefore contribute to fatigue and pain. What we have been discussing is a process that is, confusingly, sometimes called the 'central governor' model – I mention it here since it is reviewed in journals and on the internet, but Tucker's 'anticipatory regulation' is exactly the same concept using a term that is more intelligible to us newcomers to the debate. The conclusion is that the conscious or unconscious pace that an athlete sets is thought to be influenced by all these anticipatory regulation inputs rather than the body simply giving up when it reaches its limit.

Is it just mind over matter?

Talking about enduring pain in competition we've already heard the analogy Graeme Obree used, likening it to 'holding your hand in the fire … it's a case of who can deal with the pain the longest.' One might be able to imagine psyching oneself up to literally put a hand into fire: you'd have to block out the pain and fear of future life-long disfigurement … but a better analogy exists. Ross Tucker says 'you cannot commit suicide by holding your breath'.[9] While willpower is very, very powerful, you cannot overcome physiology (such as the depletion of muscle glycogen).

The implication is that champions need a burning hunger to win. Often the deep-seated need to win and to prove a point to themselves and others is a feature of breakthrough international performances. If their physiology is in top condition they can push back the barriers of acceptable levels of pain. The example of the 2004 New York Women's Marathon, which lasted 143 minutes, is a good one. Paula Radcliffe won by four seconds: she was 0.0005 per cent faster than the woman in second. What prevented the second runner from speeding up just a tiny, tiny bit more at the end? Noakes summarises his thoughts on this:

> My conclusion is that in the case of a close finish, physiology does not determine who wins. Rather somewhere in the final section of the race, the brains of the second and lower placed finishers accept their respective finishing positions …

this outcome will be strongly influenced by the manner in which the brains of the respective runners generate the sensations of fatigue during exercise. Recall that these symptoms of fatigue are entirely self-generated by each athlete's brain and so are unique to each individual ... These symptoms are unrelated to the actual amount of work done and hence the true state of bodily fatigue. Instead they are illusionary ... the winning athlete is the one whose illusionary symptoms interfere the least with the actual performance – in much the same way that the most successful golfers are those who do not consciously think when they play any of their shots. ... So the winner is the athlete for whom defeat is the least acceptable rationalization.[10]

One sentence in their jumps out at me '... the winning athlete is the one whose illusionary symptoms [of pain] interfere the least with the actual performance'. It sounds very close indeed to what Salazar was saying about your ability to deal with that pain, discomfort and fear and not have it affect your running. So Salazar's *reaffirmation and self belief in pain tolerance* perspective explains how champions are different to us. Combine this with an almost obsessional hunger to win and you have a powerful combination.

For example, Hendrick Ramaala, male winner of the same 2004 New York City marathon as Radcliffe, said:

> What I realize is that once the mind accepts anything, the body will respond ... If you don't convince yourself that you are going to win, then you aren't going to win it. For New York, I have to tell myself thousands of times that I am going to win this thing ... You have to talk to yourself otherwise you are not going to win ... You have to say: 'Whatever happens I am going to win.' In my opinion, the person who wins the race has already won it inside his head before the start of the race.[11]

You can bet that Ramaala was also in fantastic physical shape but after failure in the Olympics a few months before, this man was desperate to prove himself – it was his first major marathon win. Paula Radcliffe, who also bombed out at the Athens Games after being one of the pre-race favourites, likewise had a point to prove. Two athletes desperate to redeem themselves, they had a deep, deep need to prove their worth and achieve some inner peace from their nagging and very public Olympic failures.

Final thoughts

Some athletes talk about pain, while others don't. This is partly because it is a feature of their everyday training regime, and has become normal. Perhaps since Salazar, Wellington and Hoy so clearly articulate what pain means to them they are able to deal with it. This, combined with fulfilling deep-seated needs when competing, can result in a potent combination. When champions continually push beyond their own preconceptions of what can be endured, it provides a massive boost to their mind as much as their body.

A pothole, or worse, on the path
Depression

> At that point I was a shell. You could have taken all my kit, all my money, taken my life away. I didn't care … You lose track of what you are, and who you are …[1]

So said Marcus Trescothick, the former England cricket captain, facing career-debilitating depression while on an overseas tour in 2005. History repeated itself in 2013 as another leading English cricket player, Jonathan Trott, abandoned a tour of Australia due to long-term stress-related illness. Exploring the experiences of athletes with depression became a lot easier after Trescothick published his autobiography *Coming Back to Me* in 2007. Since then Jonny Wilkinson (rugby), Ian Thorpe (swimming), Victoria Pendleton (cycling) and others have described their dark times, providing a fascinating insight into the role of the 'black dog' in sport.

In this chapter, perhaps for the first time, I bring champions' personal stories from both sides of the Atlantic and combine them with research to try and make sense of depression in champions' sporting paths. I wanted to write about depression for three reasons. Firstly, to break down barriers, raise awareness and perhaps demystify depression. Secondly, to help demonstrate that depression is not a personal weakness – a view that often prevents athletes seeking the help they need. Thirdly, to help families, sports organisations and coaches to better support those who suffer. Most importantly, help is available and there is light at the end of the tunnel of depressive episodes.

This chapter was developed by speaking with medics and psychotherapists to confirm what circumstances prompt such episodes. To start, we need to understand the symptoms of depression.

Beyond feeling blue

It is paradoxical that exercise is believed to have a positive impact on mental health, but anecdotally it appears that mental health issues are relatively common among elite athletes, just as it is among the general population. One explanation might be that athletes are vulnerable to developing mental health issues due to the exceptional demands placed on them, or perhaps those with a propensity to develop mental health problems may be attracted to elite sport, which has a draw for people who thrive on adrenaline, perfectionism and fear of failure.

One of the difficulties for both researchers and medics is in discriminating between a period of low mood and the onset of a depressive episode. Let's use Jonny Wilkinson's description of his behaviour and feelings at the age of 26, after two years of being injured, to try to work out where to draw the line between depression and feeling down:[2]

- Sleeping is a problem … [sleeping tablets] don't seem to work.
- … [he] seem[s] to have lost the drive. Motivation has fizzled out.
- The negative thoughts won't stop.
- [His] mind is too active.
- [He doesn't] feel [he] can get up and face the day … [He doesn't] want to face the pressures … or the expectations … which [he] knows [he] can't meet.
- [He] starts turning up late [for sessions].
- [He] can't escape.
- There's simply no way [he] can concentrate enough to read a book.
- [His] mind … causes [him] to feel panic and [his] heart to beat quicker.
- Downward [thoughts], tossing endless dark, nasty images through [his] head.

You'll probably agree this sounds pretty debilitating – beyond merely feeling low. You apparently know you are depressed when you no longer want to feel anything and have no desire for experience.[3]

In medicine, symptoms for depression are compared against clinical diagnostic checklists – I'll leave you to judge how easy it is to compare Jonny's account against an online checklist relying on numbers. Take a look at this formal one for GPs from *GPnotebook*: http://www.gpnotebook.co.uk/simplepage.cfm?ID= x20091123152205182440 or this more informal one from *Netdoctor*, for the general public to use for their self-diagnosis: http://www.netdoctor.co.uk/interactive/ interactivetests/goldberg.php.

One diagnostic checklist discriminates between 'no depression' and 'mild', 'moderate' or 'severe' depression on the basis of counting the number of symptoms with the caveat that 'symptoms should be present for at least a month or more';[4] living with such symptoms for a month or more must be challenging.

It's largely down to interpretation, preferably from a professional rather than the likes of you or I, but sleep problems, inability to concentrate, feelings of emptiness, hiding away, detachment and loss of the ability to control your life all signal possible depression. In Jonny's case he eventually put out feelers in conversation with a colleague about his 'struggling a bit' and was recommended a professional to contact, with whom he then worked closely on his illness. Things improved considerably.

How widespread is depression in sport?

While the picture is becoming clearer, it is still rather vague due to the difficulties in defining depression consistently, and the likelihood of it being underreported by athletes due to potential stigma. It is something that is very difficult to define, measure and collect statistics on.

The autobiographies used in this book suggests that Ian Thorpe and Jonny Wilkinson had depression and, if you take self-harm episodes as a sign of psychological distress, then you must also count Kelly Holmes and Victoria Pendleton. This means that 10–20 per cent of our small sample of champions described depression. To that I'd add Chrissie Wellington's story of her anorexia as a young adult; although this wouldn't be classified as depression, it is still a psychological disorder.

My figure of 10–20 per cent is similar to that given in some recent new research published in France. Almost 2100 French elite athletes were investigated, a good sized sample, and it was found that just under 4 per cent of athletes had experienced at least one depressive episode in the last six months, with one in ten (10 per cent) saying they had experienced a depressive episode in their lifetime.[5] When the strict time and definitional boundaries of 'depression' are broadened it turns out that 17 per cent of the athletes had experienced at least one 'psychological disorder', with females (20 per cent) slightly more prevalent than males (15 per cent). Overall these figures are certainly higher than I imagined when I first set out to research this topic. There are then quite a number of people experiencing mental health issues in every sports changing room – in a team squad of 20 athletes about four might be vulnerable. It would help for coaches to be aware of this.

Gender differences in the likelihood of depression in athletes seem to be in line with the general population, but this might represent a greater willingness among females to seek support than males. The first step in doing something about negative feelings is admitting that you have them; men have a tendency to try and handle depression alone and, as you can imagine, it is not easy. Partly, and perhaps as a result, males are three to four times more likely to commit suicide than females.

Sadly, high profile recent cases of suicide in elite sport reflect this vulnerability later in sporting careers. Those among European sport include Robert Enke (German football goalkeeper) and Gary Speed (player and later Wales football manager).

Suicide rates

It is estimated that the figure of those who attempt suicide is more than 20 times the figure of those who succeed.[6] Young men are most at risk. In the US the overall rate is 11 deaths per 100,000 population (2006).[7] While in the UK (2011) there were 18.2 male suicides per 100,000 population compared to 5.6 female suicides. In the UK the most vulnerable group appears to be males aged 30–44 (23.5 deaths per 100,000 population), coincidently just when elite sportsmen come to the end of their careers.[8]

In the US, suicides have also drawn public attention. The suicides of two NFL players, Junior Seau and Dave Duerson, caused public comment because each man shot himself in the chest rather than the head, allowing their intact brains to be used to research the effects of severe concussion-related head injuries. It makes sobering reading – of course we'll never truly know if these and other European and US cases are linked to prolonged depression without the benefit of talking to those involved.

Coming back to known facts we have the benefit of Ian Thorpe having spoken and written about his thoughts during episodic bouts of depression, which included thinking about suicide. Here is what he said in a BBC interview:

> When you actually go through working out what the [suicide] process would be like … When you start to consider it as being solution to the way you are feeling you realise that this is a problem, that this is not just a fleeting thought, this is how you feel at the moment and this is a very clear guideline that you do need more help – you are not in control of your life and the irrational thought [of suicide being a solution] has taken over at this stage.[9]

What we can take from this and other parts of the interview is that the loss of control was the greatest signal to Thorpe that he was in severe difficulty. It is particularly debilitating to realise that you have no autonomy. One of the big questions that opened up debate about depression at the turn of the century is whether it is the nature of certain sports, or sport in general that makes athletes vulnerable.

Do some elite sports carry increased risks?

In 2001, David Frith published a seminal book, *Silence of the Heart*, which started the public conversation on depression in sport. The headline was that analysis of the characteristics of cricket – the focus of his book – suggested that mental health problems and, in particular, the rate of suicide among British ex-cricketers is higher than the rate of suicides of all British men (1.07 per cent of all male deaths), although there has been some criticism of the statistics he used.

I wonder if Marcus Trescothick, who made his international debut for England in cricket the year before the book was published, read it? Maybe, but for a long time he kept his secret pain hidden:

> Nobody knew … [he] never told anyone about the pain [he] was going through because [he] didn't understand it [himself]. It made no sense to [him] that [he] felt so bad. How could [he] explain something [he] couldn't understand?[10]

Overseas tours and the typical sport culture of 'toughing things out' were the worst aspects. On a 2005 tour of Pakistan, when captaining the national team, his father-in-law was taken seriously ill. His wife begged him to return home, but he put his team first. '[He] was congratulated on [his] decision … but inside [he] was dying a long, slow death.'[11] Eventually the story came out in his much admired autobiography.

Zack Greinke, the LA Dodgers pitcher who recently signed a $147 million deal, has also talked openly about experiencing depressive episodes in his early 20s. He is frequently asked questions on the topic, since he is one of the few baseball players who have openly admitted they had a problem. What is it about innings-based sports like cricket and baseball (which also anecdotally has a higher suicide rate than the US male average) that could lead to increased risk of depression?

I'll lay out Frith's and others' analysis and leave you to decide if you think it adds up. The argument goes something like this. These sports may trigger depression for the following reasons:

- Individual contribution: personal failure is statistically tangible. When you bat, you are given a score. Your team may win, but self-doubt can gnaw away if you don't contribute many runs. You may not even be partly responsible for a victory. This is more likely to happen in innings sports than any other team sport.
- Time scales: the time lag between failing in one innings and the opportunity to make amends in another; doubt and introspection can fester in these interludes.
- Intense schedule: no sport is 'on the road' for such extended periods; not only do cricket/baseball games take a long time but games are virtually back-to-back with a day between. It is an all-consuming schedule. When travelling, brooding athletes can be alone without home support for extended periods.
- Statistical nature: the game's statistical comparisons may attract the analytically inclined and perfectionists who will rarely be satisfied.

If you are thinking 'yes, but ...' you are doing what I hoped you would do. While it is quite a neat argument, it is very difficult to prove one way or the other, although I can see how all-consuming the game must be compared to the one or two afternoon fixtures a week in other professional team sports. Rather than dwell too much on the mental challenges of different sports it might be more useful for us to consider how athletes cope.

Coping with paths to purgatory

Now that more athletes are talking about their experiences it is fascinating to hear how many have devised different ways of coping with depression in successful careers. It reveals interesting things about the experience of depression and the contributing factors. It sounds amazing, but one of the most common coping strategies for depression is to keep on with daily routines – in sport, training and playing. One explanation might be that as we become anxious we habitually tend to seek familiarity, even if familiarity is not necessarily helpful.

Boxer Sugar Ray Leonard, Ian Thorpe and Jonny Wilkinson have each used similar metaphors of sport as a 'safe haven', 'safety blanket' or 'cloak'; they felt at their best when they were playing. Wilkinson faced his worst demons when injury meant he wasn't able to play for two years and Thorpe gave up the sport largely due to media intrusion but then came back to it. After Wilkinson's purgatory towards the end of his injury, he made a successful return and found himself sitting in the changing room afterwards not wanting the security of playing again to be lost:

> Playing rugby makes [him] feel better about [him]self; it gives [him] back a bit of self worth. And sitting there in [his] kit [while everyone else changes] extends the feeling. [He] knows that changing means having to face up to what [he] knows is waiting for [him]. It's like taking off the *cloak* of invincibility and going back to reality.[12]

But one of the very best descriptions of prolonged coping by keeping going comes from an oarsman who won Olympic gold in Los Angeles (1984) with Steve Redgrave. Martin Cross brilliantly evokes his long-term career dilemma. I asked him to tell me his story.

Martin Cross will sacrifice anything to carry on rowing

Part of my overwhelming stress during the 1990s came from realising I was coming to the end of my rowing career. By the Barcelona Olympics in 1992, I was trying to hold my place in the team against new young rowers. Now it seems obvious looking back: I should have retired. Back then, I was willing to sacrifice anything to carry on.

From the age of 13, success in rowing had seemed to give me everything: recognition, a great lifestyle, new friends. The crux of my identity came from being an international rower, and I didn't know how to change that. Getting up to push myself through the pain barrier before dawn felt like a privilege and in the 1980s, my day job, as a history teacher, felt more like a hobby. But from the early 1990s, the sport's demands changed, with increasing training loads from 12 to sometimes 16 sessions a week and more time away on overseas training camps.

I knew, deep down, I should call it a day. But doing my sport at almost any cost had become an obsession – that was the reason I had been so good at it. So rather than stop, I tried everything to stay competitive by fitting in more sessions.

It was an unsustainable lifestyle trying to balance it all. In 1997, I began to feel tired and drained, with a permanent sore throat. I convinced myself I had a serious illness. Of course, I didn't. Trying to juggle my sporting career with everything else in my life was almost impossible. I had multiple roles: a husband and father, a full-time teaching job and loads of extra responsibilities.

I thought I could keep all those plates spinning. But as the stress in my life mounted, I began to drop them, which created more stress. Over the next few years this led inexorably to a breakdown. It was an extremely painful life lesson. These days, I make sure I row just for fun.

Cross's story of staying in the sport too long while life and sporting pressures mounted to a peak, eventually leading to crippling depression points to the dilemma of keeping going or retiring. Stopping sport is a very, very difficult time for athletes (see chapter 23).

You'll also notice that Cross mentions obsessional training behaviour. His perfectionism and obsessive personality traits are viewed by many to be attributes that don't just come and go but are fixed. If you have that trait it lingers throughout your life, and if circumstances and the environment are unfavorable, as in Cross's case, it can lead to depressive episodes. We'll look at the vulnerability factors for champions in a moment but champions such as Martin Cross, Jonny Wilkinson and others with perfectionist traits certainly appear to be at risk of depression.

Another coping strategy people in all walks of life often turn to in order to dull their depressive thoughts and emotions is alcohol and substance abuse. Ian Thorpe tells of how he experimented with drinking for a while, often training through hangovers, before realising it didn't help. In professional team sport substance abuse was widespread enough to prompt the establishment of specialised sport clinics, such as Sporting Chance in the UK, to help those with mental and substance related problems.

What circumstances combine as triggers for athletes?

Beyond keeping going at sport despite diminishing ability, perfectionism and substance use, a paper in the *British Journal of Psychiatry*[13] suggests another trigger for depression in elite sport. It claims the very organisation of elite sport in itself is part of the problem because it leads to disempowerment and a loss of personal autonomy for young developing athletes. Independently, the chief executive of the Sporting Chance Clinic has said the same with reference to professional footballers:

> ... the players need to be looked after in all aspects, instead of just pampered with people carrying their bags or hotel rooms being booked and all of that, but they need to be ... if you like matured. You get a young man who at the age of 12 is told he's brilliant, what happens is he becomes the special boy in the school, the special boy in the club and then the larger local club and then a club will pick him up – he doesn't get a chance to emotionally evolve if you like ... and then bam, he's 16 and he's taken on by an academy, and in some cases at 17–18 he's playing for country and playing for a club earning vast amounts of money. Nowhere in between there or later on has he got a chance to grow emotionally.[14]

This is just storing up problems for later when their *athletic identity* is compromised. It is one thing learning how to succeed in a pressurised performance environment but quite another to learn how to lead a happy and contented life. Coaches and psychologists working with elite athletes tend to work more on the former than the latter. Threats to *athletic identity* throughout a champion's path are one of many factors that may trigger depression in sport. When a mature athlete like

Martin Cross says his whole identity came from being an international rower, and he didn't know how to change that, it points to a narrowly defined identity based around training performance, sporting relationships, public recognition and medals. This is a signal of potential trouble ahead as at some point a sportsperson's identity will need to change in order for them to move on.

All champions who talk about psychological disorders in their autobiographies have certain deeply engrained traits such as conscientiousness and introspection. Ian Thorpe goes as far to say that he thinks his depressive tendencies are part of his genetic disposition – 'it was something that I would have had to deal with whether I was a swimmer or not'.[15] It goes without saying that champions are exposed to extreme pressure and stress early in their lives, and sport may force them to cope with any dispositional traits sooner rather than later. The big question is what some of the main triggers to depression may be beyond those I have already identified. It is worth saying that often it is a combination of circumstantial triggers acting together that coalesce to prompt problematic episodes rather than one single 'cause'.

Athletic identity

As we've seen, top-level sport tends to encourage a strong athletic identity at the expense of other aspects of life. Various sportspeople have described instances of personal loss unsettling their athletic identity.

For example, injury and retirement are a form of loss that some even go as far to compare to grief. Retirement is potentially the greatest loss of identity and the risk of depression in sport increases in retirement.[16] A comprehensive 2013 survey of retired British sports professionals found that one in six (16 per cent) admitted to depression and feelings of despair in the first year of retirement with a larger proportion still (33 per cent) identifying as not feeling in control of their lives two years after they finished playing.[17]

Another example of loss occurs when relationships go sour and athletes start to see how their athletic lives may have compromised their identity as a caring partner, husband or wife. The selfishness of being an elite sport sportsman can gnaw away at you, just as Marcus Trescothick found following his wife's pleading calls for him to return home while on tour.

Ian Thorpe's lack of privacy because of media intrusion might be interpreted as a personal loss. Fame may be especially hard to handle if you are an introverted private person who is not comfortable in the limelight.

Individual patterns of behaviour

Developmental psychologists suggest that we are all a product of some hardwired behaviours deeply ingrained in early childhood, typically before the age of eight. For instance, how you interact with people in later life is partly thought to be shaped by the type of attachments you form to your primary carer as an infant. Primary caregivers who are available and responsive to an infant's needs allow the child to develop a sense of security. A child with a dependable caregiver benefits from a secure base from which the child can then explore the world. More uncertain, erratic or distant interactions with infants influence future relationship habits and dynamics.

Most people end up with fairly balanced building blocks from childhood on which their personality develops. But early disruptive patterns of behaviour can lead to future difficulties in adult life so, for instance, when psychologists are called to assist those with early signs of depression they often want to know about childhood influences. Whole books exist on this approach but here I'll just use one example of an athlete whose childhood influenced her progress to becoming a champion. One champion who has written so honestly about her past is cyclist Victoria Pendleton, who started to understand herself better with the help of a psychiatrist who probably saved her from early retirement.

Early signs of Pendleton's perfectionist tendencies or patterns were shown by a period of incessant handwashing as a teenager to try and stay germ free. A further pattern of behaviour was 'I had always feared letting down figures of authority,' Pendleton writes, 'my dad most of all'[18] who had been a cyclist himself and often set himself up as a target in the distance for his young daughter to chase in hard training. Later as a young adult in a specialised Swiss training camp she felt constantly diminished by disappointing the head coach, and as their relationship deteriorated the combination of hard training, her perception of making slow progress, dwelling on the negativity of being stuck on her own in Switzerland left her feeling like a failure – she started cutting herself with a penknife.[19] Her depressive episode had been spotted by others and the team psychiatrist, Steve Peters, turned up from England to help. Without him she says she would probably have given up the sport.

We said earlier that depression is often about people feeling they have no control over situations so he gave her options. Peters's professional experience meant he'd often seen people respond well to the invitation to take control of a situation. So he invited her to use her power and mental ability to retrain the way she thought about things to get out of the situation. He said, 'You are in control of this Vicky.'[20]

When people, take control again and understand how their childhood past might be shaping their present and learn to interpret where their emotions come from and what stimulates their anxieties, they are often able to gradually recover their self-worth. So everyone is different and trained professionals are able to identify behaviour patterns or ingrained habits that, combined with other circumstances or triggers, can lead to a disordered sense of self. One such trigger is injury.

Injury

Prolonged injury rehabilitation periods, and the resulting opportunities for introspection, increase vulnerability to depression, with an estimated 10–20 per cent of athletes requiring clinical help[21] (see also chapter 13). Jonny Wilkinson's two-year battle with injury prompted the perfectionist elements of his personality to be at their most destructive.

But Wilkinson also had another bear on his back – previous success, which always lurked in the background of his life. Kicking the winning points in the World Cup final in the dying minutes of extra time had elevated him to national hero status:

> The World Cup of 2003 was [his] moment of perfection, the realization of all [his] goals. Since then, [he has] been trying to cling on to who [he] was and what [he] had.[22]

Working away in rehabilitation rooms eroded his sense of self as a top rugby player, no matter how many times the medics advised him to be patient with his recovery.

One of the main stressors through injury is loss of affiliation or the social support system that is an important part of much athletic life: you have a separate schedule to the main team and you are often based in a different building, so injury may abruptly end feelings of belonging. For some, the loss of opportunities for self-esteem to be bolstered on the field or in the canteen or changing room is difficult to deal with in clinical surroundings and without colleagues.

Stigma

'Embarrassment' or 'shame' are words which crop up again and again in athletes' accounts of their dark times. The stigma attached to mental health issues is a key risk factor in the development of depression among athletes. Sporting cultures, particularly in teams, are such that admitting symptoms of depression or any other mental health condition would be perceived as a sign of weakness – think of Marcus Trescothick being congratulated for staying on tour despite family grief and personal pain.

If you are immersed in sporting culture, there is a tendency to avoid seeking help or talking about depression with others, often causing problems to become worse as isolation and loneliness take hold. Hopefully, now that depression is more openly talked about in sport, more athletes will feel able to be open about depression. Both Wilkinson and Thorpe first admitted their problems to sports colleagues and found professional help. Thorpe took medication, while Wilkinson talks about gaining more perspective on his life through exploring spirituality.

The impact of suicides of high-profile sportsmen in Europe and North America seems to have had an energising effect in encouraging individual athletes to come forward and confront their difficulties and sports organisations to consider how to better support athletes. Progress is starting to be made and national broadcasters, such as the BBC, are starting to make radio and TV programmes about mental health in sport. For example, Clarke Carlisle, the chairman of the Professional Footballers' Association, made a detailed documentary about his and colleagues' struggles with depression.

Three other potential factors

There is another factor that has been identified with depression and it too is a taboo subject in some sports: *sexual identity*. I'm no psychiatrist but the 'conflicted self' must be difficult to reconcile. Rugby player Gareth Thomas must have felt conflicted while being married and playing a very macho, physical sport. He was a champion athlete who also went on to captain the unique British Lions rugby team, which forms to tour overseas once every four years.

Married for five years and keeping his true sexual orientation under wraps was a torment for Thomas, who admitted to feeling alone and depressed and often standing 'on so many cliff edges' and thinking about ending it all.[23] Fortunately he had the courage to be one of the very first professional sportsmen to come out publicly as gay in 2009, having told his teammates three years previously. Statistically, he can't be the only gay person in professional sport. Certainly in terms of the sexual orientation and depression taboos his decisive action in talking about it has helped further break the mould.

Some accounts from North American sport[24] in the last decade suggest that *head injuries* in sport put athletes at risk of depression. An international medical consensus statement suggests caution, as with any head injury:

> Mental health issues (such as depression) have been reported as a consequence of all levels of traumatic brain injury including sports-related concussion. Neuroimaging studies using MRI suggest that a depressed mood following concussion may reflect an underlying pathophysiological abnormality consistent with a limbic-frontal model of depression.[25]

With the American Football League (NFL) recently agreeing a $765m settlement over head injuries with 4500 former professional players we can be sure that further research will continue in this area. But when a phenomena such as this has multifactorial causes it will always be difficult pinpoint any direct influence.

There is also some evidence[26] that biochemical changes related to *weight loss* in athletes may be linked to depression. Gymnastics, figure skating, running, combat sports, diving and swimming are among the sports where weight problems and eating disorders appear most frequently: often among female athletes. For example, the national-ranked distance runner Mary Wazeter, who thought being thin would make her run faster. She wrote about her experiences of disordered eating and depression in a book entitled *Dark Marathon*.[27] Wazeter tells of a life of extreme dieting and associated irrational thinking. We don't know what comes first, the biochemical imbalance in the brain that triggers athletes to lose weight or the behaviour associated with weight loss. The (US) National Institute of Mental Health says that nutritional deficiency may affect mood, as a variety of violent impulsive behaviours have also been linked with lower than normal levels of serotonin (this is supported by the study of brains of suicide victims).[28]

It may come as a surprise to hear that Michael Phelps has written movingly about his elder sister's battle with an eating disorder and injury, which probably prevented her from fulfilling her potential as an elite swimmer. I imagine it influenced his own motivation to achieve and realise his potential.

Final thoughts

Three main ideas stick out from this journey through the influences and debates surrounding depression in sport, these are *control*, *identity* and *isolation*.

When athletes feel that control over their lives has been lost, problems can emerge, particularly if they have a perfectionist streak. When perfectionist athletes lose control they lose the sense not only of being *in* control but also of being *able* to control, a double whammy, and this attacks their self-worth on two fronts.

The idea of a balanced personal identity, beyond one shaped solely around sport, is particularly useful in making sense of triggers to depression. An athletic identity disrupted through injury, retirement or other loss does not feel good – most elite athletes experience various shades of identity loss through and after their careers. Finally, all the accounts of depression in sport we've investigated relate to people feeling isolated, physically and/or emotionally from support networks. Sport is excellent at taking you away, forcing you to be socially competent in groups full of surface bravado, bonhomie and banter. But often all is not as it seems and fitting in can be a real struggle. To cope, many athletes employ 'impression management' to convey a happy-go-lucky athlete but often underneath they lack genuine friendships and peer understanding.

It seems that ideas around *control*, *identity* and *isolation* are useful starting points in beginning to understand depression and other mental health issues (see also chapters 11 and 23).

23 Looking back and redirecting the rocket
Retirement

Sugar Ray Leonard, the legendary American boxer, spoke to his friend Wayne Gretzky, the ice hockey star, about retirement. Leonard described:

> how you have that feeling of loss if you're not a boxer, not a hockey player ... Sometimes we don't listen to our bodies. The body says it's time, but within our hearts and minds we tell ourselves 'one more time'. It's always one more time![1]

His words suggest that champions don't realise quite how different their lives might be when they retire, and some spend their retirement longing for what they have lost. In the final chapter of their career, all champions face a period of uncertainty and reflection as they transition into a more normal life.

Similarly retrospective, in part, this final chapter looks back at what shapes champions' paths. But it also contrasts the extremes of different champions' retirement experiences – from teenage women's gymnasts to male professional boxers in their 30s and 40s.

Looking back

At the start I said that we'd explore hidden, complex and tough paths to the top that are punctuated by champions dealing with and learning from critical episodes. So what are some of the main lessons we've learnt about career obstacles and the complex interaction between physical, environmental and mental factors?

In writing this book, my own beliefs about champions' development have certainly changed. I originally thought there would be some clear patterns, but individual paths to the top are actually very different and there are numerous factors that contribute to a champion's success. However, there is one constant feature: psychology and mindset.

Mental aspects

Athletes reaching a world or Olympic final (i.e. the top eight on the planet) in a team or individual sport discipline are genetically well-suited in their physiology and anthropometric aspects to their event, have undergone intense, long-term training, avoided major injury and have often benefited from good medical, scientific and coaching input. But in this book we have emphasised that it is champions' attitudes, emotions and desires – their mental toolbox – that enables them to successfully realise their potential. Without this they cannot be considered complete.

Let's focus on that word 'desire'. A champion's drive – their rocket fuel – lies at the heart of a developing champion, keeping them going despite obstacles or plateaux in performance. Sustained determination underpins their highly finessed skills, world-class fitness and championship mental craft to achieve gold. An inner drive to succeed, combined with the right physical attributes, the appropriate opportunities and injury-free, high quality training for sustained periods leads towards the podium.

The deep-seated will to succeed varies between individuals but we've seen that some of the possible ingredients are these:

▧ A spark: something (i.e. a sporting experience or watching others) and/or someone (i.e. a teacher, parent, sibling or coach), often in childhood, that ignites an athlete's initial passion;

▧ an inner satisfaction: a growing athletic identity and/or the resolution of inner needs from sporting progress and prowess will help build self-confidence;

▧ once international success begins, champions exhibit a longing to fulfil their potential and, for some serial champions, a will to leave a record of which they can be proud – in a sense, constructing their own fitting career narrative.

For some athletes, the motivation (or 'rocket fuel') might be self-determined, but we've seen in this book that, like all fuels, there are also potent additives or circumstances that might complement the mix and add further 'zip'. We've discussed four in this book:

▧ The personality traits of persistence and conscientiousness are arguably evident in most champions. These are crucial when it comes to sticking at the demanding regime that is required over many years.

▧ Varying degrees of perfectionism that can help, but may also hinder, champions' development (see chapter 11).

▧ Early motivational energy may be provided by childhood adversity that challenges self-worth. In such cases sports training provides a safe place for enhancing self-worth and partly stimulates a desire to achieve.

▧ Setbacks: a redemptive element for previous competitive losses or embarrassments.

It is all very well articulating a list, as above, but getting deep inside champions' heads to uncover some of these complex inner drives is an ongoing challenge for coaches, athletes, authors and researchers. There is a considerable scope in the future to further unravel the puzzle of an insatiable inner drive – this may surface as more champions following different paths describe their experiences in detailed research or in a candid autobiography during retirement.

But there are also the other aspects of the mental toolbox – the multiple elements described in chapter 14 and beyond[2] (coping with pressure and anxiety, confidence, distraction control, effective goal setting, visualisation, self-control and performance evaluation). These largely develop where an athlete has the right learning orientation to negotiate and benefit from the critical episodes they face. Champions make their varied experiences count, so that in times of need they are able to draw on previous episodes or circumstances they have faced.

A key aspect of a champion's mental toolbox is the ability to understand precisely, and with clarity, what it takes to succeed and to independently take responsibility for preparation and performance. Taking responsibility is often stimulated by defeat (e.g. Usain Bolt and the Olympic hockey squads detailed in chapter 15) or a duel with another champion as we saw with Bradley Wiggins and Ben Ainslie. For some champions the vision of what it takes to succeed stemmed from a sudden realisation of the full purpose of specialised gym and conditioning sessions, which beforehand they had skimped on. The other benefits of world-class conditioning, beyond the obvious, are protection against injury and the ability to move in the most efficient way when under intense pressure (e.g. Michael Johnson, Usain Bolt and Alistair Brownlee). For other champions we saw that learning how to stay injury-free was the turning point (e.g. Kelly Holmes) or that rehabilitation from injury was a catalyst for change and renewed fresh focus (e.g. Jessica Ennis).

Another key finding was that, among the often insular world of elite sport squads, there is potential for champions to become perhaps too introspective. Champions need a means of escaping the echo chamber[3] of their sport or squad to help gain a sense of perspective. Friends and parents may provide opportunities for switching off, while family life with young children certainly acts as a grounding influence. As Chrissie Wellington said, it is partly about discovering an identity beyond athletic performances that helps keep a balance in a sportsperson's unusual life.

A curiosity and fascination with the process

Continuing the mental theme I want to focus on one attitude in particular: the idea of embracing and enjoying learning which in the early part of this book I termed a learning orientation. As I have completed this book I can now add more explanation and examples. As six times Olympic gold medalist Chris Hoy said – 'one of the things you can do as an athlete is to constantly ask questions: it is a healthy curiosity and a constant quest for answers that produces a lot of the drive'.[4] Then, in 2014, Peter Keen who lead the transformation of British Cycling outlined his thoughts about champions, including Chris Hoy, who was a leading member of his squad. Keen describes champions needing to have 'a fascination with the process'[5] Notice neither Hoy or Keen use the word 'obsession' (see chapter 11), which perhaps has more negative connotations while curiosity and fascination describe a deep excited engagement with, not winning per se, but the *process* of *how* you become the best in the world and then deliver on the day under pressure. They get deep satisfaction of the forensic examination of what it takes and the subsequent preparation. Perhaps it is partly a personality trait. For example, not only does Chris Hoy have a degree in applied sports science but he shows similar fascination and curiosity for another love – making coffee – he is a trained barista and often travels with his coffee machine. The big question is how this special type of learning interest might be encouraged by coaches and families or whether it can be spotted and nurtured with the right training environment.

The timing of elite training and specialisation

In the early part of this book we explored the challenges inherent in accurately predicting future sporting potential via childhood selection. Sports organisations with finite resources understandably want to focus their efforts by attempting to identify talent for elite training and specialisation. We've seen that identifying young talent becomes more efficient with age, particularly after maturation when growth and change are over. The implications are that ideally champions are developed – trained, coached and exposed to appropriate competitive opportunities – to achieve their potential for as long as possible, without prematurely being assigned labels (e.g. 'you're too small/big to succeed at the top') that attempt to predict their ability as adults.

Most sports currently use selection for elite training before maturation. There are a very small number of sports in which international success can be achieved before maturity, principally female gymnastics and diving. These sports often select at a very tender age indeed (i.e. under eight) and, for some observers, this helps perpetuate the myth that early selection is standard and part of normal practice.

Sports organisations, coaches and parents need to strike a balance then – to encourage both 'early engagement *and* late specialisation in the sport'.[6] Numerous examples in this book call for young athletes to sample and acquire valuable skills from a wide range of playful activities and sports, combined with focused advice from coaches in those sports they are most passionate about. In highly professionalised sports such as football, tennis and golf, early specialisation is sadly becoming normalised. Starting early elite training can indeed lead to early success – despite the research evidence and two sports medicine organisations issuing position statements about the risk this represents for sustained careers.[7]

Social and family hinterlands

Each champion brings their own past and social influences (e.g. parents, resources, where they grew up and inspiring figures – I call this the 'social hinterland') with them as they climb towards the podium, and this is why it is often such an emotional and poignant moment when the medal is placed around their neck for the first time. Consider judokas Kayla Harrison's and Gemma Gibbons's (from chapter 1) thoughts as they stood there on the podium of the London 2012 Olympics. For both Kayla and Gemma their mothers must surely have featured in their minds as they climbed the podium steps and watched their national flags raised in their honour. All champions talk of early successful experiences in sport sparked by an encouraging early environment or person.

Once their passion is sparked, a champion's social hinterland then largely determines what opportunities are available to them in the sports in which they show promise. As champions approach retirement it is perhaps easier for them to appreciate the good fortune they experienced along the way – not only individuals that helped them but also where they lived and the local club that allowed an early environment in which to thrive. Whenever you hear an emerging sporting champion interviewed or profiled now, carefully tune in to where they grew up; you'll hopefully have become sensitised to the small-town 'big fish small pond' phenomenon we considered in chapter 9.

The starkest illustration of an influential personal hinterland recently has been Mo Farah who moved to London in his childhood revealing his separation from his identical twin who stayed, and still lives, in Somalia. The same genes but a different social, cultural and family hinterland led to two completely different paths. Ultimately, it was Mo's determination and long-term drive that saw him eventually convert his promise and opportunities into world and Olympic success. We've returned to the mental side again – what else would stimulate him to relocate to Kenya, for long periods of training, and eventually to the USA to pursue his podium dream?

The four podium themes (mental aspects, fascination with the process, age of specialisation and hinterlands) can only really be understood in the wider context of their connection to all the other factors we have discussed in this book.

The retirement experiences of champions are equally diverse. Let's apply these themes to world champion boxer, Joe Calzaghe, and look at how he contemplated his retirement.

Joe Calzaghe: Looking back

Unusually, Calzaghe was trained by his father; they lived in the small town of Newbridge (population 6000) in Wales. For over a decade and 21 fights he held the WBO Super Middleweight title: a remarkable record. His story is particularly interesting in how he kept on striving to construct a fitting legacy – a record of which he could be proud. He ticked off ever more demanding and ambitious goals and eventually he fought at the Welsh national stadium in Cardiff, unifying all the different world championship belts (or 'brands'), at the age of 35. But he found one more ultimate goal: a fight in the States:

> ... the thing is with the Americans, they don't recognise you as the best unless you go out there and beat one of them.
> So I went out there and fought against Bernard Hopkins ... And I just had this dream and this wish to finish off my career at Madison Square Garden. So I decided probably twelve months before the [final] Roy Jones fight, this was it.[8]

He won and stuck to his word of stopping at the age of 36 having achieved all his ambitions. Here then is an example of a distinctive family and small town hinterland, a genetic predisposition with the right mix of slow and fast-twitch muscle fibres and a physiology that responded to training. But what of the inner drive that helped him learn his craft in the gym?

In retirement he became the figurehead for a national anti-bullying campaign, admitting that he had suffered at the hands of peers as a scrawny 13-year-old. He admitted to becoming an 'introverted wreck' because of bullies – an early humiliating episode which acted as a catalyst – and took refuge by immersing himself in boxing. He has described his two personalities during that period: the introvert at school and the extrovert at the boxing club. His specialisation in boxing was relatively early and 12 years after his bullying episodes he won his first world title. You don't keep plugging away at the same activity for 23 years without a deep hunger to succeed and taking satisfaction from the process, and perhaps he was also pursuing his financial future. It was an increasingly well-paid job.

In Calzaghe's retirement process we get a glimpse of a deliberate, planned episode. Post-boxing he has sampled boxing promoting, TV appearances, some acting training and charity work for the anti-bullying organisation. Let's see how his retirement compares to others.

The latest research on sporting retirement

An echo that has resonated throughout the book is the extent to which champions experience and personally attribute some phenomena (e.g. anxiety, pain, challenges) differently to other athletes and the general population as a whole. Our final question then is: how do champions' sporting retirements differ to the traditional working life retirement that most of us face in our 60s?

The common narrative of athletes' sense of loss and struggling in retirement hinted at by Sugar Ray Leonard's words at the top of this chapter is not entirely accurate. Shortly before completing this book a unique piece of major research about the well-being of retired professional sportsmen was announced. It reveals, combined with other data, that whenever you retire, either from sport or work, roughly one in three people face difficulties (see the box overleaf).

So retirement is never easy, but it can be particularly harsh for some athletes due to timing. Retirement from sport at the top level is distinct from that of almost every other profession since it occurs 30–45 years earlier and is a transition into adult life and often their first job role; a transition from a very public life to a more private one.[9] To explore sporting retirements we start by looking at teenage female gymnasts.

After Shawn Johnson won Olympic gold in Beijing on the balance beam, aged 16, she was catapulted into the limelight of American celebrity, appearing on numerous chat shows and winning 'Dancing with the Stars'. Her attempt to come back from celebrity life to defend her Olympic title in 2012 ended when a serious knee injury prevented full training: she retired at the tender age of 20. Notice once again the necessity of avoiding serious injury in order to become a multiple champion.

During the retirement process, Johnson reflected that she felt unfortunate at having participated in a sport where it was ingrained that athletes had to be

---

The latest research on sporting retirement[10]

When 1200 retired professional cricketers, footballers, rugby players and jockeys were surveyed in the UK, ranging in age from 22 to 95, the results were eagerly anticipated, since it was the largest survey of its kind. These were mostly professional career team sport athletes rather than serial world or Olympic champions.

Happily, most retired professional sportspeople are living relatively contented, normal lives, with 79 per cent satisfied with their lives as a whole, slightly higher than the figure (76 per cent) for the population in general. Contrary to popular myth, 90 per cent need to work after retirement from sport, and most are in 'normal' jobs, earning a wage above the national average of between £30,000–£40,000.

However, *a third* of those surveyed identified not feeling in control of their lives two years after they finished playing with one in six (16 per cent) admitting to depression and feelings of despair in the first year.

But those retiring from traditional working life also face the same difficult transition. In Canada, an identical proportion face 'short term difficulties adjusting' with some 10–15 per cent of seniors suffering from depressive symptoms.[11]

In Britain the warning for those approaching traditional retirement is even more stark – the likelihood of being in very good or excellent health decreases by 40 per cent and the likelihood of suffering from clinical depression increases by 40 per cent.[12]

---

perfect, and that perfectionism, like an addictive drug, is hard to get rid of. When she stopped her sport she returned to a sort of normalcy and admitted to 'still trying to break that [perfectionist] mentality'. Body image and food can be prominent in an elite gymnast's life and it took a while for her to work out an appropriate diet when she stopped training. She admitted to slight difficulties in finding a healthy balance mentally and physically in her new life 'since the elite mentality was so embedded'.[13]

Breaking out of the mentality she'd lived with for over a decade and realising she no longer had to be perfect, Johnson showed how she had the self-awareness, skills and mental tools to support her transition to a more normal life. Not all athletes demonstrate such subtle awareness – qualities such as circumspection, temperance, compromise, self-reflection and equanimity.[14]

It's worth considering whether the millions of dollars earned from sponsorships and endorsements, as with Joe Calzaghe, help or hinder their transition to retirement. We'll come back to this.

Sticking with gymnasts, interviews with seven young British international gymnasts (admittedly *not* serial champions), with an average retirement age of 18, reveals some strong reactions to post-gymnastics life.[15] Six of the seven gymnasts' disengagement from gymnastics was profoundly traumatic: they viewed it as being 'a nightmare' and described feeling 'empty' and 'hopeless' and comparing retirement to 'the loss of a close friend'. Here is more:

> ... gymnastics gives you a security ... a gymnast is who you are, and when you leave you're not a gymnast anymore. I guess I still haven't found what that other bit of me is.

> ... suddenly adjusting to having to run your own life by yourself ... that's a major challenge ... because you really haven't been running your own life for all the years you've been involved in gymnastics.

Top young athletes like these are mostly ill prepared for the exit from their sport, even though they know it is coming. One of the biggest aspects is loss of athletic identity – this is particularly acute with teenagers. The International Olympic Committee (IOC) realises all retiring Olympians face similar challenges. They have a fact sheet entitled 'Athletic identity and sport transition'.[16] It makes for interesting reading.

The IOC describes how every person has different identities. Some perceive themselves as colleagues or friends (the social self), others educational classmates (the academic self) while others view themselves as the younger sibling (the family self) and so on. For many Olympians, athletic identity is central, as they dedicate 100 per cent of their resources to the pursuit of their sporting goals. The risk is that an exclusive identification with an athletic role and goals makes athletes vulnerable when this identity is lost during prolonged injury or retirement. The IOC counsels Olympians to expand horizons and their competence at other activities; to nurture supportive relationships; and preparation to minimise the shock experienced from leaving top-level sport.

But retirement cannot always be planned. Injury accounts for 14–24 per cent of sporting retirements[17] (e.g. Shawn Johnson). Other examples of shock retirements are those resulting from deselection, financial problems and family crisis. Those who face the shock of being 'made redundant' from sport are almost twice as likely to face difficulties in the first two years of their retirement compared to those who had the benefit of retiring on their own terms.[18] As with life in general, a shock event is far harder to deal with.

One would expect a mature champion near the age of 40 to fare better when they stop their sport. Certainly, they've had more opportunity to develop other interests and a more balanced perspective. For instance, Steve Redgrave had five Olympics cycles to consider his final retirement, aged 38, and has gone on to raise considerable funds for charity and enjoy family life.

A smooth but eventful transition

I want to counter the oft-told doom and gloom of the sport retirement stories that tend to make the headlines and consider how a different narrative might apply to serial champions. The recent UK retirement research identified four key factors which determine how well athletes adapt to life after sport. We address each in turn.

1. *Satisfaction with their sporting career*: most serial champions will have had largely fulfilling careers. In research, those who reported dissatisfaction with their sporting career were twice as likely to have difficulties with health, addiction or financial problems than those who said they were satisfied.[19] Satisfaction and financial resources that allow choice and freedom probably help (for example, Shawn Johnson and Joe Calzaghe) unless there are compulsive aspects of a champion's personality that draw them back to their sport (e.g. see Sugar Ray Leonard's story opposite or the Diego Maradona / Paul Gascoigne personality type discussed in chapter 6).

2. *Preparation for the future while competing*: this is easier said than done as competing and training are so all consuming, perhaps even more so for the serial champions featured in this book. Champions who think about what they might do after sport are often deeply worried. Consider this anxious commentary from Victoria Pendleton some 10 months before her planned retirement after her home Olympic Games in London, 2012:

    > I am terrified, really terrified, about life after cycling because that is all I have done. Apart from a job over the Christmas holidays where I did some part-time work at my local pub and restaurant to earn some extra cash in between university, I haven't really had any jobs. It's quite daunting. What will I be good at? What do I want to do? I think I am going to take a year out and try everything. I am going to take up as many opportunities as I can with the people I have met along the way and just try a load of stuff.[20]

    She was deep in training at the time, so limited preparation was possible beyond keeping an open mind about the possibilities. (She, like other champions, tried *Strictly Come Dancing*, but it turns out that gymnasts like Shawn Johnson (USA) and Louis Smith (UK) have learnt how to move far better than top cyclists – who train in a static position. Both gymnasts dominated their dancing contests!)

3. *Retiring on their own terms, as opposed to being forced to retire*: serial champions have often been in their sport for a while and they know when their prowess and/or hunger is waning and often do retire on their own terms. Those in this situation tend to keep going for one last championship, often picking an event on home soil in front of their own supporters. Interpreting Victoria Pendleton's autobiography, it is likely that without the temptation of appearing at a home Olympics she may well have retired earlier. In contrast, we know how the shock of being 'made redundant' puts athletes at higher risk of difficulties.[21]

4. *The support athletes receive during the first two years of the transition period*: the importance of cultivating a family and sporting culture that reinforces the

benefits of asking for help is becoming more widely understood. Serial champions are likely to have forged strong support networks over long careers, and to have developed coping strategies and mental tools to have overcome the numerous obstacles they have faced. They are likely to be better placed, in terms of support and coping skills, than many other athletes.

It is interesting that the UK research was largely led by the Professional Cricketers Association – a sport whose all-consuming lifestyle has been subject to considerable scrutiny in recent years (see chapter 22) and which is working hard at cultivating a supportive culture in the game.

Knowing when to retire: Boxing

Professional boxing, despite a far older age profile compared to gymnastics, is also not easy to retire from, for different reasons. Boxing is full of comebacks and pledges of 'one last fight'. The contrast with gymnastics could not be stronger: male professional boxing is full of bravado, swagger and big paydays. Minute age-related decrements in speed, reactions, fitness and drive sometimes cause painful defeats, and it is perhaps this uncertainty of outcome that spectators are seeking. Is it the lure of money that makes boxing comebacks so common or is there more to it? Sugar Ray Leonard was clear in a BBC interview[22] that nothing could satisfy him outside the ring. 'There is nothing in life that can compare to becoming a world champion, having your hand raised in that moment of glory ...'

He described when he came back 'I felt safer in the ring. I could defeat those demons that possessed me outside the ring'. He talks of training for a comeback acting as 'a release' as immediately he was clean from cocaine, alcohol and depression, resulting in a serene sense of calm. This is why he became known for his multiple comebacks, four (depending on how you count them), finally stopping at the age of 40.

His reasons for returning to the sport reminded me of the 34-year-old British fighter and world champion Ricky Hatton who described similar motivations for returning in a memorable interview. A sweating and beaten Hatton, with a bloodied and swollen face said: 'I needed to find out if I still have it, and I haven't'. Three months later he elaborated:

> It was something that I very much needed to do ... The main thing about the whole [comeback] performance was about redeeming myself, because I felt like I let down a lot of people, with how I behaved in my personal life ... I [now] feel really content.[23]

From Leonard's sporadic retirement and Hatton's redemptive comeback, to Joe Calzaghe's planned final exit. But it is perhaps fitting that one of our final champions, George Foreman, had podium experiences spanning 26 years – the longest of all those we have looked at in this book.

Foreman became an Olympic heavyweight boxing champion, at the age of 19, at the Mexico City Games. He went on to become the heavyweight champion of the world as a professional. He then lost to Muhammad Ali in the momentous Rumble in the Jungle, in Zaire. He only lost one more fight in that first part of his career. But something happened that caused him to retire – he found religion.

Ten years later Foreman came back claiming that he needed to fund his charity:

> I'd put all of my effort into the George Foreman Youth Centre. I started helping kids go to college. And I'd run out of money. And I just couldn't let this place close. I had to find a way to keep the George Foreman Centre going. And I had to go to work. And I had one profession. It was boxing.[24]

Remarkably, in 1994, he regained the world title, 20 years after winning his first, at the age of 45. Foreman explains the role his wife took in encouraging him to retire three years later.

> We [boxers] don't know when to quit ... You just have to have someone in your life to tell you enough is enough. Most boxers can't find that person. There's always that one purse, and that one punch you think you can land ... My wife told me [to stop]. And I said, I can still do it. Don't you believe in me? She said, isn't that the way you want to leave the sport, believing that you can still do it. I said, yeah. She said leave it. And I left it [aged 48].

These boxing examples show the different sides of retirement.

The added purpose that champions gain in their later competitive years in philanthropic pursuits for a cherished charity or working directly to help others is often the focus of successful retirement adjustments – for example, Andre Agassi's renewed zeal for playing and subsequent retirement after he focused on his educational academy (see chapter 6).

Looking more generally at what serial champions do in their retirement to redirect their rocket has been illuminating. Charity and/or media work top the lists of most popular activities, followed by coaching roles or public service of some sort. The inner drive rocket that gets champions to the top can be redirected by creating new meaning in their lives. Meaning is often found through working in a profession that they are fortunate enough to have the transferable skills and education for, or in helping the next generation or in a new hobby.

Following his retirement, English shot-putter Geoff Capes (twice European champion and 'World's Strongest Man'), an ex-policeman, directed his passion towards keeping birds. Beware the former champion who takes up a hobby; they tend to do it with great gusto and attention to detail. Capes ended up with another world title with his yellow/green Recessive Pied budgies and became president of the Budgerigar Society.

Final thoughts

While writing I have often been asked 'what are the best autobiographies you've read?' Perhaps the most engaging was Andre Agassi's, which was enhanced by the style and tone of a Pulitzer Prize-winning author – there was a lot about his childhood, father, use of a long wig, divorce, his subsequent marriage to Steffi Graf and a journey to a number 1 world ranking, a fall to 141st and then back to first – lots of twists and turns.

There were also two stories that revealed a great deal about individual paths beyond sport; Seb Coe's description of his role in government and delivering the 2012 Olympics after athletics, and Chrissie Wellington's international development career and obsessions before Ironman. Finally, there were compelling parts of champions' stories, often a three to five year period, from close failure to standing at the top of their sport: Bradley Wiggins's rise to secure victory in the Tour de France (spanning two books) and Usain Bolt's evolution from a promising, gangly 15-year-old to emergence as a world-beater in Beijing were the most memorable.

One of the difficulties with biographical accounts and research is that peoples' recall of their childhood experiences is rather fuzzy or rosy: not surprising since it is often decades later. But two contributions from experts in this book stuck out for me – both about childhood. The first was about letting athletes make mistakes and learn for themselves, characterised by this advice from chapter 6:

> We [parents] can't just pass on all our skills and knowledge, we have to be able to stand back and let them [young athletes] experience it for themselves and then be there to pick up the pieces without even a hint of, 'I told you so'!

The second was about taking responsibility at a young age, which I took from the use of structured challenges in chapter 18. It suggested that young people can get dispirited very easily with only a modest amount of effort applied – they benefit most if they quickly learn how to negotiate challenges and the consequences of their actions.

Perhaps smoothing out career progress into straight line paths and providing lots of caring support might actually be doing young athletes a disservice as negative episodes in life and sport are all part of the learning process. The balance is in providing appropriate challenges for developing athletes without these experiences being harmful.[25] For coaches and parents, the balancing act is a difficult one.

In writing this book and perhaps by you reading it, we have started to make sense of the many influences and balances that contribute to shaping a champion. One outcome is clear: I will never ever read about a champion's podium backstory or listen to an in-depth interview again without starting to consider how it reverberates with one or more of the themes of this book. If you have developed your own tentative theories along the way then the book has done its job in provoking deeper thought on a complex but fascinating topic: the path of champions to the podium.

Notes

1 Behind the lines

1. www.bbc.co.uk/sport/0/olympics/19164072
2. olympics.time.com/2012/08/02/kayla-harrisons-winning-spirit-takes-first-u-s-gold-in-judo-speaks-out-on-sexual-abuse/
3. I took inspiration from this article for these words: www.bbc.co.uk/sport/0/olympics/19229223
4. Malcolm Gladwell, in his 2008 book *Outliers*, drew on Anders Ericsson's (1993) research of musical expertise and deliberate practice to come up with the figure of 10,000 hours – it has since been disputed by many. Later in the book I explore some of these critiques, including Ericsson's own rebuttal of this oversimplification of his original research. Gladwell, M., *Outliers* (Penguin, 2008).
5. *Moneyball* is the book and film account of how talent scouts' opinions were supplemented with statistical analysis to underpin the buying and selling decisions of professional baseball players by the Oakland Athletics team. They subsequently outperformed their limited spending budget.
6. Agassi, A., *Open: An Autobiography* (HarperCollins, 2010).
7. Holmes, K., with Blake, F.. *Black, White and Gold: My Autobiography* (Virgin Books, 2008).
8. Nick Townsend is the co-author of both these autobiographies.
9. At the time of writing Roger Federer looks to be coming to the end of his career.
10. Taken from the following research article: Van Yperen, N., 'Why some make it and others do not: Identifying psychological factors that predict career success in professional adult soccer', *Sport Psychologist*, 23:3 (2009), pp. 317–29.
11. Collins, D., and MacNamara, Á., 'The Rocky Road to the Top; Why Talent Needs Trauma', *Sports Medicine*, 42:11 (2012), pp. 907–14.
12. Simonton, D. K. 'Talent Development as a Multidimensional, Multiplicative, and Dynamic Process', *Current Directions in Psychological Science*, 10 (2001), pp. 39–43, p. 39.
13. Howe, M. J. A., Davidson, J. W., Sloboda, J. A., 'Innate Talents: Reality Or Myth?', *Behavioural and Brain Sciences*, 21 (1998), pp. 399–442.
14. Ericsson, K. A. (ed.), *The Road to Excellence: The Acquisition of Expert Performance in the Arts and Sciences, Sports, and Games* (Erlbaum, 1996).
15. Bolt, U., *Usain Bolt: Faster than Lightning: My Autobiography* (HarperCollins, 2013), p. 60.

2 How could I have got it so wrong?

1. Bailey, R., Toms, M., Collins, D., Ford, P., MacNamara, A., and Pearce, G., 'Models of Young Player Development in Sport', in Stafford, I. (ed.), *Coaching Children in Sport* (Routledge, 2010), pp. 38–56.
2. Wojciechowski, G., 'College Sports: Survival of the fittest', *ESPN Sports*, available from: sports.espn.go.com/espn/columns/story?columnist=wojciechowski_gene&page=wojciechowski-110918&sportCat=ncf, accessed 25 February 2013.

3. www.bbc.co.uk/sport/0/tennis/22902803
4. Mens' professional ranking are from www.atpworldtour.com/Rankings/Singles.aspx, womens' from www.wtatennis.com/singles-rankings
5. International Tennis Federation, *Selling the Tennis Idea*, 2009, presentation as part of the ITF Coaches Education Programme with national data, Miguel Crespo & Machar Reid, available from www.itftennis.com/media/113963/113963.pdf
6. International Rugby Board: www.irb.com/unions/index.html
7. www.rwcsevens.com/home/news/newsid=2065240.html#england+nz+rwc+sevens+seedings
8. 2007 www.ausport.gov.au/sportscoachmag/development_and_maturation2/where_id_the_talent
9. *Financial Times*, 27 October 1997.
10. Abbott, A. and Collins, D., 'A Theoretical and Empirical Analysis of a "State of the Art" Talent Identification Model', *High Ability Studies*, 13:2 (2002), pp. 157–78.
11. Ibid., pp. 172–3.
12. Vaeyens, R., Lenoir, M., Williams, A. M., and Philippaerts, R. M., 'Talent Identification and Development Programmes in Sport', *Sports Medicine*, 38:9 (2008), pp. 703–14.
13. Caioli, L., *Messi: The Inside Story of the Boy who Became a Legend* (Corinthian Books, 2010), p. 295.
14. Vaeyens, R., Güllich, A., Chelsea, R., Philippaerts, R. and Philippaerts, W., 'Talent Identification and Promotion Programmes of Olympic Athletes', *Journal of Sports Sciences*, 27:13 (2009), pp. 1367–80.
15. Barreiros, A., Côté, J., and Fonseca, A. M., 'From Early to Adult Sport Success: Analysing Athletes' Progression in National Squads', *European Journal of Sport Science* (forthcoming), pp. 1–5.
16. Ibid., and Vaeyens et al., 'Talent Identification', p. 1370.
17. Tucker, R., 'Long-Term Athlete Development Foundations and Challenges, *Science of Sport Website*, www.sportsscientists.com/2013/02/long-term-athlete-development.html?utm_source=feedburner&utm_medium=email&utm_campaign=Feed%3A+blogspot%2FcJKs+%28The+Science+of+Sport%29, accessed 13 February 2013.
18. This section is drawn from material I wrote in 2013 for an Open University module E313, 'Exploring Psychological Aspects of Athletic Development'.
19. Dweck, C.S., 'The Mindset of a Champion, Stanford University Home of Champions', Campus Perspectives, available from champions.stanford.edu/perspectives/the-mindset-of-a-champion/, accessed 8 January 2013.
20. Dweck, C. S., *Mindset* (Random House, 2006); Biddle, S. J. H., Wang, C. K. J., Chatzisarantis, N. L. D., Spray, C. M., 'Motivation for Physical Activity in Young People: Entity and Incremental Beliefs about Athletic Ability', *Journal of Sports Sciences*, 21 (2003), pp. 973–89; Ommundsen, Y., 'Implicit Theories of Ability and Self-regulation Strategies in Physical Education Classes', *Educational Psychology*, 23:2 (2003), pp. 141–57.
21. Mueller, C. M., and Dweck, C. S., 'Intelligence Praise can Undermine Motivation and Performance', *Journal of Personality and Social Psychology*, 75 (1998), pp. 33–52.

3 Champion DNA?

1. Norton, K., and Olds, T., 'Morphological Evolution of Athletes Over the 20th Century; Causes and Consequences', *Sports Medicine*, 31:11 (2001), p. 775.
2. Hollis, B., 'What Makes the Perfect Swimmer?', English Institute of Sport (EIS) report (2012).
3. Thorpe, I., with Wainwright, R., *This Is Me* (Simon & Schuster, 2012), p. 85.
4. Ibid., p. 198.
5. Ibid., p. 119.

6.   Tucker, R., and Collins, M., 'What Makes Champions? A Review of the Relative Contribution of Genes and Training to Sporting Success', *British Journal of Sports Medicine*, 46 (2012), pp. 555–61.
7.   Ibid.
8.   www.newscientist.com/article/dn6705-endurance-running-is-in-east-africans-genes.html
9.   Ibid.
10. Tsainos, G., Eleftheriou, K. I., Hawe, E., Woolrich, L., Watt, M., Watt, I., Peacock, A., Montgomery, H., Grant, S., 'Performance at Altitude and Angiotensin I-Converting Enzyme Genotype', *European Journal of Applied Physiology*, 93:5–6 (2005), pp. 630–3.
11. University College London, Institute of Sport, Exercise and Health Seminar: 'Optimising Performance: Success for our Athletes, Health for our Nation', 10 July 2012, available from: www.youtube.com/watch?v=0ZtkcYvhnVI
12. www.yvanc.com/abstract%20003.htm
13. 'Fitness Gene', *Competition Science Vision* magazine, October 1998, p. 1101.
14. The same professor has written and talked about his work here: Tucker, R., and Collins, M., 'Athletic Performance and Risk of Injury: Can Genes Explain All?', *Dialogues in Cardiovascular Medicine*, 17:1 (2012), pp. 31–9. See following note for the same author on a similar topic.
15. Collins, M., 'Professor Malcolm Collins on Genomics in Sports Medicine: A Role in Talent Identification or a Role in Sports Injury Prevention?', *British Journal of Sports Medicine* podcast, 15 February 2013.
16. Mark Hirst, Senior Lecturer in Human Genetics, The Open University.
17. www.abc.net.au/tv/life/stories/s2994579.htm
18. Moshe Szyf and Michael Meaney (2003).
19. 'My Perfect Weekend – Joanna Rowsell', *Daily Telegraph*, 2 March 2013, available from www.telegraph.co.uk/news/celebritynews/my-perfect-weekend/9900612/My-perfect-weekend-Joanna-Rowsell-Olympic-cyclist.html
20. www.telegraph.co.uk/sport/olympics/cycling/9095307/London-2012-Olympics-GB-cycling-champion-Joanna-Rowsell-reveals-how-alopecia-spurred-her-to-gold-success.html

4 How do champions' paths differ?

1.   Bolt, *Faster than Lightning*, p. 60.
2.   Ibid, p. 79.
3.   Ibid, p. 81.
4.   Ibid, p. 101.
5.   Ibid, p. 106.
6.   Ibid, p. 117.
7.   In tennis, winning a Grand Slam event. In team sport, becoming a consistent member of the senior international team.
8.   www.theguardian.com/sport/2012/may/23/london-olympics-2012-helen-glover-heather-stanning
9.   Ericsson, A., 'The Danger of Delegating Education to Journalists: Why the APS Observer Needs Peer Review When Summarizing New Scientific Developments' (2012), available from: www.psy.fsu.edu/faculty/ericsson/ericsson.hp.html
10. www.bbc.co.uk/blogs/paulfletcher/2011/02/football_league_fears_over_pla.html

5 From playground to podium: Playing then specialising

1.   McGeechan, I., *Lion Man: The Autobiography* (Simon and Schuster, 2010), pp. 19–20.
2.   I admit to an obvious adaption of the title of this sporting initiative: www.efds.co.uk/our_work_in_sport/playground_to_podium

3. Côté, J., Erickson, K., and Abernethy, B., 'Play and Practice during Childhood', in Côté, J., and Lidor, R. (eds), *Conditions of Children's Talent Development in Sport* (Fitness Information Technology, Inc, 2013), ch. 2, pp. 9–20, p. 10.
4. www.bbc.co.uk/iplayer/episode/p00p6rxf/Health_Check_The_Human_Race_Lifecycle_Of_An_Athlete/
5. Côté, Erickson, and Abernethy, 'Play and Practice'.
6. Johnson, M., *Gold Rush: What makes an Olympic Champion?* (HarperSport, 2010), p. 55.
7. Brewer, C., 'Physical and Movement Skill Development', in Stafford (ed.) *Coaching Children in Sport* (Routledge, 2011), ch. 10, p. 157.
8. Moore, L. L., Lombardi, D. A., White, M. J., Campbell, J. L., Oliveria, S. A. and Ellison, R. C. 'Influence of parents' physical activity levels on activity levels of young children', *Journal of. Pediatrics,* 118 (1991), pp. 215–219.
9. Güllich, A., and Emrich, E., 'Considering Long-Term Sustainability in the Development of World-Class Success', *European Journal of Sport Science* (2012) DOI: 10.1080/17461391. 2012.706320.
10. Johnson, *Gold Rush*, pp. 77–8.
11. www.inthewinningzone.com/wz/Magazine/Commonwealth-Youth-Games-Special/Chris-Hoy-s-No-1-Fan/363/
12. Bridge, M. W., and Toms, M. R., 'The Specialising or Sampling Debate: a Retrospective Analysis of Adolescent Sports Participation in the UK', *Journal of Sports Sciences* (2012), DOI: 10.1080/02640414.2012.721560.
13. www.nytimes.com/2006/12/17/nyregion/nyregionspecial2/17Rsports.html?pagewanted=all&_r=0
14. American College of Sports Medicine (Malina, R. M., 'Early Sport Specialization: Roots, Effectiveness, Risks', *Current Sports Medicine Reports,* 9(6) (2010), pp. 364–71) and American Orthopaedic Society for Sports Medicine (Jayanthi, N., Pinkham, C., Dugas, L., Patrick, B., and LaBella, C. 'Sports Specialization in Young Athletes Evidence-Based Recommendations', *Sports Health: A Multidisciplinary Approach*, 5(3) (2013), pp. 251–7).
15. Ankerson, R., *The Gold Mine Effect; Crack the Secrets of High Performance* (Icon Books, 2012).
16. Gogarty, P., and Williamson, I., *Winning at all Costs: Sporting Gods and their Demons* (JR Books, 2009).
17. Ibid., pp. 114–15.
18. Gulbin, J., Weissensteiner, J., Oldenziel, K., and Gagné, F., 'Patterns of Performance Development in Elite Athletes', *European Journal of Sport Science* (2013), pp. 1–10.
19. Mageau, G. A., and Vallerand, R. J., 'The Coach–Athlete Relationship: A Motivational Model', *Journal of Sports Science,* 21 (2013), pp. 883–904.
20. Deci, E. L., and Ryan, R. M., 'The "what" and "why" of Goal Pursuits: Human Needs and the Self-Determination of Behavior, *Psychological Enquiry*, 11 (2000), pp. 227–68.
21. Phelps, M., with Cazeneuve, B., *Beneath the Surface: My Story* (Sports Publishing, 2012), p. 55.
22. Phelps with Cazeneuve, *Beneath the Surface*, pp. 21–2.

6 Winning parents: Getting the balance right

1. Agassi, *Open*, p. 28.
2. Peters, S., *The Chimp Paradox: The Mind Management Programme for Confidence, Success and Happiness* (Vermilion, 2012), p. 80.
3. Ibid., pp. 80–1.
4. Peters, K., Dyslexia and learning specialist, personal communication with author (2013).
5. Winnicott, D. W., *The Maturational Process and the Facilitative Environment* (International Universities Press, 1965).
6. Gogarty and Williamson, *Winning at all Costs*.

7.   Fredricks, J. A., and Eccles, J. S., 'Parental Influences on Youth Involvement in Sports', in Weiss, M. (ed.), *Developmental Sport and Exercise Psychology: A Lifespan Perspective* (Information Technology, 2004).

8.   Redgrave, S., with Townsend, N., *A Golden Age* (BBC Books, 2000), p. 25.

9.   Collins, M. F., and Buller, J. R., 'Social Exclusion from High-Performance Sport: Are all Talented Young Sports People being given an Equal Opportunity of Reaching the Olympic Podium?', *Journal of Sport and Social Issues*, 27:4 (2013), pp. 420–42.

10.   Cited in Harwood, C., Douglas, J., and Minniti, A. 'Talent Development: The Role of the Family', in Murphy, S. (ed.), *The Oxford Handbook of Sport and Performance Psychology* (Oxford University Press, 2012), p. 482.

11.   Johnson, M., *Slaying the Dragon* (HarperCollins, 1996), pp. xv, 5–7.

12.   With thanks to Kate Peters for her input to this conclusion.

7 Are younger siblings more likely to become champions?

1.   Hemery, D., *Sporting Excellence: What Makes a Champion?* (Collins Willow, 1991) pp. 47–8.

2.   Phelps, M. with Cazeneuve B., (2012) *Beneath the Surface: My Story*, p. 72.

3.   Syed, M., *Bounce: How Champions are Made* (Fourth Estate, 2010).

4.   'Faster, Higher, Stronger … and Younger? Birth Order, Sibling Sport Participation, and Sport Expertise', *North American Society for the Psychology of Sport and Physical Activity Conference* (June 2012).

5.   Usain Bolt was also the only child of his mother but had half sisters and brothers.

6.   Hodge, K., Pierce, S., Taylor, M., Button, A., *Talent Development in the New Zealand Context* (University of Otago, 2012).

7.   Fraser-Thomas, J., Côté, J., and Deakin, J., 'Understanding Dropout and Prolonged Engagement in Adolescent Competitive Sport, *Psychology of Sport and Exercise*, 9:5 (2008), pp. 645–62.

8.   www.bbc.co.uk/news/uk-19175322

9.   Davis, N. W., and Meyer, B. B., 'When Sibling Becomes Competitor: A Qualitative Investigation of Same-Sex Sibling Competition in Elite Sport', *Journal of Applied Sport Psychology*, 20: 2 (2008), pp. 220–35.

10.   Ibid.

11.   MacNamara, A., Button, A., and Collins, D., 'The Role of Psychological Characteristics in Facilitating the Pathway to Elite Performance-Part 1: Identifying Mental Skills and Behaviors', *Sport Psychologist*, 24:1 (2010), p. 52.

12.   Carette, B., Anseel, F., and Van Yperen, N. W., 'Born to Learn or Born to Win? Birth Order Effects on Achievement Goals', *Journal of Research in Personality*, 45:5 (2011), pp. 500–3.

13.   Ibid.

14.   www.tes.co.uk/article.aspx?storycode=6090264

15.   A blend of three sources:
      ▪ www.huffingtonpost.co.uk/2011/08/06/interview-olympian-rebecc_n_920176.html
      ▪ www.telegraph.co.uk/sport/olympics/2540541/Rebecca-Adlingtons-swimming-gold-down-to-sibling-rivalry.html
      ▪ www.telegraph.co.uk/sport/olympics/9059514/Rebecca-Adlington-my-sisters-brush-with-death-inspires-me.html

16.   Klissouras, V., Casini, B., Di Salvo, V., Faina, M., Marini, C., Pigozzi, F., Pittaluga, M., Spataro, A., Taddei, F., Parisi, P., 'Genes and Olympic Performance: A Co-Twin Study', *International Journal Sports Medicine*, 22:4, 2001), pp. 250–5.

8 Selection myths and compromises revealed

1.   www.time.com/time/magazine/article/0,9171,836963,00.html#ixzz2NKm68lSw

2.   Overman, M., *Living out of Bounds: The Male Athlete's Everyday Life* (University of Nebraska Press 2010), p. 14.

3. www.optimumperformanceconsulting.co.uk/why-sport-psychology.html

4. Sharp, C., *Some Features of the Anatomy and Exercise Physiology of Children Related to Training* (Brunel University, undated) available from: www.coachr.org/ythtrng.htm

5. McKie, R., 'Puberty For Girls Is Now Starting Five Years Earlier Than It Did In 1920', *Guardian*, 23 October 2012.

6. Smitherman, L., Reiter, E. O., Hussey, S. A., Dowshen, R., Wasserman, J., R., Serwint, L. M., Herman-Giddens, E., Steffes, J., Harris, D., E., Slora, M., 'Secondary Sexual Characteristics in Boys: Data From the Pediatric Research in Office Settings Network', DOI: 10.1542/peds.2011–3291, *Pediatrics* (2012); 130;e1058; originally published online 20 October 2012.

7. Read more: www.smh.com.au/rugby-league/league-news/call-for-weight-limits-in-school-rugby-20130408-2hhdy.html#ixzz2fAlPMwDP and www.brisbanetimes.com.au/sport/union/rugby-codes-can-only-gain-from-junior-weight-restrictions-says-cornelsen-20090424-agx3.html#ixzz2fAkMCcxl

8. Seminar conversation at RFU Talent Symposium, The Royal Society, London, May 2013.

9. www.usatoday.com/story/sports/nfl/2013/02/03/polynesian-super-bowl/1882001/

10. Folley, M., *A Time to Jump: An Authorised Biography of an Olympic Champion*, (HarperCollins, 2001), p. 79.

11. Gladwell, *Outliers*.

12. Pankhurst, A., Presentation at RFU Talent Symposium, May 2013, Royal Society, London.

13. Berstein, D., 'I Doubt whether Lionel Messi would have Prospered in my Team', *The Times*, 2 April 2012.

14. Caioli, *Messi*, p. 46.

15. MacDonald, D. and Baker, J. 'Circumstantial Development: Birthdate and Birthplace Effects on Athlete Development', in Côté, J. and Lidor, R. (eds). *Conditions of Children's Talent Development in Sport*. (Fitness Information Technology, 2013), pp. 197–204.

16. Romaneiro, C., Folgado, H., Batalha, N., and Duarte, R., 'Relative Age Effect of Olympic Athletes in Beijing 2008', Department of Sport and Health, University of Évora, Portugal (2009). Available from: http://www.skillteam.se/wp-content/uploads/2012/01/f%C3%B6delsem%C3%A5n-os-beijing.pdf

17. Baker, J., and Logan, A. J., 'Developmental Contexts and Sporting success: Birth Date and Birthplace Effects in National Hockey League Draftees 2000–2005', *British Journal of Sports Medicine*, 41:8 (2007), pp. 515–7.

18. Each year, recruitment to professional teams in North America is determined by the draft, in which those players progressing to the professional level – typically after college years – are 'picked' by teams in a number of rounds. In a league of 30 teams, there are over 10 rounds of picks with each team selecting a player in turn resulting in a ranking list of 1st pick to 300th pick. It is like an annual soccer transfer system for new entrants, typically aged 18, but strictly controlled over one day with considerable research done by teams to try to identify who they want to pick in each round. Those considered the most attractive buys are picked early with less attractive players lower down each team's ranking list. Note that 45 per cent of those drafted end up not playing a major league game and are likely to be released from any contract – a similar proportion (39 per cent) exists in English professional soccer (those at UK Premier League academies who don't later play for the club's first team).

19. Deaner, R., Lowen, A., Cobley, S. 'Born at the Wrong Time: Selection Bias in the NHL Draft': www.plosone.org/article/info%Adoi%2F10.1371%2F/journal.pone.0057753.

20. Ibid.

21. Dhuey E., and Lipscomb S., 'What Makes a Leader? Relative Age and High School Leadership', *Economic Education Review*, 27 (2008), pp. 173–83, DOI: 10.1016/j.econedurev.2006.08.005. and also Thompson, A. H., Barnsley, R. H., Battle, J. (2004), 'The Relative Age Effect and the Development of Self-Esteem', *Eductional Research*, 46:313–320, DOI: 10.1080/0013188042000277368.

22. Sample selection policy:

    The aim of selection is to prepare athletes for international success at junior level (U15 and U19) and encourage developmental experiences that support transition to the senior programme.

    World Championships – the selection will be based on two criteria:

    ▪ One athlete will be selected who leads the result list by a clear margin of at least 1 point.

    ▪ The second athlete may be selected from the ranking list positions 2 to 4 who in the opinion of the selectors indicates future potential within the under-15 category (i.e. aged 13 yrs /11 months or under).

    Junior International – the selection will be based on three criteria:

    ▪ The top two aged 14 athletes from the result list positions 1 to 4 will be selected.

    ▪ The top two athletes aged 13 yrs, 11 months or under from the ranking list positions 1 to 6 will be selected.

    ▪ Further discretionary places may be awarded to those who in the opinion of the selectors indicate future development potential as a senior or within the under-15 category (i.e. aged 13 yrs, 11 months or under).

23. Mills, A., Butt, J., Maynard, I., and Harwood, C., 'Identifying Factors Perceived to Influence the Development of Elite Youth Football Academy Players', *Journal of Sports Sciences*, 30:15 (2012), 1593–1604, DOI: 10.1080/02640414.2012.710753.

24. Ibid., p. 1600.

25. 'All I Care About is W's and L's', in N. Silver (ed.), *The Signal and the Noise; the Art and Science of Prediction* (Allen Lane, 2012), pp. 74–107.

9 Location, location, location: Revealing the geography of success

1. Côté, J., Macdonald, D. J., Baker, J., and Abernethy, B., 'When "where" is more Important than "when": Birthplace and Birthdate Effects on the Achievement of Sporting Expertise', *Journal of Sports Sciences*, 24:10 (2006), pp. 1065–73.

2. Marsh, H. W., and Parker, J. W., 'Determinants of Student Self-Concept: Is it Better to be a Relatively Large Fish in a Small Pond Even if you Don't Learn to Swim as Well?', *Journal of Personality and Social Psychology*, 47:1 (1984), p. 213.

3. Côté, Macdonald, Baker and Abernethy, 'When "where" is more Important', p. 1071.

4. www.wired.com/wiredscience/2010/08/how-to-raise-a-superstar/

5. Murray, J., 'From Playing for Fun to World Beating Performances', UK Sport Talent Masterclass: High Performance Parenting (April 2012), Rugby School.

6. Laing, S., Lead Talent Scientist, UK Sport, personal communication, 11 April 2013.

7. Redgrave, *A Golden Age*, pp. 29 and 32.

8. www.monthehoops.co.uk/showthread.php?t=18653

9. Bale, J., and Sang, J., *Kenyan Running: Movement Culture, Geography and Global Change* (Routledge, 1996).

10. www.telegraph.co.uk/sport/othersports/cycling/tour-de-france/10144509/Tour-de-France-2013-the-incredible-rise-of-Chris-Froome-and-how-he-was-almost-killed-by-a-hippo.html

11. www.theguardian.com/sport/2013/jan/25/chris-froome-sky-tour-de-france

12. Bolt, *Faster than Lightning*, p. 16.

13. Ibid., pp. 31–2.

14. Ibid., p. 32.

10 Fitness and recovery epiphanies

1. Johnson, *Gold Rush*, p. 105.

2. Stauffer, R. *Roger Federer: Quest for Perfection* (New Chapter Press, 2006), p. 45.

3. Ibid., p. 137.
4. Ibid., p. 155.
5. Coe, S., *Running My Time: The Autobiography* (Hodder and Stoughton, 2012), p. 33.
6. Jarvis, M., *Strength and Conditioning for Triathlon: the Fourth Discipline* (Bloomsbury, 2013).
7. Bass, S., Pearce, G., Bradney, M., Hendrich, E,. Delmas, P. D., Harding, A., Seeman, E., 'Exercise before puberty may confer residual benefits in bone density in adulthood: studies in active prepubertal and retired female gymnasts', *Journal of Bone and Mineral Research*, 13:3 (1998), pp. 500–7.
8. Janz, K. F., Burns, T. L., Levy, S. M., Torner, J. C., Willing, M. C., Beck, T. J., Gilmore, J. M., Marshall, T. A., 'Everyday Activity Predicts Bone Geometry in Children: The Iowa Bone Development Study', *Medicine and Science in Sports and Exercise*, 36 (2004), pp. 1124–31.
9. running.competitor.com/2010/01/training/the-lactic-acid-myths_7938
10. Brooks, G. A., 'Cell–Cell and Intracellular Lactate Shuttles', *Journal of Physiology*, 587:23 (2009), pp. 5591–600.
11. Leeder, J., Gissane, C., van Someren, K., Gregson, W., and Howatson, G., 'Cold Water Immersion and Recovery from Strenuous Exercise: A Meta-Analysis', *British Journal of Sports Medicine*, 46:4 (2012), pp. 233–40.
12. Wellington, C., *A Life without Limits: A World Champion's Journey* (Constable, 2012).
13. steveingham.blogspot.co.uk/2012/06/top-10-applications-no-5-adapting.html
14. Jarvis, *Strength and Conditioning*.
15. Hoy, C., *Chris Hoy: The Autobiography* (HarperSport, 2009).
16. Wiggins, B., *My Time* (Yellow Jersey Press, 2012), p. 46.
17. Roberts, M., Case Study Presentation: UK Sport Talent Masterclass, Bisham Abbey, 25 January 2012.
18. M. Jarvis, personal communication with the author, 2013.
19. Brink, M. S., Visscher, C., Coutts, A. J. and Lemmink, K. A. P. M. 'Changes in Perceived Stress and Recovery in Overreached Young Elite Soccer Players', *Scandinavian Journal of Medicine & Science in Sports*, 22 (2012), pp. 285–92. DOI: 10.1111/j.1600-0838.2010.01237.x.
20. Sinnerton, S., and Reilly, T., 'Effects of Sleep Loss and Time of Day in Swimmers', *Biomechanics and Medicine in Swimming: Swimming Science IV*, in Maclaren, D., Reilly, T., and Lees, A. (E and F.N. Spon, 1992), pp. 399–405.
21. Weston, N., *Learning to Cope in Extreme Environments: Solo Endurance Ocean Sailing*, in Thatcher, J., Jones, M. and Lavallee, D. (eds), *Coping and Emotion in Sport* (Routledge, 2012), pp. 300–55.
22. Leeder, J., Glaister, M., Pizzoferro, K., Dawson, J., and Pedlar, C., 'Sleep Duration and Quality in Elite Athletes Measured using Wristwatch Actigraphy'. *Journal of Sports Science*, 30 (2012), pp. 541–5.

11 From passion to persistence, perfection and obsession: How does personality shape champions' paths?

1. UK Sport Talent Team, UK Sport (no date) Stage 5 of Talent Development, *Talent Master Class: characteristics, skills and talent presentation.*
2. Mageau, G. A., Vallerand, R. J., Charest, J., Salvy, S.-J., Lacaille, N., Bouffard, T., and Koestner, R., 'On the Development of Harmonious and Obsessive Passion: The Role of Autonomy Support, Activity Specialization, and Identification with the Activity', *Journal of Personality*, 77 (2009), pp. 601–46. DOI: 10.1111/j.1467-6494.2009.00559.x.
3. BBC 2, 'Olympic Spark: Fire Up Your Future' (2013), available from: www.bbc.co.uk/programmes/p016dhd7
4. Vallerand, R. J., 'From Motivation to Passion: In Search of the Motivational Processes Involved in a Meaningful Life', *Canadian Psychology/Psychologie canadienne*, 53:1 (2012), pp. 42, 47.
5. Kieron Sheehy, Senior Lecturer in Child Development, The Open University.
6. Vallerand, 'From Motivation to Passion', pp. 42, 47.

7. Wellington, C., *A Life Without Limits*, pp. 25–6.
8. These six characteristics have been abridged from Hall, H. K., Jowett, G, E. and Hill, A. P., 'Perfectionism: The Role of Personality in Shaping an Athlete's Sporting Experience', in Papaioannou, A., and Hackfort, D. (eds), *Routledge Companion to Sport and Exercise Psychology: Global Perspectives and Fundamental Concepts* (Routledge. 2014).
9. Adapted from original ideas presented ibid.
10. Hall, H. K., Hill, A. P. and Appleton, P. R., 'Perfectionism: A Foundation for Sporting Excellence or an Uneasy Pathway to Purgatory?', in Roberts, G. C., and Treasure, D. C. (eds), *Advances in Motivation in Sport and Exercise*, 3 (2012), pp. 129–68.
11. Wilkinson, J., *Jonny: My Autobiography* (Headline, 2011), p. 241.
12. Ibid., p. 102.
13. Hill, A. P., 'Perfectionism and Burnout in Junior Soccer Players: A Test of the 2 x 2 Model of Dispositional Perfectionism', *Journal of Sport and Exercise Psychology*, 35:1 (2013), pp. 18–29.
14. www.skysports.com/watch/video/7965424/sporting-chapters-martin-cross
15. Hall, Jowett and Hill, 'Perfectionism', p. 4.
16. Wellington, *A Life without Limits*, p. 41.
17. Hall, Jowett and Hill, 'Perfectionism', p. 11.
18. www.yorku.ca/yfile/archive/index.asp?Article=2893
19. Wilkinson, *Jonny*, p. 296.
20. www.open.edu/openlearn/body-mind/psychology/what-obsessive-compulsive-disorder-ocd
21. Adapted from an article by my Open University colleague, Dr Danial Nettle: www.open.edu/openlearn/body-mind/psychology/personality-user-guide.
22. Costa, P. T. and McCrae, R. R., *NEO PI-R Professional Manual* (Psychological Assessment Resources, 1992).
23. Stoeber, J., Otto, K., and Dalbert, C., 'Perfectionism and the Big Five: Conscientiousness Predicts Longitudinal Increases in Self-Oriented Perfectionism', *Personality and Individual Differences*, 47 (2009), pp. 363–8.
24. Duckworth, A., and Eskreis-Winkler, L., 'True Grit', *Observer* (April 2013), available from www.psychologicalscience.org/index.php/publications/observer/2013/april-13/true-grit.html
25. Duckworth, A. L., and Quinn, P. D., 'Development and Validation of the Short Grit Scale (GRIT–S)', *Journal of Personality Assessment*, 91:2 (2009), pp. 166–74.
26. Duckworth and Eskreis-Winkler, 'True Grit'.

12 How do critical episodes shape champions?

1. www.telegraph.co.uk/sport/tennis/wimbledon/2361351/The-making-of-a-champion.html
2. Ibid.
3. Stauffer, *Roger Federer*.
4. Hodge, K., Pierce, S., Taylor, M., Button, A., *Talent Development in the New Zealand Context* (University of Otago, 2012).
5. Davidson, M. (2011) *Fields of Courage: The Bravest Chapters in Sport* (Little Brown, 2011), p. 58.
6. Youth Sports Trust (2012) Performance Parent Resource: Ellie Simmonds case study.
7. Davidson, *Fields of Courage*, p. 57.
8. Caioli, *Messi*, p. 295.
9. web.archive.org/web/20061118073910/www.cbc.ca/greatest/top_ten/nominee/gretzky-wayne.html
10. MacNamara, Á., and Collins, D., 'The Role of Psychological Characteristics in managing the Transition to University, *Psychology of Sport and Exercise*, 11:5 (2010), pp. 353–62.
11. In this case the job title was 'Talent Development Manager'.

12. I have excluded 'academic transitions' since we want to focus mainly on the sporting issues – not all athletes attend university.
13. MacNamara and Collins, pp. 359–60.
14. Pendleton, V., with McRae, D. (2012) *Between the Lines: The Autobiography* (HarperSport, 2012) p. 63.
15. Ibid., p. 65.
16. Ibid., p. 72.
17. Ibid., p. 71.
18. Ibid., p. 72.
19. Ibid., p. 75.
20. Debois, N., Ledon, A., Argiolas, C., and Rosnet, E., 'A Lifespan Perspective on Transitions During a Top Sports Career: A Case of an Elite Female Fencer', *Psychology of Sport and Exercise*, 13:5 (2012), pp. 660–8.
21. Agassi, *Open*, p. 74.
22. A similar distinction is made by researchers investigating sporting career transitions.
23. Tamminen, K. A., Holt, N. L., and Neely, K. C., 'Exploring Adversity and the Potential for Growth Among Elite Female Athletes', *Psychology of Sport and Exercise*, 14 (2013), pp. 28–36.
24. Gogarty and Williamson, *Winning at all Costs*.
25. Armstong, L., *Every Second Counts*, Yellow Jersey Press (2003), p. 25.
26. Ainslie, B., *Close to the Wind, Ben Ainslie: Britain's Greatest Olympic Sailor* (Yellow Jersey Press, 2012), p. 28.
27. Van Yperen, 'Why some make it and others do not', p. 317.
28. Meacham, J., 'I Had to Learn to Fight', *Newsweek* (1 September 2008).

13 Broken bodies, broken minds?

1. Richardson, H., *Celebration Event for Olympic 2012 OU students*, Open University, 30 November 2012.
2. Natalie Walker co-author of Arvinen-Barrow, A., and Walker, N., *The Psychology of Sport Injury and Rehabilitation* (Routledge, 2013).
3. Martin Cross's book *Olympic Obsession: The Inside Story of Britain's Most Successful Sport* (Derby Publishing 2012) recounts this time. He had rowed with Steve in the 1984 gold medal crew.
4. In conversation with Natalie Walker.
5. Cross, *Olympic Obsession*, p. 302.
6. Redgrave, S., *A Golden Age*, p. 239.
7. Ibid., p. 187.
8. Ibid., p. 186.
9. From a BBC Radio 5 interview *Track and Field: US Super Coaches*, 18 December 2012.
10. Kyndt, T., and Rowell, S., *Achieving Excellence in High Performance Sport. The Experiences and Skills Behind the Medals* (Bloomsbury, 2012), p. 75.
11. Ibid., p. 80.
12. Interview with Alison Rose, *The Triathlon Coach*: www.thetriathloncoach.com/coaches/healthy-running-an-interview-with-olympic-physiotherapist-alison-rose/
13. Ibid.
14. Ennis, J., *Unbelievable: From My Childhood Dreams to Winning Olympic Gold* (Hodder and Stoughton, 2012), p. 100.
15. www.open.edu/openlearn/body-mind/health/sport-and-fitness/sport/olympic-dreams-when-the-going-gets-tough
16. Wellington, *A Life Without Limits*.
17. Arvinen-Barrow and Walker, *The Psychology of Sport Injury and Rehabilitation*, p. 23.
18. www.open.edu/openlearn/body-mind/health/sport-and-fitness/sport/olympic-dreams-when-the-going-gets-tough

14 What is in a champion's mental toolbox?

1. Gould, D., Dieffenbach, K., and Moffett, A., 'Psychological Characteristics and their Development in Olympic Champions', *Journal of Applied Sport Psychology*, 14:3 (2002), pp. 172–204.
2. MacNamara, Á., Button, A., and Collins, D., 'The Role of Psychological Characteristics in Facilitating the Pathway to Elite Performance, Part 2: Examining Environmental and Stage-Related Differences in Skills and Behaviours', *Sport Psychologist*, 24 (2010), pp. 74–96.
3. Ibid.
4. Ibid.
5. Phelps with Cazeneuve, *Beneath the Surface*, p. 152.
6. Ibid.
7. Sweetenham, B., 'Case Study: Strategies for Preparing International Winning Teams and Athletes, in Sotiriadou, P., and De Bosscher, V. (eds), *Managing High Performance Sport* (Routledge, 2013).
8. Johnson, *Gold Rush*, p. 112.
9. Cited in Moran, A., 'Concentration Attention and Performance', in Murphy, S. (ed.) *Oxford Handbook of Performance Psychology*, p. 128.
10. BBC programme 'The Making of Me', available from video.yandex.ru/users/undz/view/4/#
11. Ibid.
12. Gould et al., 'Psychological Characteristics', p. 199.
13. Hoy, C ., *Chris Hoy: The Autobiography* (Harper Sport, 2009), p. 164.
14. Ibid, p. 168.
15. Johnson, *Gold Rush*, p. 153.
16. Phelps with Cazeneuve, *Beneath the Surface*, p. 50.
17. MacNamara, Button and Collins, 'The Role of Psychological Characteristics in Facilitating the Pathway to Elite Performance'.
18. Ibid.
19. Johnson, *Gold Rush*, p. 65.
20. Wiggins, *My Time*, p. 43.
21. MacNamara, Button and Collins, 'The Role of Psychological Characteristics in Facilitating the Pathway to Elite Performance', Part 2.
22. Wellington, *A Life Without Limits*, p. 144.
23. Johnson, *Gold Rush*, p. 165.
24. Murphy, S., Jowdy, D., and Durtschi, S., 'Report on the US Olympic Committee Survey on Imagery use in Sport' (US Olympic Training Center, 1990).
25. Johnson, *Slaying the Dragon*.
26. Wiggins, B., *In Pursuit of Glory* (Orion, 2008), p. 177.
27. Collins, D. and Collins, L., 'Optimising your development environment: Optimising progress, exploiting/countering stress and developing personal resilience', Session 2 of Talent Developmnent Symposium, University of Central Lancashire, Preston, 14 April 2014.

15 Learning from defeat: Rhetoric or reality?

1. Coe, *Running My Time*, p. 152.
2. Reid, C., 'Losing to Win: A Clinical Perspective on the Experience of Loss among Elite Athletes', *Coping and Emotion in Sport* (Routledge, 2012), pp. 261–83.
3. Ibid.
4. Danson, A., Celebration event for Olympic 2012 Open University students, 30 November 2012.
5. Kyndt and Rowell, 'Case Study: Danny Kerry', pp. 198–207.
6. Ibid.
7. Wiggins, *In Pursuit of Glory*, p. 93.

8. Ainslie, *Close to the Wind*, p. 93.
9. Wiggins, *In Pursuit of Glory*, p. 82.
10. Ainslie, *Close to the Wind*, p. 56.
11. Ibid., p. 78.
12. Ibid., p. 109.
13. www.bbc.co.uk/sport/0/olympics/18893044
14. Ibid.

16 Confidence

1. Barnes, S., 'Rusedski Sinks from the Sublime to the Ridiculed', *The Times*, 1 July 1999.
2. Freeman, C., *Born to Run; My Story* (Penguin, 2007), p. 33.
3. Ibid., pp. 34–5.
4. Phelps with Cazeneuve, *Beneath the Surface*, p. 87.
5. Thorpe with Wainwright, *This is Me*.
6. BBC interview at the time of his retirement: downloads.bbc.co.uk/podcasts/5live/5lspeci als/5lspecials_20130323-1616a.mp3
7. Wiggins, *In Pursuit of Glory*.
8. Ibid., p. 259.
9. Wiggins, *My Time*, p. 124.
10. Ibid., pp. 274, 277.
11. Hays, K., Maynard, I., Thomas, O., and Bawden, M., 'Sources and Types of Confidence Identified by World Class Sport Performers', *Journal of Applied Sport Psychology*, 19:4 (2007), pp. 434–56.
12. Ibid.
13. Steve Peters talking on BBC *Hardtalk*: www.youtube.com/watch?v=X_NIgp8GGps
14. Folley, M., *A Time to Jump*, p. 284.
15. Woodman, T., Akehurst, S., Hardy, L., and Beattie, S., 'Self-Confidence and Performance: A Little Self-Doubt Helps', *Psychology of Sport and Exercise*, 11:6, (2010), 467–70.
16. From a BBC Radio 5 interview 'Track and Field: US Super Coaches', 18 December 2012.
17. Post-match on-court interview with BBC: www.bbc.co.uk/sport/0/olympics/19135381
18. McCullagh, P., Law, B. and Ste-Marie, D., 'Modelling and Performance', in Murphy (ed.) *The Oxford Handbook of Sport and Performance Psychology*, ch. 13.
19. Ibid.
20. Will Carling, quoted from Open University module 'Sport and Exercise Science; a case study approach'.

17 Keeping it all together: Nerves

1. Grey-Thompson, T., *Aim High* (Accent Press, 2007), pp. 42 and 44.
2. Murray, A., *Andy Murray: Seventy-Seven: My Road to Wimbledon Glory* (Headline, 2013).
3. This title is taken from Hanton, S., and Jones, G., 'The Acquisition and Development of Cognitive Skills and Strategies. I: Making the Butterflies Fly in Formation', *Sport Psychologist*, 13 (1999), pp. 1–21.
4. Hanton, S., Cropley, B., Neil, R., Mellalieu, S., and Miles, A., 'Experience in Sport and its Relationship with Competitive Anxiety', *International Journal of Sport and Exercise Psychology*, 5:1 (2008), pp. 28–53, p. 32.
5. Thatcher et al., *Coping and Emotion in Sport*, p. 143.
6. Hanton et al., 'Experience in Sport and its Relationship with Competitive Anxiety', *International Journal of Sport and Exercise Psychology*, 5:1 (2008), pp. 28–53,
7. Syed, *Bounce*, pp. 169–70.
8. Oudejans, R. R. D., Kuijpers, W., Kooijman, C. C., and Bakker, F. C., 'Thoughts and Attention of Athletes under Pressure: Skill-Focus or Performance Worries?', *Anxiety, Stress & Coping: An International Journal*, 24:1 (2011), pp. 59–73.

9. Jackson, R., Beilock, S., and Kinrade, N., '"Choking" in Sport; Research Implications', in Farrow, D., Baker, J., and MacMahon, C. (eds), *Developing Sport Expertise: Enhancing the Coach–Scientist Relationship* (Routledge, 2013), ch. 10.

10. Oudejans, R. R. D., and Pijpers, J. R., 'Training with Anxiety has a Positive Effect on Expert Perceptual–Motor Performance under Pressure', *Quarterly Journal of Experimental Psychology*, 62:8 (2009), pp. 1631–47,

11. UK Sport, *Creating Champions*, (UK Sport, 2004), p. 70.

12. Marc Jones (a Reader at Staffordshire University) has cited this author when explaining this: Seery, M. D., 'Challenge or Threat? Cardiovascular Indexes of Resilience and Vulnerability to Potential Stress in Humans', *Neuroscience and Biobehavioral Reviews*, 35:7 (2012), pp. 1603–10.

13. This was reported in Williams, R., 'Its all in the Hands', *Guardian*, 20 November 2003.

14. Wilkinson, *Jonny*, p. 144.

15. Jackson et al., '"Choking"'.

16. Ibid.

17. Ibid., p. 193.

18. Murray, *Seventy-Seven*, p. 17.

19. Jackson et al., '"Choking"', p. 192.

20. Jones, M and Turner, M., 'Will my Emotions Choke Me?', in Totterdell, P., and Niven, K. (eds), *Should I Strap a Battery to my Head? (And Other Questions about Emotion)* (CreateSpace, 2012), p. 79.

21. Wiggins, *My Time*, p. 150.

18 Under pressure: New approaches

1. Hardy, L., Bell, J., and Beattie, S., 'A Neuropsychological Model of Mentally Tough Behaviour', *Journal of Personality*, 25 February 2013, DOI: 10.1111/jopy.12034.

2. Ibid.

3. Bell, J. J., Hardy, L., and Beattie, S., 'Enhancing Mental Toughness and Performance Under Pressure in Elite Young cricketers: A 2-Year Longitudinal Intervention' *Sport, Exercise, and Performance Psychology*, advance online publication (17 June 2013) DOI: 10.1037/a0033129.

4. Ibid.

5. Lew Hardy explains his ideas on choking for the British Psychological Society: www.youtube.com/watch?v=UiA00Om_gXc&feature=youtu.be

6. Stuart Lancaster, England Manager quoted at the RFU talent symposium, 17–19 May 2013, The Royal Society, London.

7. Müller, S., Abernethy, B., and Farrow, D., 'How do World-Class Cricket Batsmen Anticipate a Bowler's Intention?', *Quarterly Journal of Experimental Psychology*, 59:12 (2006), pp. 2162–86.

8. Epstein, D., *The Sports Gene: Inside the Science of Extraordinary Athletic Performance* (Penguin Books, 2013).

9. Ibid., p. 5.

10. Wilson, M., 'Anxiety, The Brain, The Body and Performance', in Murphy, S. (ed.), *The Oxford Handbook of Sport and Performance Psychology* (Oxford University Press, 2012), ch. 9.

11. Panchuk, D., and Vickers, J. (2013) 'Expert Visual Perception; Why Having a Quiet Eye Matters in Sport', Farrow et al., *Developing Sport Expertise*, chapter. 11.

12. Moore, L. J., Vine, S. J., Cooke, A., Ring, C., and Wilson, M. R., 'Quiet Eye Training Expedites Motor Learning and Aids Performance under Heightened Anxiety: The Roles of response Programming and External Attention', *Psychophysiology*, 49:7 (2012), pp. 1005–15.

13. Ibid., p. 202.

14. Panchuk and Vickers,'Expert Visual Perception'.

19 What I wish I'd known about Olympic coaching when I started

1. LeUnes, A., 'Modelling the Complexity of the Coaching Process: A Commentary', *International Journal of Sports Science & Coaching*, 2:4 (2007), pp. 403–7, p. 404.
2. Olympisize Me! will respond to a search engine or is available from: www2.open.ac.uk/openlearn/olympisize_html/#?state=0&_suid=138385690595307348858299611636
3. Agassi, A., *Open*, p. 187.
4. Murray, *Seventy-Seven*.
5. Ibid., p. 45.
6. Briggs, S., 'Murray Faces Toughest Task', *Daily Telegraph*, 12 January 2013.
7. Linklater, M., 'Andy's Fans were Saying "You Look so Scary on Television!"', *The Times*, 29 December 2012.
8. Ibid.
9. Ibid.
10. Abridged from an Open University module 'Working and Learning in Sport and Fitness' (E113).
11. Bolman, L. G., and Deal, T. E., *Reframing Organisations* (Jossey-Bass, 1997), p. 13.
12. Jones, R. L., Armour, K. M., and Potrac, P., *Sports Coaching Cultures: From Practice to Theory* (Routledge, 2004), p. 50.
13. Thaler, R. H., and Sunstein, C. R. (2008). *Nudge: Improving Decisions about Health, Wealth, and Happiness* (Yale University Press, 2008) pp. 3–4.
14. Johnson, *Slaying the Dragon*, p. 83.
15. Côté, J., Erickson, K., and Duffy, P., 'Developing the Expert Performance Coach', in Farrow et al. (eds), *Developing Sport Expertise*.
16. Olusoga, P., Maynard, I., Hays, K. and Butt, J., 'Coaching under Pressure: A Study of Olympic Coaches', *Journal of Sports Sciences*, 30:3 (2012), pp. 229–39.
17. Høigaard, R., Jones, G. W., and Peters, D. M., 'Preferred Coach Leadership Behaviour in Elite Soccer in Relation to Success and Failure', *International Journal of Sports Science and Coaching*, 3:2 (2008), pp. 241–50, p. 247.
18. Tucker, R., 'Upton is New Breed of Coach', *Times* (Johannesburg, South Africa), October 2013, available from: www.timeslive.co.za/thetimes/2013/10/29/upton-is-new-breed-of-coach
19. This is adapted from: Côté, J., and Gilbert, W., 'An Integrative Definition of Coaching Effectiveness and Expertise', *International Journal of Sports Science and Coaching*, 4:3 (2009), pp. 307–23.
20. Ibid.
21. Johnson, *Slaying the Dragon*.

20 Learning from behind the lines: Coaching stories

1. From a BBC Radio 5 interview: 'Track and Field: US Super Coaches', 18 December 2012.
2. Ibid.
3. 'Elite Athletes Push the Frontiers of Pain', English Institute of Sport website: http://www.eis2win.co.uk/pages/news_eliteathletespushthefrontiersofpain.aspx
4. Syed, *Bounce*, p. 98.
5. Patterson, J., and Lee, T. D., 'Organizing Practice: Effective Practice is more than just Reps', in Farrow et al. (eds), *Developing Elite Sports Performers*, pp. 132–53, p. 142.
6. Ibid.
7. This example of judo is cited in Cushion, C., Ford, P. and Williams, M., 'Coach Behaviours and Practice Structures in Youth Soccer: Implications for Talent Development', *Journal of Sports Sciences*, 30:15 (2012), pp. 1631–41.
8. Potrac, P., Jones, R., and Cushion, C., 'Understanding Power and the Coach's Role in Professional English Soccer: A Preliminary Investigation of Coach Behaviour', *Soccer and Society*, 8:1 (2007), pp. 33–49.

9. Kroenke Sports Enterprises has interests in the Denver Nuggets of the NBA, Colorado Rapids of Major League Soccer, Colorado Avalanche of the NHL, Colorado Mammoth of the National Lacrosse League and St Louis Rams of the NFL.
10. Carson, M., *The Manager: Inside the Mind of Football's Leaders* (Bloomsbury, 2013) p. 80.
11. Ibid., p. 86.
12. The leadership expert Mike Carson interviewed Wenger for his book *The Manager*.
13. Ibid., p. 70.
14. Ibid., p. 74.
15. Comments by Arsène Wenger at a 2013 conference question and answer session in Japan reported in a number of newspapers e.g.: www.dailymail.co.uk/sport/football/article-2380477/Arsene-Wenger-interview-management-Japan--transcript.html#ixzz2hV6sPUAo
16. Carson, *The Manager*.
17. Stauffer, R. (2006) *Roger Federer*, p. 11.
18. Ibid.
19. *The Times*, 29 December 2012, p. 15.
20. Ibid.

21 Do champions think differently about pain?

1. Hoy, C., *Chris Hoy the Autobiography* (Harper Sport, 2009).
2. Ibid., pp. 99–100.
3. Wellington, *A Life Without Limits*, pp. 142–3.
4. sportsillustrated.cnn.com/2010/writers/david_epstein/11/05/Alberto.Salazar/index.html#ixzz2aVskuIID
5. Tucker, R., 'Fatigue Series Introduction', *Science of Sport* website (2008), available at: www.sportsscientists.com/2008/04/fatigue-series-introduction.html
6. Tucker, R., 'Fatigue and Exercise: Part I B', *Science of Sport* website (2008), available at: www.sportsscientists.com/2008/05/fatigue-and-exercise-part-i-b-the-pacing-strategy-continued/
7. Tucker, R., Rauch, L., Harley, Y. X., and Noakes, T. D., 'Impaired Exercise Performance in the Heat is Associated with an Anticipatory Reduction in Skeletal Muscle Recruitment', *Pflügers Archiv*, 448:4, pp. 422–30.
8. From a BBC Radio 5 interview: 'Track and Field: US Super Coaches', 18 December 2012.
9. Tucker, 'Fatigue Series Introduction'.
10. Noakes, T., 'Fatigue Is A Brain-Derived Emotion That Regulates the Exercise Behaviour to Ensure the Protection of Whole Body Homeostasis', *Frontiers in Psychology*, 3 (2012), p. 82.
11. Cited in Noakes, T., 'In Sport is it all Mind over Matter?', *Dialogues in Cardiovascular Medicine*, 17:1, p. 52.

22 A pothole, or worse, on the path: Depression

1. An interview with the English International cricketer in the *Independent* newspaper about his autobiography *Coming Back to Me*: www.independent.co.uk/sport/cricket/marcus-trescothick-i-thought-i-was-going-to-die-942688.html
2. Wilkinson, *Jonny*, pp. 241 and 242.
3. Cited in Wallace, C. 'Sports: Time Out', *Paris Revue*, 10 July 2012, available at: www.theparisreview.org/blog/2012/07/10/time-out/
4. www.gpnotebook.co.uk/simplepage.cfm?ID=x20091123152205182440
5. Schaal, K., Tafflet, M., Nassif, H., Thibault, V., Pichard, C., Alcotte, M., Guillet, T., Helou, N. E., Berthelot, G., Simon, S. and Toussaint, J., 'Psychological Balance in High Level Athletes: Gender-Based Differences and Sport-Specific Patterns', *PLoS ONE*, 6:5, pp. 1–9.

6. Marcus, M., Yasamy, M. T., van-Ommeren, M. and Chisholm, D., 'Depression – a global public health concern' (2012), available at: www.who.int/mental_health/management/depression/who_paper_depression_wfmh_2012.pdf.
7. www.nimh.nih.gov/health/publications/the-numbers-count-mental-disorders-in-america/index.shtml#Suicide
8. Office for National Statistics, 'Suicides in the United Kingdom 2011' (2013), available at: www.ons.gov.uk/ons/rel/subnational-health4/suicides-in-the-united-kingdom/2011/index.html
9. Thorpe, I., 'BBC Radio 5 Live Sports Special', 13 November 2012.
10. Davidson, *Fields of Courage*, p. 250.
11. Ibid.
12. Wilkinson, *Jonny*, p. 246.
13. Hughes, L., and Leavey, G., 'Setting the Bar: Athletes and Vulnerability to Mental Illness', *British Journal of Psychiatry: The Journal of Mental Science*, 200:2 (2012), pp. 95–6.
14. BBC, *Life After Football*, BBC 1, 16 May 2005.
15. Thorpe, 'BBC Radio 5 Live Sports Special' (2012).
16. www.bbc.co.uk/sport/0/football/23226524
17. Professional Players Assoication, *Press Release: Research Results – Life after Sport*, 12 September 2013: www.ppf.org.uk/index.php5?action=press#press51
18. Pendleton with McRae, *Between the Lines*.
19. Ibid., p. 75.
20. Cochrane, K., 'Victoria Pendleton: I'm not the perfect model of what an athlete should be', the *Guardian*, 9 September 2012, available at: www.theguardian.com/sport/2012/sep/09/victoria-pendleton-not-perfect-athlete
21. Walker, N., Thatcher, J., Lavallee D., 'Psychological Responses to Injury in Competitive Sport: A Critical Review', *Society for Promotion Health*, 127 (2007), pp. 174–80.
22. Wilkinson, *Jonny*, p. 250.
23. www.dailymail.co.uk/femail/article-1237035/
24. Henderson, J. C., 'Suicide in Sport: Athletes at Risk', in Parman, D. (ed.), *Psychological Basis of Sport Injuries*, 3rd edn (Fitness Information Technology, 2007), pp. 267–85.
25. McCrory, P., Meeuwisse, W. H., Aubry M., et al., (2013) 'Consensus Statement on Concussion in Sport: The 4th International Conference on Concussion in Sport held in Zurich', *British Journal of Sports Medicine*, 47 (2013), pp. 250–8.
26. Henderson, 'Suicide in Sport'.
27. Wazeter, M., and Lewis, C., *Dark Marathon* (Zondervan Publishing, 1989).
28. Arango, V., Huang, Y. Y., Underwood, M. D., Mann, J. J., 'Genetics of the Serotonergic System in Suicidal Behavior', *Journal of Psychiatric Research*, 37 (2003), pp. 375–86.

23 Looking back and redirecting the rocket: Retirement

1. www.bbc.co.uk/sport/0/20646102
2. Derived largely from Aine MacNamara and colleagues work e.g. MacNamara, Button and Collins, 'The Role of Psychological Characteristics in Facilitating the Pathway to Elite Performance, Part 2'.
3. This turn of phrase comes from of Owen Shears's book *Calon; A Journey to Heart of Welsh Rugby* (Faber and Faber, 2013), p. 169.
4. Hoy, C., *Chris Hoy: The Autobiography* (Harper Sport, 2009), p. 173.
5. For example: Keen, P. (2014) 'Ordinary People Do Extraordinary Things: What Do the Lives of Olympians Tell Us about the Champion in Us All?', Tyranny of the Normal Lecture 4, Green Templeton College, Oxford, 24 Febuary 2014.
6. English Rugby Football Union (RFU) *Summary notes from the RFU Talent Symposium*, The Royal Society, 17–19 May 2013.
7. American College of Sports Medicine (Malina, 2010) and American Orthopaedic Society for Sports Medicine (Jayanthi, Pinkham, Dugas, Patrick and LaBella, 2012).

8. BBC Radio Wales, 'What Sport Stars do Next', 24 March 2012.
9. Overman, S., *Living Out of Bounds*, p. 179.
10. Professional Players Association (2013) *Press Release: Research Results – Life after Sport*, 12 September 2013: www.ppf.org.uk/index.php5?action=press#press51
11. The Retirement Planning Institute's (RPI) *Depression in Retirement*, February 2011 Newsletter: www.rpi-ipr.com/pssa/en/newsletter/2011/2/news_short.cfm?year=2011& month=2&item=2
12. www.iea.org.uk/publications/research/work-longer-live-healthier-the-relationship -between-economic-activity-health-a
13. articles.chicagotribune.com/2013-03-08/health/chi-olympic-gold-medal-gymnast-shawn-johnson-talks-running-fitness-and-weight-gain-20130308_1_shawn-johnson-gymnast-62-mile-race
14. Gogarty and Williamson, *Winning at all Costs*, p. 193.
15. Lavallee, D. and Robinson, H. K., 'In Pursuit of an Identity: A Qualitative Exploration of Retirement from Women's Artistic Gymnastics', *Psychology of Sport and Exercise*, 8:1 (2007), pp. 119–41.
16. www.olympic.org/Documents/elite_athletes/ATHLETIC_IDENTITY.pdf
17. Peterson, K., 'Overtraining, Burnout, Injury, and Retirement', in Hays, K. (ed.), *Performance Psychology in Action: A Casebook for Working with Athletes, Performing Artists, Business Leaders, and Professionals in High-Risk Occupations* (American Psychological Association, 2009), pp. 225–43.
18. Twenty-three per cent of those who retired on their own terms took more than two years to come to terms with the ending of their career, with this figure being significantly higher (42 per cent) among those 'made redundant'.
19. One in 10 of all players report that they were disappointed with their playing careers, but this increases to 1 in 5 among those who have experienced health, addiction or financial problems.
20. CyclingNews, 'Pendleton Daunted by Retirement Plan', *CyclingNews*, 28 November 2011, available at: www.cyclingnews.com/news/pendleton-daunted-by-retirement-plan (Accessed 15 November 2013).
21. See footnote 18 above.
22. www.bbc.co.uk/sport/0/boxing/20757358
23. On the ropes, Boxing Radio: otrboxingradio.com/?p=568
24. BBC, 'Sporting Heroes: After The Final Whistle', with Michael Vaughan, 9 May 2012.
25. As a number of researchers (including Collins and MacNamara) and coaching practitioners argued at the Talent Development Symposium, University of Central Lancashire, Preston, 14 April 2014.

Index